STUDY GUIDE

John V. Thill
Chief Executive Officer, Communication Specialists of America
Courtland L. Bovée
Professor of Business Communication, Grossmont College
Murray Johnston
Partner, skopus WEBdesign
James D. Weare
Partner, skopus WEBdesign

Excellence in Business Communication

Canadian Edition

John V. Thill
Courtland L. Bovée
Ava Cross

Prentice
Hall

Toronto

© 2002 Pearson Education Canada Inc., Toronto, Ontario

ISBN 0-13-065287-3

Acquisitions Editor: Sophia Fortier
Developmental Editor: Laura Paterson Forbes
Production Editor: Sherry Torchinsky
Production Coordinator: Peggy Brown

1 2 3 4 5   05 04 03 02 01

Printed and bound in Canada.

CONTENTS

vi   Contents

ENGLISH ESSENTIALS   162

Practice, Practice, Practice ...

A college course in business communication can teach quite a lot about how people in business write and speak, read and listen. The textbook, the instructor, and eager students all contribute to the educational process, but if you really want to master communication in business, you must practice and get feedback on your work. You must actually write letters, memos and reports and speak in small meetings and before large groups. Your first attempts will be less than perfect; however, they are the price you pay for the ability to produce quality work, quickly and accurately.

"Great," you say, "I know I need practice, but how can I get it? Many employers hire only people who already have on-the-job experience." We'd like to propose a solution to this dilemma. First, be aware that going through the application and interview process will demonstrate your communication skills to potential employers. Your writing skills show in your résumé and application letters; your speaking skills, in interviews and other conversations. Secondly, if you take every opportunity to practice business communication while you're still a student, you will enter the job market with skills comparable to those of people already working. In addition, your proven ability to communicate will increase your confidence, and improve your presentation of your other skills and abilities, during the hiring process.

This Study Guide has been designed to guide your practice. Used in conjunction with its companion textbook, *Excellence in Business Communication,* First Canadian Edition, this guide can help you accomplish important goals:

- Understand the content of textbook chapters

- Prepare for quizzes, tests and assignments

- Apply what you have learned to practical problems

- Understand related issues in business communications

- Improve your spelling and expand your vocabulary

- Improve your knowledge of grammar, punctuation and mechanics

These goals are attained through a wide variety of exercises. Simply by reading, you can gain a new perspective on the chapters in the textbook, and new insights into peripheral issues. Fill-in and short essay exercises test your recall and understanding of chapter content, and vocabulary activities test your ability to spell and use words correctly. (Because the answers to these exercises are provided at the end of each chapter, you can check your own work and get immediate feedback.) Crossword puzzles included in each chapter in the appendices section further test your ability to spell and use words correctly. Application exercises in each chapter allow you to take the role of professional communicator—whether writer, editor or speaker. The English Essentials section at the end of this book contains 20 lessons covering basic grammar, punctuation and mechanics, with explanations and exercises interwoven.

To use all these exercises to best advantage, we propose the following study program:

1. Read the one-paragraph summary/statement of objectives at the beginning of each chapter in the Study Guide.

2. Read the corresponding chapter in *Excellence in Business Communication*

3. Immediately complete two sections of the Study Guide—Master Key Concepts and Quiz Yourself—checking your answers right away and rereading any portion of the textbook that seems to have given you trouble. (Textbook page numbers are provided to make this step easier.)

4. When you feel comfortable with the textbook's content, do the application exercise in Build Your Skills; then check the suggested answers at the end of the chapter.

5. Work through Develop Your Word Power. (The answers are at the end of the chapter, but keep a dictionary at hand so you can look up any the spelling or definition of any troublesome words.)

6. Do one of the English Essentials lessons at the back of this book.

If you work at this program consistently and diligently, you will improve many of the skills important to business communicators.*

---

* *The Canadian Oxford Dictionary* is the authority for the vocabulary sections of this Study Guide. The hard cover version of the COD includes a brief, but very useful style guide.

PART ONE
FOUNDATIONS OF BUSINESS COMMUNICATION

Chapter 1
Communicating Successfully in an Organization

The main point of Chapter 1 is that communication is the glue that holds organizations together. As you read the chapter, think of the many ways that people in business communicate. Also think about the role that communication plays in the various activities of organizations. When you finish reading, analyze your own communication skills and preferences, and plan how you can improve your weak areas.

Master Key Concepts

Use the following terms to fill in the blanks in the outline. All terms are used, but none is used more than once.

approach	effective	grapevine	link
audience-centered	efficiently	horizontally	power
climate	ethical	information	technology
communication	external	intercultural	
crises	formal		

I. Organizations cannot function without effective communication (p. 2)
    A. Every member of an organization is a ___link___ (p. 3) in the information chain.
    B. The flow of information is essential to a company's operations. Outsiders provide the fuel—information, people, raw materials, and capital—which the organization transforms into goods and services that can be sold to customers.
    C. Within the company, you and your co-workers use the information you obtain from outsiders and from one another to guide your activities.
    D. In making and implementing decisions, managers must gather and evaluate information (p. 3) and must communicate their decisions to others in the organization.

II. The ___approach___ (p. 3) to communication varies from organization to organization.
    A. Through ___formal___ (p. 5) communication channels, information flows upward and downward following the official chain of command; official channels also permit messages to flow ___horizontally___ (p. 6) from department to department.
    B. Informal communication channels, also called the ___grapevine___ (p. 7), are an important source of information, both accurate and inaccurate.
    C. In many cases, the informal communication network is the real ___power___ (p. 7) structure of the company.

1

III. The marketing department and the public relations department play an important role in managing the flow of _external_ (p. 8) messages.
   A. One of the public relations department's most visible functions is to help management plan for and respond to _crises_ (p. 8).
   B. The way a company handles a crisis can have a profound impact on the organization's subsequent performance.

IV. _Effective_ (p. 11) communication exhibits six important characteristics.
   A. An organization's communication _climate_ (p. 11) affects the quantity and quality of the information transmitted.
   B. _Ethical_ (p. 12) communication includes all relevant information, is true in every sense, and is not deceptive in any way.
   C. Both internationally and domestically, firms are working with an increasingly diverse work force and paying more attention to _intercultural_ (p. 15) communication.
   D. The growing amount of information and increasing speed of communication are making it necessary for all businesspeople to understand and adapt to _technology_ (p. 13).
   E. When you use an _audience centered_ (p. 16) approach, you focus on the person or persons who will be receiving your message.
   F. Messages can be handled more _efficiently_ (p. 16) by reducing the number of messages making instructions and assignments clearer, distributing communication responsibility more evenly, and training employees to be better writers and speakers.

Check your answers at the end of this chapter.

Quiz Yourself

1. What is the key risk facing managers who depend too heavily on formal communication channels? What is one way of reducing this problem? *key risk is encountering distortion or misunderstanding. A way of reducing this problem is to reduce the number of levels in the organizational structure*

2. Give three examples of downward information flow in an organization.
   1) casual conversation
   2) formal interview between a supervisor & ind. employee
   3) communicating orally in a meeting, workshop, videotape or voice mail

pg. 6 3. Give three examples of upward information flow in organization.
   1) e-mail or group meetings
   2) interviews w/ employees who are leaving the company
   3) formal procedures for resolving grievances.

pg. 6 4. Give one example of horizontal communication flow.
   from one dept. to another
   ex) plant manager phones director of advertising to discuss changes in production schedule.

5. What is the major advantage of informal communication channels? What is the major disadvantage?
   Advantage - no barriers between co-workers

   Disadvantage - threatens executives power to control flow of information.

6. Which two functional units of an organization are particularly important in managing the flow of external messages? How do their functions differ?

pg. 8   *the marketing dept. & the public relations dept. Their functions differ*

7. Give two examples of recommended actions to take when a crisis occurs, and two examples of actions to be avoided.

pg. 10
table 1.1   *do: get top management involved, be prepared for trouble*
don't: blame anyone for anything, refuse to answer questions.

8. What six organizational characteristics contribute to effective communication?

pg. 11   *fostering an open communication climate, committing to ethical comm, understanding difficulties involved in intercultural comm, becoming proficient in comm, tech., using an audience-centered approach to com, creating & processing messages effectively*

9. Communicators at times face ethical dilemmas. Give examples of questions to ask yourself in order to resolve such dilemmas.

10. Give three measures that a manager can take to more efficiently handle the flow of routine messages.

Check your answers at the end of this chapter.

Build Your Skills: What Are Your Strengths And Weaknesses As A Communicator?

Knowing your strengths and weaknesses as a communicator helps you set priorities for self-improvement. Ask yourself the following questions. Then Put a *W* by the items that require the most work, a *P* by those that need polishing, and a *U* by those you can use to the fullest right away.

Reading

P   Do you read fast enough for your work?

P   Are you able to pick out and remember key points?

P   Can you vary your approach to reading to match different types of reading situations?

Listening

U   Are you able to focus your attention on what a speaker is saying?

P   Can you identify and recall key points of a speech to your satisfaction?

U   Are you able to put aside your preconceptions and judge the speaker's message on its merits, regardless of whether you agree or disagree with the ideas or like or dislike the speaker as an individual?

4 Chapter Checkups

P Are you able to analyze a speaker's message and ask questions to test its logic and accuracy? Are you satisfied with your ability to take notes during a lecture?

Engaging in Casual Conversation

U Are you confident in conducting casual social conversations?

P Can you think of interesting things to say to keep up your end of a conversation?

P Do you ask good questions?

U Do you listen empathetically to the other person and draw her or him out?

P Are you comfortable talking with a wide range of people, including those who differ from you in background, age, and interests?

U Do you give the other person a chance to talk as well?

U Are you sensitive to the other person's reactions?

Interviewing

___ Do you prepare adequately for interviews by developing a list of anticipated questions and by preparing answers to those questions?

___ Are you confident in interview situations?

___ Are you able to remain objective in difficult interviews?

___ Can you use different types of questions to obtain the information you want?

___ Are you able to match your interview style to the situation?

___ Can you draw out the other person?

___ Are you able to give and receive criticism effectively?

___ Are you relaxed in interviews with people who outrank you or have more power than you do?

___ Are you considerate in interviews with people in a subordinate position?

Dealing with Small Groups

___ If you are in charge, do you lay the proper groundwork for the meeting by preparing an agenda and making necessary arrangements well in advance?

___ As the leader, are you able to keep the group focused on the business at hand?

___ Are you familiar with the rules of parliamentary procedure?

___ Can you facilitate interaction by balancing the contributions of group members?

___ Are you able to build consensus among group members?

____ Are you able to summarize results and assign responsibilities?

____ As a group participant, do you make useful and constructive comments?

____ Are you sensitive to the needs and concerns of other group members?

Delivering Speeches and Presentations

____ Are you able to plan a speech or presentation that is suitable for various situations and times?

____ Are you able to control your stage fright?

____ Can you speak clearly and distinctly so that people understand you?

____ Do you sound natural and engaging?

____ Are you able to use visual aids effectively in a speech or presentation?

____ Can you handle unexpected or hostile comments effectively?

____ Can you deliver a speech from notes?

Writing Letters, Memos, and Reports

____ Do you have an adequate command of basic grammar and punctuation?

____ Are you able to vary the style and tone of your writing to suit different situations?

____ Can you write clearly, accurately, and concisely?

____ Are you able to organize messages logically and persuasively?

____ Are you familiar with different formats and their uses?

____ Can you construct tables, charts, and other illustrations to supplement your writing?

____ Are you careful about editing and proofreading your work?

Develop Your Word Power

Spelling Challenge   Identify the misspelled word in each of the following sentences, and spell it correctly in the space provided. If all the words in a sentence are spelled correctly write C in the space.

achievements 1. Congratulations on your many acheivements over the past year.

____C____ 2. Our building is adjacent to the hospital.

____C____ 3. They plan to aquire a small manufacturing company.

____C____ 4. In Mark's absense, you can assist me.

____C____ 5. Refinancing would be an acceptable alternative.

_____ 6. How many new workers can that plant accomodate?

_____ 7. His skills are not adaquate for the position.

_____ 8. You are absolutely right!

_____ 9. Jennifer accidently sent those memos to all staff members.

_____ 10. Speed and acuracy are the two qualities most valuable in a typist.

Vocabulary Challenge Match the words in the first column with the definitions in the second column.

_____ 11. acumen   A. opponent

_____ 12. adversary   B. something not in its correct historical time

_____ 13. antecedent   C. something going before

___B___ 14. affinity   D. keen insight

_____ 15. anachronism   E. natural likeness or agreement

Circle the best definition of the highlighted word in each of the following sentences.

16. We should make computers **accessible** to all office workers.

    A. easily modified   B. extra   C. available

17. Some modest people prefer to work in **anonymity**.

    A. without recognition   B. loose-fitting clothing   C. solitude

18. George volunteered with **alacrity** to take on the new project.

    A. willingness   B. reluctance   C. ignorance

19. The customer was **adamant** about getting a refund.

    A. angry   B. unyielding   C. unsure

20. An **ambiguous** answer will only postpone resolution of the problem.

    A. two-sided   B. small-minded   C. indefinite

Select one of these words to complete each of the following sentences, and write the word in the space provided.

acrimonious   **adroit**   **amicable**   **acute**   **aloof**

21. Contrary to her claims that she wants to get involved, Stacey has remained _____ from all the group's activities.

22. Thanks to Deborah Sweeney's _____ handling of the malfunctioning control mechanism, a disastrous accident has been avoided.

23. After an _____ exchange between Eric and his boss, Eric stormed out.

24. To maintain goodwill, we train all our customer-service representatives to seek _____ settlement of complaints.

25. An _____ shortage of petroleum products would have severe effects on our ability to keep the plant open.

Follow-up Word Study Check your answers at the end of this chapter. In the spaces below, write the words that you spelled or used incorrectly. (Use a separate piece of paper if you missed more than five words.) Then use your dictionary to carefully study the spelling, pronunciation, definition, and history (etymology) of each word. Finally, to help fix the word in your memory, write it in a sentence.

Word   *Sentence*

_____   _____

_____   _____

_____   _____

_____   _____

_____   _____

Check Your Answers

Master Key Concepts

I. communication
   A. link
   D. information

II. approach
   A. formal, horizontally
   B. grapevine
   C. power

III. external
   A. crises

IV. effective
   A. climate
   B. ethical
   C. intercultural
   D. technology
   E. audience-centered
   F. efficiently

Quiz Yourself

1. Depending too heavily on formal communication channels carries the risk of messages becoming distorted or misunderstood. One way to reduce distortion is to reduce the number of levels in the organizational structure. (p. 4)

2. Examples of downward information flow would include any communications from executives, managers, or supervisors to those below them in the organizational hierarchy, such as memos to

employees, instructions on how to perform various jobs, policy directives to all employees, or motivational pep talks. (p. 5)

3. Examples of upward information flow would include any communications from lower-level employees to supervisors, managers, or executives, such as written or oral reports, employee exit interviews, grievance filings, or group meetings. (p. 6)

4. One example of horizontal communication is a memo sent from the director of marketing to the head of production. (p. 7)

5. The main advantage of informal communication channels is that they provide employees with their major sources of information. The main disadvantage of informal communication channels is that they are often sources of misinformation. (pp. 7-8)

6. The two most important functional units for managing the flow of information to outsiders are the marketing department and the public relations department. The two differ in their central focus: Marketing is focused on selling goods and services, whereas public relations is more concerned with developing the organization's overall reputation. (p. 8)

7. When a crisis occurs, be prepared for trouble and get top management involved as soon as the crisis occurs. Avoid blaming anyone for anything and avoid speculating in public about unknown facts. (pp. 10-11)

8. The factors that contribute to effective communication are as follows:
    *   Management fosters an open communication climate
    *   The organization is committed to ethical communication
    *   Employees understand the difficulties involved in intercultural communication
    *   Employees are proficient in communication technology
    *   Employees use an audience-centered approach
    *   Messages are created and processed in a timely, efficient manner. (p. 13)

9. Questions to ask to ensure ethical decisions:
    *   Is this decision legal?
    *   Is it balanced?
    *   Can you live with it?
    *   Is it feasible? (p. 13)

10. Managers can facilitate the flow of routine messages by
    *   Reducing the number of messages being produced
    *   Speeding up the preparation of messages
    *   Making writers and speakers better at their jobs through training programs (pp. 16-17)

Build Your Skills: What Are Your Strengths and Weaknesses as a Communicator?

The checklist in this exercise is designed to make students think about their own abilities in reading, listening, engaging in casual conversation, interviewing, dealing with small groups, delivering speeches and presentations, and writing memos, letters, and reports. You might suggest that they follow up by preparing a list of goals as well as action plans for building their skills in areas that need the most attention.

Develop Your Word Power

1. achievements	6. accommodate	11. D	16. C	21. aloof
2. adjacent	7. adequate	12. A	17. A	22. adroit
3. acquire	8. C	13. C	18. A	23. acrimonious
4. absence	9. accidentally	14. E	19. B	24. amicable
5. C	10. accuracy	15. B	20. C	25. acute

Chapter 2
Understanding Business Communication

The main point of Chapter 2 is that the communication process consists of a series of steps and is effective only when each step is successful. As you read the chapter, think about how misunderstandings can arise, especially in business communication. When you finish reading, mentally review some personal experiences with misunderstandings and try to figure out how they could have been overcome or avoided.

Master Key Concepts

Use the following terms to fill the blanks in the outline. All terms are used, but none is used more than once.

audience	credibility	key points	perception
~~barriers~~	~~decoding~~	~~listening~~	repeating
~~channel~~	~~encoding~~	media richness	~~sender~~
complexity	~~feedback~~	~~medium~~	specific and accurate
control	~~filtering~~	~~nonverbal~~	~~time and space~~

I. Communication occurs in two basic forms: verbal and _nonverbal_ (p. 25).
    A. Nonverbal communication, which conveys most of the emotional meaning of a message, can be grouped into six main categories: facial expressions and eye behavior, gestures and postures, vocal characteristics, personal appearance, touching behavior, and use of _time & space_ (p. 26).
    B. Verbal communication involves speaking and writing to send messages and _listening_ (p. 27) and reading to receive messages.

II. Communication takes place in a _repeating_ (p. 28) process of six phases.
    A. The _sender_ (p. 28) has an idea.
    B. The idea is put into a message the receiver will understand. This phase is called _encoding_ (p. 28).
    C. In order to transmit the message, the sender selects a communication _channel_ (p. 28) and _a medium_ (p. 28).
    D. Once the receiver gets the message, that person absorbs and understands the information by _decoding_ (p. 28) the message.
    E. Finally, the receiver sends _feedback_ (p. 29) to the sender.

III. Misunderstandings are common, and they may arise at any point in the communication process.
    A. Problems in _formulating_ (pp. 29-30) a message may result when the sender can't decide what to include in a message, isn't sure about how the information will be used or who will use it, or finds it difficult to express ideas.
    B. If you communicate well, other people will understand you, whether they agree with you or not.

10

IV. Communication _barriers_ (p. 30) can exist between people and within organizations.
  A. To overcome incorrect _filtering_ (p. 31), establish more than one communication channel so that information can be verified through multiple sources. Also try to eliminate as many intermediaries as possible.
  B. To overcome language barriers, use the most _specific & accurate_ (p. 31) words possible.
  C. To overcome message _complexity_ (p. 33), use strong organization and be sure to ask for feedback.
  D. _media Richness_ (p. 34) is determined by a medium's ability to use more than one informational cue, facilitate feedback, and establish personal focus.

V. Successful communicators have several traits in common.
  A. Because of their _perception_ (p. 36), they are able to predict how you'll receive their message.
  B. Because of their _credibility_ (p. 36), you have faith in the substance of their message.
  C. Their _control_ (p. 36) allows them to shape your responses.

VI. One of the ways effective communicators overcome communication barriers is by creating the message carefully.
  A. The first thing to do to create messages carefully is to focus on your _audience_ (p. 37).
  B. Another way to create careful messages is to call attention to your _Key points_ (p. 37).

Check your answers at the end of this chapter.

Quiz Yourself

1. List six types of nonverbal messages.

2. Identify the five phases involved in the communication process.

3. Which phase in the communication process allows you to evaluate the effectiveness of your message?

4. List three problems that may arise when a message is being developed.

5. List six kinds of communication barriers that can occur between people.

6. Every message contains both a _____ meaning, which deals with the subject of the message, and a _____ meaning, which suggests the nature of the interaction between the sender and the receiver.

7. Describe three ways business messages are particularly complex.

8. What can you do to overcome competition barriers?

9. Briefly summarize six steps you can take to create your message carefully.

10. List four ways that you can make feedback more useful.

Check your answers at the end of this chapter.

Build Your Skills: Can You Read Body Language?

Turn on the TV—the local News, Weather, and Sports, for instance. Now turn the sound off and just watch. Observe the facial expressions, eye behaviour, gestures, and postures of each announcer. See if you can answer the following questions:

- Was the lead story good or bad news?
- Will you need an umbrella tomorrow?
- Did the home team win?

Give some attention to physical appearance and personal style of the announcers. Of course, their appearance is part of the job requirement. But imagine them switching roles: if the Sports guy or gal were reading the News, would she or he need to dress differently, or change hair style?

Develop Your Word Power

Spelling Challenge   Identify the misspelled word in each of the following sentences, and spell it correctly in the space provided. If all the words in a sentence are spelled correctly, write *C* in the space.

_____   1.   What would it cost to advertize in *Maclean's?*

_____   2.   Bill is anxous because he has *not* heard from his associate yet.

_____   3.   Ms. Hansen will analyse your income statement.

_____   4.   Standish Corp.'s anual meeting will be held on August 17.

_____   5.   That typewriter is ancient!

_____   6.   We will issue stock when it is advantageous to do so.

_____   7.   What kinds of returns are allowible?

_____   8.   I must apologise, Mike, for being unable to attend your meeting.

_____   9.   What did you think of her analisis?

_____   10.   It is not adviseable to wear your Sport watch while swimming.

Vocabulary Challenge Match the words in the first column with the definitions in the second column.

_____   11. benign   A. gentle

_____   12. apathetic   B. independent

_____   13. bilateral   C. haughty

_____   14. arrogant   D. two-sided

_____   15. autonomous   E. uninterested

Circle the best definition of the highlighted word in each of the following sentences.

16. Her remarks about market trends were **apropos** because we are considering a major change in our marketing approach.

    A. pertinent   B. spooky   C. positive

17. We can **avert** future disaster only by taking precautions against accidents now.

    A. predict   B. lessen   C. prevent

18. I **ascribe** our poor sales last month to consumer uncertainty about the economy.

    A. assume   B. credit   C. report

19. We should not purchase any business until we **audit** its books.

    A. examine   B. read   C. hear

20. All Persian carpets from the House of Nasseri are **authentic**.

    A. original   B. genuine   C. high quality

Select one of these words to complete each of the following sentences, and write the word in the space provided.

anticlimax   **antipathy**   **antithesis**   **apathy**   **attrition**

21. Because of his _____ toward office work, he has decided on a career that will seldom require him to sit behind a desk.

22. Her _____ may infect the other programmers, who might then lose their enthusiasm for the project.

23. The _____ of right is wrong.

24. After all the talk about changing store operations, the minor change in store hours seems an _____.

25. She doesn't like to fire anybody, so she'll whittle her staff through _____.

Follow-up Word Study Check your answers at the end of this chapter In the spaces below, write the words that you spelled or used incorrectly. (Use a separate piece of paper if you missed more than five words.) Then use your dictionary to carefully study the spelling, pronunciation, definition, and history (etymology) of each word. Finally, to help fix the word in your memory, write it in a sentence.

Word   *Sentence*

_____   _____

_____   _____

_____   _____

_____   _____

Check Your Answers

Master Key Concepts

I. nonverbal
 A. time and space
 B. Listening

II. repeating
 A. sender
 B. encoding
 C. channel, medium
 D. decoding
 E. feedback

III. A. formulating

IV. barriers
 A. filtering
 B. specific and accurate
 C. complexity
 D. media richness

V. A. perception
 B. credibility
 C. control

VI. A. audience
 B. key points

Quiz Yourself

1. The six main types of nonverbal messages are facial expressions and eye behavior, gestures and postures, vocal characteristics, personal appearance, touching behavior, and use of time and space. (p. 26)

2. The six phases involved in the communication process are:
 a) The sender has an idea.
 b) The idea becomes a message.
 c) The message is transmitted.
 d) The receiver gets the message.
 e) The receiver interprets the message.
 f) The receiver reacts and sends feedback to the sender (pp. 28-29)

3. The final step, when the receiver sends feedback to the source, is what allows you to evaluate the effectiveness of your message. (p. 29)

4. Three common problems that may occur when a message is being developed are
   - Indecision about the message content
   - Lack of familiarity with the situation or the audience
   - Difficulty in expressing ideas (p. 30)

5. Communication barriers that can occur between people include
   - Differences in perception
   - Incorrect filtering
   - Language problems
   - Poor listening
   - Differing emotional states
   - Differing backgrounds (pp. 30-32)

6. Every message contains both a *content* meaning, which deals with the subject of the message, and a *relationship* meaning, which suggests the nature of the interaction between the sender and the receiver. (p. 31)

7. Business messages are complex in a number of ways. Here are two:
   - The sender of the message may not always completely agree with the ideas that have to be expressed or may be emotionally reluctant to send the message.
   - The subject is often inherently dry or difficult to explain. (p. 33)

8. To overcome competition barriers, you can try the following:
   - Avoid making demands on a receiver who doesn't have the time to pay attention.
   - Make written messages visually appealing and easy to understand.
   - Deliver oral messages by speaking directly to your receiver. (p. 33)

9. Here are some of the things you can do to create your message carefully:
   - Tell your audience what to expect.
   - Balance general concepts with concrete examples.
   - Keep messages as brief and clear as possible.
   - Connect new information to information the audience is already familiar with.
   - Emphasize key ideas.
   - In concluding the message, review the key points. (p. 37)

10. Feedback can be made more useful if you:
    - Plan how you want to obtain feedback and choose an appropriate method of transmission.
    - Encourage people to be open with you
    - Listen to and value the feedback you get.
    - Use feedback to revise your message in order to overcome misunderstandings. (pp. 38-39)

Build Your Skills: Can You Read Body Language?

You were probably able to answer at least some of the questions, without the verbal component. You might even have concluded that the lead story involved a death, or other tragedy. You might understand that the home team lost, and lost badly. But body language alone would not tell you what tragedy, or the final score in the game.

Body language conveys most of the emotional content of the message. We also believe that body language transmits reliable information. If we perceive a conflict between the verbal and non-verbal components of a message, we almost always believe the non-verbal aspect.

Good communicators reinforce the verbal message with appropriate facial expressions, gestures, and tone of voice. Observe any public figure with a reputation for honesty and accuracy, and you will see close agreement between the verbal and non-verbal parts of the presentation.

Develop Your Word Power

1. advertise	6. *C*	11. A	16. A	21. antipathy
2. anxious	7. allowable	12. E	17. C	22. apathy
3. analyze	8. apologize	13. D	18. B	23. antithesis
4. annual	9. analysis	14. C	19. A	24. anticlimax
5. *C*	10. advisable	15. B	20. B	25. attrition

Chapter 3
Communicating Interculturally

The main point of Chapter 3 is that communication with people who are from other cultures and other countries requires special sensitivity and enhanced skills. As you read the chapter, think about not only the language barriers that often exist but also the cultural barriers that affect communication. When you finish reading, seek opportunities to communicate with people from cultures other than your own and take note of the accommodations you must make to communicate well.

Master Key Concepts

Use the following terms to fill in the blanks in the outline. All terms are used, but none is used more than once.

advertisements	direct	globalization	sales
context	ethical	judgment	status
cultural diversity	ethnocentrism	persistent	subculture
culture	flexible	pronunciation	time
customers			

I. The _____ (p.48) of business is accelerating as more companies cross national borders to find customers, materials, and capital.
   A. With the expansion of international business, companies are finding that good communication skills are essential for meeting _____ (p.48), making _____ (p. 38), and working more effectively with colleagues in other countries.
   B. The _____ (p. 48) in Canada has resulted from immigration trends, differing ethnic backgrounds, active hiring of more ethnic minorities, and common differences such as gender, age, physical ability, and educational background.

II. We all belong to many different cultures.
   A. A _____ (p. 50) is a shared system of symbols, beliefs, attitudes, values, expectations, and norms for behavior; a cultural group that exists within a major culture is called a _____ (p. 50).
   B. Cultures vary in social values, roles and _____ (p. 51), decision-making customs, concepts of _____ (p. 52), concepts of personal space, cultural _____ (p. 52), body language, social behavior and manners, and legal and _____ (pp. 53-54) behavior.

III. When you deal with people who don't speak your language at all, you have three options: learn their language, use a translator, or teach them your language.
   A. Although many international business letters are written in English, many other forms of communication must be translated, including _____ (p. 56), warranties, maintenance manuals, product labels, policy and procedure manuals, and reports.
   B. Several sources of confusion in oral communication are _____ (p. 56-57), the way people use their voices, and idiomatic expression.

IV. The tendency to judge all other groups according to our own group's standards, behaviors, and customs is called _____ (p. 57).

V. Tips for developing intercultural communication skills include:
- taking responsibility for communication
- withholding _____ (p. 61)
- showing respect
- empathizing
- tolerating ambiguity
- looking beyond the superficial
- recognizing your own cultural biases
- being _____ (p. 61)
- emphasizing common ground
- sending clear messages
- increasing your cultural sensitivity
- dealing with the individual
- learning when to be _____ (p. 61)

Check your answers at the end of this chapter.

Quiz Yourself

1. List the nine areas of cultural differences that can give rise to misunderstanding in international business communication.

2. In Canada and the U.S., business people try to reach decisions as quickly and efficiently as possible. The top people concern themselves with reaching agreement on the main points, then leave the details to others. Give examples of cultures with different decision making styles.

3. Give an example illustrating how body language that is meaningful in one country can be misconstrued by a person from another culture.

4. When you deal with people who don't speak your language at all, what options do you have?

5. Which forms of written communication from North American firms to foreign countries are most likely to require translation?

6. What language barriers might you encounter in a conversation with a person for whom English is a second language?

7. Briefly discuss the implications of ethnocentrism.

8. Explain several factors that could cause problems when negotiating with someone from another culture.

9. Give some tips on how to achieve clarity in letters written in English to people from other cultures.

10. List four ways in which you might overcome language and cultural barriers in oral communication.

Check your answers at the end of this chapter.

Build Your Skills: Plan Your Business Trip Abroad

Your boss has asked you to spend two weeks scouting for business opportunities in a foreign country. Your assignment is to find a good location for a new resort hotel. Where you go is up to you, so pick a county that you have never seen before and plan your two-week trip. Make a list of all the things you will need to do or learn before you go.

Develop Your Word Power

Spelling Challenge Identify the misspelled word in each of the following sentences, and spell it correctly in the space provided. If all the words in a sentence are spelled correctly, write *C* in the space.

_____	1.	Seize the opportunity to profit from others' mistakes!
_____	2.	The most sensable course is to build slowly
_____	3.	These serviceable tablecloths will give you many years of wear.
_____	4.	Our sales representatives receive a strait commission.
_____	5.	Compare the strenth of Grit detergent with that of your current brand.
_____	6.	This policy supercedes your old one.
_____	7.	Donna desperately wants to succede in sales.
_____	8.	The replacement we are sending is simmilar to the umbrella you bought.
_____	9.	Keep yesterday's receipts seperate from today's.
_____	10.	Each day has a certain rythem from start to finish.

Vocabulary Challenge Match the words in the first column with the definitions in the second column.

_____	11.	tacit	A.	implied
_____	12.	tedious	B.	succinct
_____	13.	tenacious	C.	persistent
_____	14.	terse	D.	hackneyed
_____	15.	trite	E.	monotonous

Circle the best definition of the highlighted word in each of the following sentences.

16. Be careful not to **subvert** your own authority by appearing too playful.

    A.   undermine   B.   increase   C.   mock

17. Five temporary clerks will be **sufficient** during the holidays.

    A.   enough   B.   employed   C.   absent

18. Professor Buckalew will be one of the panelists at the **symposium.**

    A.   inquiry   B.   trade show   C.   conference

19. This move will require us to **synchronize** many people and things.

    A.   weed out   B.   coordinate   C.   notify.

20. Include a **synopsis** at the beginning of the report.

    A.   outline   B.   introduction   C.   summary

Select one of these words to complete each of the following sentences, and write the word in the space provided.

superficial   **superfluous**   **susceptible**   **symbolic**   **synonymous**

21. Unfortunately, our sophisticated new equipment is _____ to breakdown.

22. See if you can flesh out this _____ analysis.

23. The name Pearson's is _____ with value.

24. The statue in front of the building is _____ of our role in the world of health care.

25. Jane already realizes her mistake; your criticism is _____ .

Follow-up Word Study Check your answers at the end of this chapter. In the spaces below, write the words that you spelled or used incorrectly. (Use a separate piece of paper if you missed more than five words.) Then use your dictionary to carefully study the spelling, pronunciation, definition, and history (etymology) of each word. Finally, to help fix the word in your memory, write it in a sentence.

Word   *Sentence*

_____   _____

_____   _____

_____   _____

_____   _____

_____   _____

Check Your Answers

Master Key Concepts

I. globalization
   A. customers, sales
   B. cultural diversity

II.   A. culture, subculture
    B. status, time, context, ethical

III.   A. advertisements
     B. pronunciation

IV. ethnocentrism

V. judgment, persistent, flexible, direct

Quiz Yourself

1. Misunderstandings are especially likely to occur because of differences in
    - Social values
    - Roles and status
    - Decision-making customs
    - Concepts of time
    - Concepts of personal space
    - Cultural context
    - Body language
    - Social behavior and manners
    - Legal and ethical behavior (pp. 51-54)

2. Greek executives assume that anyone who ignores details is evasive and untrustworthy. Latin Americans prefer to make deals slowly, under much discussion. Japanese negotiating teams strive for consensus, an elaborate, time-consuming process from a North American perspective. (p. 53)

3. Here are two examples that illustrate how body language that is considered meaningful in one country can be misconstrued by a person from another culture:
    a) A Western executive crosses his legs so that the sole of his shoe is showing, unaware that this gesture is viewed as an insult by an Egyptian businessperson.

   b)   North Americans assume that a person who doesn't make frequent eye contact is evasive or dishonest: however, in many parts of Latin America and Asia, keeping your eyes lowered is a sign of respect. (p. 53)

4.   When you deal with people who don't speak your language at all, your options are:
   • Learn their language
   • Use an intermediary or translator
   • Teach them your language (p. 55)

5.   The following types of written communication are likely to require translation:
   • Advertisements
   • Warranties
   • Repair and maintenance manuals
   • Product labels
   • Policy and procedure manuals and benefit plans used by foreign subsidiaries of Canadian companies
   • Reports passed between foreign subsidiaries and Canadian headquarters (p. 56)

6.   When conversing with someone for whom English is a second language, barriers arise from pronunciation problems, speech patterns, idiomatic expressions, and variations in the meaning of some words and phrases. (pp. 56—57)

7.   Ethnocentric people are prone to stereotyping and prejudice. They generalize about entire groups of people on the basis of sketchy evidence, and then develop biased attitudes toward the group. As a consequence, they fail to see people as they really are. They ignore the personal qualities of individuals. (pp. 57-58)

8.   When negotiating with someone from another culture, you're likely to encounter a number of differences.
   • Your approach to negotiation may differ (such as preferring an impersonal or a sociable atmosphere).
   • Your tolerance for disagreement may differ.
   • Your problem-solving techniques may differ.
   • Your protocol may differ.
   • Your attitudes about schedules may differ.
   • Your decision-making methods may differ. (pp. 61-62)

9.   When writing letters to people from other cultures:
   • Use short, precise words.
   • Rely on specific terms; avoid abstractions.
   • Stay away from slang, jargon, buzzwords, idioms, acronyms, and North American product names.
   • Use shorter and simpler sentences than usual.
   • Use short paragraphs.
   • Use many transitional devices.
   • Use numbers, visual aids, and preprinted forms. (p. 62)

10.   Any four of the following suggestions would help overcome language and cultural barriers in oral communication:
   • Clarify your message by using repetition and example.
   • Listen patiently and carefully.
   • Be aware of cultural differences in the meanings assigned to specific gestures and expressions.
   • Adapt your conversation style to that of the person or persons with whom you are conversing.

- When your conversation ends, be certain that you and the other participants agree on what has been discussed and decided.
- When appropriate, follow up an oral conversation with a letter or memo. (pp. 64-65)

Build Your Skills: Plan Your Business Trip Abroad

Plans for the trip should involve such logistical considerations as making travel arrangements, booking hotels and rental cars, getting a passport and visa, buying suitable clothing, converting currency and the like.

In addition, the plan should involve learning about the culture of the other country, through various types of research. From a business standpoint, there are many things you should investigate to get an idea of the suitability of the country as a site for a tourist resort. Issues to consider might include the political structure of the country, its religion and social customs, the weather, health-care facilities, economic conditions, laws regarding foreign investment and foreign visitors, police protection, scenic attractions, shopping facilities, and transportation.

Another thing that might be useful in preparing for the trip would be to compile a list of people, in this country and in the foreign country, who might be able to facilitate the study of possible locations.

Develop Your Word Power

1. *C*	6. supersedes	11. A	16. A	21. susceptible
2. sensible	7. succeed	12. E	17. A	22. superficial
3. *C*	8. similar	13. C	18. C	23. synonymous
4. straight	9. separate	14. B	19. B	24. symbolic
5. strength	10. rhythm	15. D	20. C	25. superfluous

Chapter 4
Communicating Through Technology

The main point of Chapter 4 is to emphasize how important it is for today's business people to understand, use, and adapt to technological tools of communication. The chapter emphasizes how technology affects communication, offers guidance about when it is appropriate to use various technological tools, introduces the ways technology can help produce messages, and introduces proper formats for various technological media.

Master Key Concepts

Use the following terms to fill in the blanks in the outline. All terms are used, but none is used more than once.

audience expectations	electronic	presentation	voice recognition
boilerplates	fax	scanner	work processing software
cost	graphics	spell checkers	work environment
databases	nature	teleconferencing	work life
desktop publishing	networks	time	World Wide Web
e-mail	overload	voice mail	

I. Because technology keeps changing, no hard rules dictate when it's appropriate to use a particular technological tool for communicating. The decision is based on several factors:
   A. _____ (p. 72) determine the methods that are acceptable to the people who will receive your message.
   B. Often the biggest factor in your technology choice is _____ (p. 73), although _____ (p. 73) will also have an impact, not only on how much you can afford to spend but also on how much is appropriate for the situation.
   C. What you need to say in the document, the _____ (p. 73) of the message, also affects what technological tool you will choose.
   D. Your _____ (p. 73) needs dictate for instance, whether you will use typeset printing and color graphics or electronic mail.
   E. Where you conduct your communication—your _____ (pg. 73)—can range from the traditional office to home, hotel rooms, and even cars.

II. The dominant tool for creating printed documents is _____ (p. 73). Of course, you can use group authoring tools (sometimes called groupware) when two or more people are working together on a document.
   A. To computerize the process of assembling finished pages, _____ (p. 74) software was created.
   B. When researching information for a document, you can consult _____ (p. 74), which are collections of facts ranging from financial figures to the text of reports.
   C. In addition to keyboarding, you can enter text into a computer using a pen-based or a _____ (p. 75) system.
   D. Prewritten text often used in business messages can range from standard blocks of text called _____ (p. 75) to already printed versions of material that you want to enter into your computer using a device known as a _____ (p. 76).
   E. The software for creating business visuals falls into two basic groups: presentation software and _____ (p. 76) software.

24

F. _____ (p. 77) are handy tools for catching typos, but they cannot replace strong spelling skills.

G. Using regular phone lines, you can transmit an exact reproduction of a document from one _____ (p. 79) machine to another.

III. An increasing number of documents are never placed on paper, being written on computer, transmitted along telephone lines or other connections, and read on computer. These _____ (p. 79) documents can save the amount of paper a business uses.

A. _____ (p. 79) connect people within a single company, across town, across the country., and around the world.

B. Documents created, transmitted, and read entirely on computer are referred to as _____ (p. 80).

C. The _____ (p. 82), a powerful system of interconnections on the Internet, is an exploding means for companies and individuals to provide information and disseminate PR and advertising messages.

IV. Technology can also improve oral communication between individuals and groups.

A. Similar to e-mail in concept, _____ (p. 85) doesn't require each user to have a computer, only a touch-tone phone, letting you send, store, and retrieve spoken messages.

B. Through _____ (p. 85) and videoconferencing, you can conduct meetings via phone lines and satellite with people who are scattered around the world.

V. Technology can speed the exchange of information, improve teamwork, overcome organizational structure, and decrease communication costs; however, it can also lead to information _____ (p. 87), burden people with unwanted messages, isolate some people from employment opportunities, and blur the line between _____ (p. 88) and home life.

Check your answers at the end of this chapter.

Quiz Yourself

1. When might it be a good idea to send your message on videotape?

2. Give an example of external sources of information you might want to use when researching a business document.

3. What is a CD-ROM? Give an example of this recent technology.

4. Name two functions that help you revise your document, and explain what these functions do.

5. What are some limitations of a grammar checker?

6. In what three ways can word processing and desktop publishing software help you produce a business document?

7. Explain what mail merge can do for document distribution.

8. What two benefits can fax machines provide businesspeople?

9. List at least six benefits of e-mail, along with at least two drawbacks.

10. What is the main advantage of intranets?

Check your answers at the end of this chapter.

Build Your Skills: Suppose You Were Equipping An Office ...

Let's say that you have decided to go into business for yourself by opening a one-person real estate office in your hometown. You have rented space in a new building. Now you must obtain the furnishings, equipment, and supplies you need to get started. Make a list of all the items you need. Remember, you're on a tight budget.

Develop Your Word Power

Spelling Challenge Identify the misspelled word in each of the following sentences, and spell it correctly in the space provided. If all the words in a sentence are spelled correctly, write *C* in the space.

_____   1.   Reserve the meeting room for next Wensday.

_____   2.   For a long report, a table of contents is useful.

_____   3.   A deposit is unecessary for orders under $50.

_____   4.   This year our researchers discovered a twelfth-century townsite.

_____   5.   While I'm on the road, you can reach me threw the main office.

_____   6.   Midday tempratures are in the high 70s.

_____   7.   The store needs a through, floor-to-ceiling cleaning.

_____   8.   We are truely sorry for any inconvenience you have experienced.

_____   9.   After only a week, the thermometer is no longer useable.

_____   10.   Store your valuables in our security vaults.

Vocabulary Challenge Match the words in the first column with the definitions in the second column.

_____   11. ulterior   A. one-sided

_____   12. uncompromising   B. firm

_____   13. unilateral   C. unparalleled

_____   14. unprecedented   D. sophisticated

_____   15. urbane   E. concealed

Circle the best definition of the highlighted word in each of the following sentences.

16. After working with Richard for five years, I have learned to cope with his **vagaries.**

　　A. abstractions   B. bad moods   C. whims

17. The **vicissitudes** of the restaurant business parallel the state of the general economy.

　　A. ups and downs   B. facts   C. truths

18. Before our new product line comes out, we will be **vulnerable** to the competition.

　　A. bothersome   B. attractive   C. defenseless

19. Many of our customers are **wary** because they have been disappointed.

　　A. combative   B. tired   C. on guard

20. Many new inspectors are overly **zealous.**

　　A. sensitive   B. diligent   C. trained

Select one of these words to complete each of the following sentences, and write the word in the space provided.

vacillating   **vapid**   **versatile**   **vigilant**   **vindictive**

21. Protect your home with a _____ watchdog.

22. We have enough specialists; let's try to find someone who is _____.

23. Don't be in a hurry to write up a contract for a _____ client; his mind will change before the ink is dry.

24. A _____ commercial is unlikely to build anyone's enthusiasm.

25. Julia is _____ and will not hesitate to pay you back for insulting her.

Follow-up Word Study Check your answers at the end of this chapter. In the spaces below, write the words that you spelled or used incorrectly. (Use a separate piece of paper if you missed more than five words.) Then use your dictionary to carefully study the spelling, pronunciation, definition, and history (etymology) of each word. Finally, to help fix the word in your memory, write it in a sentence.

Word   *Sentence*

_____   _____

_____   _____

_____   _____

_____   _____

_____   _____

Check Your Answers

Master Key Concepts

I. A. audience expectations
    B. time, cost
    C. nature
    D. presentation
    E. work environment

II. word processing software
    A. desktop publishing
    B. databases
    C. voice recognition
    D. boilerplates, scanner
    E. graphics
    F. spell checkers
    G. fax

III. electronic
    A. networks
    B. e-mail
    C. World Wide Web

IV. A. voice mail
     B. teleconferencing

V. overload, work life

Quiz Yourself

1. You might want to send your message on videotape when you need to convey emotion and excitement but you don't have the time to visit every member of your audience. (p. 73)

2. An example of external information is Statistics Canada's Web site. *The Tax Page* explains many recent government taxation actions. (p. 74)

3. A CD-ROM is a type of compact disk that can be read by special computer equipment. An example is Microsoft's *Encarta,* an encyclopedia on CD-ROM. (p. 75)

4. When revising a document, *cut and paste* is a function that allows you to cut a block of text out of one section and paste it in somewhere else. The *find and replace* function helps you track down words or phrases and change them if you need to. (p. 77)

5. Since the computer doesn't have a clue about what you're trying to say, determining whether you've said it correctly is difficult. Moreover, even if you've used all the rules correctly, a grammar checker still can't tell whether your document communicates clearly. (p. 77)

6. Word processing and desktop publishing software can help you produce business documents in the following ways:
    - Adding a first-class finish (by providing attractive typefaces or by adding color graphics)
    - Managing document style (by insuring consistency with such features as style sheets)
    - Generating supporting elements (such as footnotes, endnotes, index, or table of contents). (pp. 77-79)

7. Mail merge automatically combines a standard version of a document with a list of names and addresses. It will produce one copy for each person on your mailing list, saving you the trouble of inserting the name and address each time. (p. 79)

8. Fax machines offer business people two distinct advantages: overcoming the delay problems of regular mail and overcoming the time-zone problems of trying to contact someone by phone. (p. 79)

9. The benefits of e-mail include
    - Speed
    - Low cost
    - Portability
    - Convenience
    - Ease of record keeping
    - Access to news services
    - Egalitarianism
    - Openness of communication
    - Distribution lists
    - Automated mail

    The drawbacks of e-mail include
    - Overuse
    - Electronic junk mail
    - Overloads and crashes
    - Lack of privacy (pp. 80-82)

10. The biggest advantage of intranets is that they eliminate the problem of employees' using different types of computers within a company. Other advantages include saving paper; saving time for employees, who don't have to dig through files; easy updating of company materials and manuals; ease of collaboration; and ease of interacting with other employees in remote locations. (p. 84)

Build Your Skills: Suppose You Were Equipping an Office . . .

One good way to approach this exercise is to visit a real-estate office and look around or, better yet, explain the assignment to one of the real-estate agents.

At a minimum, the office should have some basic furniture: a desk, several chairs, a filing cabinet, a computer table, and a lamp or two.

The equipment should include a personal computer with a letter-quality printer. A simple photocopier would also be a plus, and these days a fax machine (or fax built in to the computer) is a must. Or you might consider an "all-in-one" fax/scanner/printer/copier. In addition, the office would require a telephone with several lines as well as an answering machine or service to record incoming calls when no one was in the office. Other possible items might include a postage meter and an electric coffee maker.

The supplies required would include letterhead stationery and envelopes for correspondence, paper for the copy machine and the computer printer, manila envelopes, file folders, various labels, an appointment calendar, pens and pencils, scratch pads, and copies of preprinted forms required in completing real-estate transactions. Another useful item would be a wall map of the area and smaller maps that could be handed out to potential clients. In addition, assorted miscellaneous items like Post-It notes, paper clips, rubber bands, and scissors might be required.

Develop Your Word Power

1. Wednesday	6. temperatures	11. E	16. C	21. vigilant
2. *C*	7. thorough	12. B	17. A	22. versatile
3. unnecessary	8. truly	13. A	18. C	23. vacillating
4. twelfth	9. usable	14. C	19. C	24. vapid
5. through	10. *C*	15. D	20. B	25. vindictive

PART TWO
THE WRITING PROCESS

Chapter 5
Planning Business Messages

The main point of Chapter 5 is that the most effective business messages are planned. As you read the chapter, think about why it is important to have a clear purpose when you communicate and why it is important to keep your audience's needs in mind. When you finish reading, think about some written and oral messages you have sent that would have benefited from .greater advance planning.

Master Key Concepts

Use the following terms to fill in the blanks in the outline. All terms are used, but none is used more than once.

accurate	collaborating	motivational	reaction
audience	idea	practical	specific
brainstorming	informational	purpose	teleconferencing
channel			

I.   The composition process consists of three main steps: planning, composing, and revising.

II. The first step in planning a business message is defining your _____ (p. 95).
   A.   There are three general purposes to business communication: informing, persuading, and
        _____ (p. 97) with the audience.
   B.   Within the general purpose, a message also has a _____ (p. 97) purpose.
   C.   A message should not be sent if the purpose is not realistic, the timing isn't right, you are not the right person to deliver the message, or the purpose is not acceptable to the organization.

III. The second step in planning a business message is analyzing the _____ (p. 98).
   A.   Developing an audience profile involves asking several questions: What is the size and composition of the audience? Who is the primary audience? What is the audience's probable _____ (p. 97)? What is the audience's level of understanding? What is your relationship with the audience?
   B.   To satisfy the audience's _____ (pp. 99-100) needs, you need to find out what the audience wants to know, anticipate unstated questions, provide all the required information, be sure the information is _____ (p. 99), and emphasize ideas of greatest interest to the audience.
   C.   To satisfy the audience's _____ (p. 100) needs, you need to use either a rational or an emotional approach or a combination of the two.
   D.   To satisfy, the audience's _____ (p. 100) needs, you need to make the information easy to grasp.

IV. The third step in planning a business message is establishing the main _____ (p. 101).
   A. One way to come up with a main idea is to use _____ (p. 101) techniques, such as the storyteller's tour, the random list, the FCR worksheet, the journalistic approach, and the question-and-answer chain.
   B. Limit the scope of your message to three or four major points, no matter what the message length.

V. The fourth step in planning a business message is selecting the _____ (p. 104) and the medium.
   A. Use oral communication if your purpose is to collaborate with the audience.
   B. The most common types of written communication used in business are letters, memos, reports, and proposals.
   C. Both oral and written messages can be communicated electronically. For instance, oral messages can be sent via voice mail, _____ (p. 109), or videotape. Written messages can be sent via fax, e-mail, or computer conferencing.

Check your answers at the end of this chapter.

Quiz Yourself

1. What are the three main steps involved in preparing business messages?

2. List at least two advantages of collaborative writing.

3. What are the three general purposes common to business communication?

4. What four questions should you ask yourself to test your purpose?

5. What five steps can you take to develop an audience profile?

6. When trying to satisfy your audience's information needs, what five steps should you take?

7. What steps can you take to make a long oral message easier for an audience to grasp?

8. What is the difference between the topic of a message and the main idea of a message?

9. List and briefly describe five brainstorming techniques.

10. List five situations in which an oral message would be more appropriate than a written one.

Check your answers at the end of this chapter.

Build Your Skills: Developing Audience Profiles

For each of the following communication situations, develop an audience profile (probable size and composition, probable reaction to the message, likely level of understanding):

a) A speech to seniors at a large downtown high school about careers in accounting
b) A speech to business majors at a large university about careers in accounting
c) A letter to all persons who bought a Mercedes in Palm Springs, Florida last month, urging them to purchase a service contract
d) A letter to all persons who bought a television set at a discount TV warehouse in Hamilton, Ontario last month, urging them to purchase a service contract

Develop Your Word Power

Spelling Challenge   Identify the misspelled word in each of the following sentences, and spell it correctly in the space provided. If all the words in a sentence are spelled correctly, write *C* in the space.

_____1. How large is the balance in my account?

_____2. The applicant was an outstanding athelete in high school.

_____3. Would you please handle the arangements for the open house?

_____4. Mr. Blevins apreciates loyalty.

_____5. There were no apparent cracks in the housing.

_____6. Patrick's carries an extensive line of fine apparrel for men.

_____7. All apllicable equal opportunity laws will be observed during the hiring process.

_____8. Avoid arguements with all customers.

_____9. Her decision was based on the assumtion that Louise is retiring.

_____10. See how well the applicants handle akward encounters.

Vocabulary Challenge   Match the words in the first column with the definitions in the second column.

_____11. blasé   A. obvious

_____12. blatant   B. inclusive

_____13. cogent   C. unimpressed

_____14. comprehensible   D. understandable

_____15. comprehensive   E. to the point

Circle the best definition of the highlighted word in each of the following sentences.

16. They will accept any **bona fide** offer for the company.

      A. high   B. from the loyal   C. genuine

17. Take the criticisms of a **chronic** complainer with a grain of salt.

      A. timely B. grouchy   C. habitual

18. We answer letters in **chronological** order.

      A. customary B. by time   C. haphazard

19. Only the most **circumspect** middle managers should be given a copy of this report.

      A. discreet B. overweight   C. around for a long time

20. The expression "What goes up must come down" is a **cliché**.

      A. puzzle B. trite saying   C. metaphor

Select one of these words to complete each of the following sentences, and write the word in the space provided.

capitulate chide   circumvent   compel   compromise

21. If we insist, they will eventually _____ to our demands.

22. We cannot _____ any employee to contribute to this fund drive.

23. Attendance at that meeting will _____ your reputation for objectivity.

24. You can _____ health and safety regulations for only so long before a serious accident occurs.

25. Do not _____ your employees if they fail to read your mind.

Follow-up Word Study Check your answers at the end of this chapter. In the spaces below, write the words that you spelled or used incorrectly. (Use a separate piece of paper if you missed more than five words.) Then use your dictionary to carefully study the spelling, pronunciation, definition, and history (etymology) of each word. Finally, to help fix the word in your memory, write it in a sentence.

Word   *Sentence*

_____   _____

_____   _____

_____   _____

_____   _____

_____   _____

Check Your Answers

Master Key Concepts

II. purpose
    A. collaborating
    B. specific

III. audience
    A. reaction
    B. informational, accurate
    C. motivational
    D. practical

IV. idea
    A. brainstorming

V. channel
    C. teleconferencing

Quiz Yourself

1. The three main steps in preparing a business message are planning, composing, and revising. (p. 95)

2. Among the advantages of collaborative writing are that it:
    - Brings multiple skills and perspectives to a project
    - Increases productivity
    - Enriches knowledge
    - Enhances personal relationships (p. 95)

3. The three general purposes of messages are to inform, to persuade, and to collaborate. (p. 97)

4. To test your purpose, ask yourself:
    a) Is the purpose realistic?
    b) Is this the right time?
    c) Is the right person delivering the message?
    d) Is the purpose acceptable to the organization? (pp. 97-98)

5. When developing an audience profile,
    a) Determine the size and composition of the audience?
    b) Identify the primary audience?
    c) Estimate the audience's probable response?
    d) Gauge the audience's level of understanding?
    e) Define your relationship with the audience? (p. 98)

6. The steps you need to take to satisfy the audience's information needs are:
    a) Find out what the audience needs to know.
    b) Anticipate unstated questions.
    c) Provide all the required information.
    d) Be sure the information is accurate.
    e) Emphasize ideas of greatest interest to the audience. (p. 99)

7. Among the steps you can take to make a long oral message acceptable are
    a) Give your listeners an overview of the structure of the message.
    b) Express your thoughts clearly and logically.
    c) Use flip charts, slides, or handouts to highlight key points.
    d) Lead your audience through your message. (p. 101)

8. The topic is the broad subject of the message, such as "Barbie's image." The main idea makes a statement about the topic that provides a rationale and explains the purpose of the message in terms the audience can accept, such as "Barbie's careers have made the character a more rounded person." (p. 101)

9. Brainstorming techniques include:
   - Storyteller's tour-talking into a tape recorder, pretending you are giving an overview of your message to someone you run into on the street
   - Random list-making a list of everything that pops into your head pertaining to your message
   - FCR worksheet-dividing a sheet of paper into three columns, one each for findings, conclusions, and recommendations
   - Journalistic approach-answering the questions of who, what, when, where, why, and how
   - Question-and-answer chain-following a chain of questions your audience might ask and coming up with replies for them (pp. 101-102)

10. An oral message is more appropriate when:
    - You want immediate feedback from your audience.
    - Your message is relatively simple and easy to accept.
    - You do not need a permanent record.
    - You can assemble the audience conveniently and economically.
    - You want to encourage interaction to solve a problem or reach a decision. (p. 105)

Build Your Skills: Developing Audience Profiles

Here are the audience profiles requested:

a) The audience would be made up of 400 to 500 teenagers, probably of mixed origins, both male and female. Although many would be interested in hearing about careers, most would not be very interested in accounting. The level of understanding would be low for many, although some might have a basic grasp of the topic from high school accounting classes.

b) The audience would be made up of perhaps several hundred men and women of various ages and backgrounds. As business majors, most would probably be interested in the topic, and their level of understanding would be high.

c) The audience would be small but affluent, consisting primarily of older (retired) men and women. Receptivity to the message would probably vary, and level of understanding would be medium to high.

d) The audience would be large and diverse, perhaps with a preponderance of blue-collar families. Receptivity and understanding would both vary greatly.

Develop Your Word Power

1. *C*	6. apparel	11. C	16. C	21. capitulate
2. athlete	7. applicable	12. A	17. C	22. compel
3. arrangements	8. arguments	13. E	18. B	23. compromise
4. appreciates	9. assumption	14. D	19. A	24. circumvent
5. *C*	10. awkward	15. B	20. B	25. chide

Chapter 6
Composing Business Messages

The main point of Chapter 6 is that any message has more impact when the facts and ideas have been carefully organized. As you read the chapter, think about the various purposes of business messages and the organizational patterns that are most effective for each purpose. When you finish reading, see whether you can classify the business messages you receive according to their organizational patterns.

Master Key Concepts

Use the following terms to fill in the blanks in the outline. All terms are used, but none is used more than once.

company	evidence	polite	tone
credibility	goodwill	positive	understand
direct	indirect	purpose	*"you"*
disorganized	outline	sequence	

I. Good organization is a hallmark of good communication.
    A. Messages seem _____ (p. 117) when the sender takes too long to get to the point, includes irrelevant information, gets ideas mixed up, or leaves out necessary information.
    B. Good organization can be achieved by ensuring that the subject and _____ (p. 117) are clear, relating all information in the message to the subject and purpose, grouping ideas in a logical way, and including all necessary information.
    C. Good organization is important because it helps the audience _____ (pp. 118-119) the message, helps the audience accept the message, saves the audience's time, and simplifies the communicator's job.

II. Good organization is a two-step process: defining and grouping the ideas, and establishing the _____ (p. 119-122) of ideas through organizational patterns.
    A. An _____ (p. 119) is a systematic way of grouping ideas; an organization chart can also be used to identify the main idea, the major points, and the supporting _____ (p. 121).
    B. There are two approaches for sequencing the main ideas in a message: _____ (p. 122), in which the main idea is placed first and followed by the evidence, and _____ (p. 122), in which the evidence is first and the main idea is later.
    C. The four basic plans for short messages are those for direct requests; routine, good-news, or _____ (p. 122) messages; bad-news messages; and persuasive messages.
    D. Longer messages may follow an informational or analytical pattern, depending on the purpose of the message.

III. When preparing the first draft of a message, try to establish the appropriate style and tone, depending on the nature of your message and your relationship with the reader.
    A. The first step toward getting the right _____ (pp. 128-129) is to think about the relationship you want to establish with your audience.
    B. Project the _____ (p. 129) attitude by talking in terms of the audience's interests and referring when possible to the audience instead of yourself.
    C. Emphasize the _____ (p. 129) by focusing on opportunities for improvement instead of criticizing or trying to assess blame.

D. Establish your _____ (p. 129) by showing that you understand the other person's situation, are competent, can back up your claims with evidence, and are confident.

E. The best tone for business messages is almost always a _____ (p. 135) one.

F. In addition to writing for the reader, you are also writing for the _____ (p. 136), so be sure that your words are acceptable to the organization and that your style is compatible with the image it wants to project.

Check your answers at the end of this chapter.

Quiz Yourself

1. What are four common sources of disorganization in business communication?

2. What are the four basic advantages of a well-organized document?

3. List six types of details that can be used to present evidence in a report.

4. Describe the four basic types of letters, memos, and other brief messages and explain how the audience is likely to react to each. Which basic organizational approach (direct or indirect) is best for each?

5. What is the best way to begin a bad-news message?

6. How does the choice of organizational pattern for a longer message relate to the purpose?

7. What are five specific things to avoid if you want to establish a businesslike tone?

8. Name five specific things you can do to emphasize the positive aspects of your message.

9. List four ways you can exhibit courtesy in business communications.

10. Discuss what it means to "write for the company."

Check your answers at the end of this chapter.

Build Your Skills: How Should These Messages Be Organized?

For each of the messages described below, select one of the following four organizational plans:

a) Direct approach for direct requests
b) Direct approach for routine or good-news messages
c) Indirect approach for bad-news messages
d) Indirect approach for persuasive messages

Here are the situations that require some sort of communication. How should each message be organized?

1. You are the manager of a restaurant. A disgruntled customer has complained about the slow service at dinner on a recent evening. You are assuring the customer that you are concerned about the complaint and have taken appropriate action.
2. You are a market-research analyst who has been assigned to study the hospital-products industry. You are asking hospital administrators to allow you to interview them.
3. You are a buyer for a large department store. You are complaining to one of your suppliers about the quality of the last shipment of merchandise you received.
4. You're a stock broker, and you have recently moved from one brokerage firm to another. You are letting your clients know of the change and encouraging them to continue doing business with you at your new firm.
5. You have opened a gift store in a new shopping mall. Because your initial sales have been below expectations, you are unable to pay your rent on time. You are asking the shopping-center owner for an extension.
6. As the shipping clerk for a building-supply company, you are informing a customer that her order has been received and that her merchandise is being shipped according to her instructions.
7. You are making arrangements with a resort hotel for your firm's annual sales convention.
8. You have been asked to speak at a luncheon meeting of a professional association, but you are unable to accept and are declining the invitation.

Develop Your Word Power

Spelling Challenge   Identify the misspelled word in each of the following sentences, and spell it correctly in the space provided. If all the words in a sentence are spelled correctly, write *C* in the space.

_____1.   The problem is basicly one of quality.

_____2.   Please send a broshure on your kitchen lighting fixtures.

_____3.   We can make your bisness more profitable.

_____4.   Mark January 15 on your calender.

_____5.   When you practice your speech, strive to make it believeable.

_____6.   Schedule a meeting to unveil the new advertising campain.

_____7.   He has 12 years' experience as a bookeeper.

_____8.   Jason has a strong belief in himself.

_____9.   Another course in personnel management would be benefical.

_____10.   How have you benefited from the program?

Vocabulary Challenge Match the words in the first column with the definitions in the second column.

_____11. concede   A.   to approve

_____12. concur   B.   to squeeze

_____13. condone   C.   to discuss

_____14. confer   D.   to agree

_____15. constrict   E.   to admit

Circle the best definition of the highlighted word in each of the following sentences.

16. This job requires the ability to **conceptualize.**

     A. form a mental image   B. agree with others   C. convince others

17. Annette has **concocted** another excuse for skipping the meeting.

     A. conspired   B. rejected   C. devised

18. Ms. Buracond will serve as the **conduit** for all suggestions from the staff.

     A. recorder   B. judge   C. channel

19. **Conjecture** about Dr. Drandall's successor is premature.

     A. gossip   B. uninformed guesses   C. strong feeling

20. He is a **consummate** speaker and much in demand.

     A. superb   B. exciting   C. bawdy

Select one of these words to complete each of the following sentences, and write the word in the space provided.

compulsive   **compulsory**   **concise**   **conducive**   **contemporary**

21. I will need only five minutes to present a _____ overview of the year's accomplishments.

22. The _____ family consists of two breadwinners and one or two children.

23. Attendance at Monday's staff meeting is _____ for all clerks.

24. Brian has _____ need to correct everyone's grammar.

25. A supportive atmosphere is _____ to creativity and initiative.

Follow-up Word Study Check your answers at the end of this chapter. In the spaces below, write the words that you spelled or used incorrectly. (Use a separate piece of paper if you missed more than five words.) Then use your dictionary to carefully study the spelling, pronunciation, definition, and history (etymology) of each word. Finally, to help fix the word in your memory, write it in a sentence.

Word   *Sentence*

_____   _____

_____   _____

_____   _____

_____   _____

_____   _____

Check Your Answers

Master Key Concepts

I. A. disorganized
    B. purpose
    C. understand

II. sequence
    A. outline, evidence
    B. direct, indirect
    C. goodwill

III. A. tone
     B. "you"
     C. positive
     D. credibility
     E. polite
     F. company

Quiz Yourself

1. Business writing seems disorganized when the writer:
    a) Takes too long to get to the point
    b) Includes irrelevant material
    c) Groups ideas in a confusing way
    d) Leaves out necessary information (p. 117)

2. A well-organized document:
    a) Helps the audience understand the message
    b) Helps the audience accept the message
    c) Saves the audience time
    d) Simplifies the communicator's job (p. 119)

3. Type of details that can be used to present evidence in a report include:
    a) Facts and figures
    b) Examples or illustrations
    c) Description
    d) Narration
    e) Reference to authority
    f) Visual aids (p. 123)

4. Here are the four most common types of brief messages, the reader's most likely reaction to each, and the best organizational approach for each:
    a) A direct request is a simple, routine inquiry. The recipient is likely to be interested and willing. Use the direct approach.
    b) A routine, good-news, or goodwill message provides basic, everyday information. The audience is likely to be neutral, interested, or pleased. Use the direct approach.
    c) A bad-news message conveys disappointing information. The audience is likely to be displeased. Use the direct approach.
    d) A persuasive message asks the audience to do something that will benefit the sender. The audience may be uninterested in complying or unwilling to comply. Use the indirect approach. (pp. 124-126)

5. Begin a bad-news message by putting the sincere explanation before the refusal to focus attention on your reasons. (p. 126)

6. When the purpose of a long message is to inform, the major points are based on a natural order, with the main idea presented first and then the subtopics. When the purpose of a long message is to persuade or collaborate, the organizational pattern should be analytical, focusing either on the conclusions and recommendations or on logical arguments. (p. 126)

7. To achieve a businesslike tone:
    a) Don't be too familiar.
    b) Don't be excessive in your use of humor.
    c) Don't flatter the audience.
    d) Don't preach to the audience.
    e) Don't brag. (p. 130)

8. To emphasize the positive aspects of your message:
    a) Stress what is or will be, not what isn't or won't be.
    b) In offering criticism or advice, emphasize what the other person can do to improve.
    c) Point out how the reader will benefit from your message.
    d) Avoid words with negative connotations.
    e) Avoid superlatives and exaggerations. (pp. 132-133)

9. You can demonstrate your courtesy in the following ways:
    a) Use tactful language rather than blunt terms.
    b) Adjust your language so it is appropriate to the relationship between you and the reader.
    c) Do or say something special to demonstrate your person interest in the reader.
    d) Be prompt in your correspondence. (pp. 135-136)

10. Writing for the company means that you must handle your correspondence in a way that is compatible with the interests and style of the organization. Your own personality and views should be adjusted to project an image that is acceptable to the company, and your way of expressing yourself should conform to the company's wishes. (p. 135)

Build Your Skills: How Should These Messages Be Organized?

The messages should be organized as follows:

1. b (direct approach for routine or good-news messages)
2. a (direct approach for direct requests)
3. c (indirect approach for bad-news messages)
4. d (indirect approach for persuasive messages)
5. d
6. b
7. a
8. c

Develop Your Word Power

1. basically	6. campaign	11. E	16. A	21. concise
2. brochure	7. bookkeeper	12. D	17. C	22. contemporary
3. business	8. *C*	13. A	18. C	23. compulsory
4. calendar	9. beneficial	14. C	19. B	24. compulsive
5. believable	10. *C*	15. B	20. A	25. conducive`

Chapter 7
Revising Business Messages

The main point of Chapter 7 is that making an effort to revise and refine your messages helps your audience understand what you mean, in exactly the way you mean it. As you read the chapter, think about the ways the readability of your message is affected by word choice, sentence construction, paragraph development, design decisions, and accuracy of mechanics. When you finish reading, analyze the weaknesses in your own writing style and develop an approach to revising your written messages.

Master Key Concepts

Use the following terms to fill in the blanks in the outline. All terms are used, but none is used more than once.

beginning	ending	obsolete	transitional
classification	functional	predicate	verbs
compound	illustration	pronoun	white space
content	modifiers	proofreading	
dependent	nouns	topic	

I.   When revising your document, plan to go over it three times: once for content and organization, once for style and readability, and once for mechanics and format.
   A.   When editing for content and organization, see what might be added or cut, and pay special attention to the _____ and the _____ (p. 148).
   B.   When editing for style and readability, check your vocabulary and sentence structure, and apply a readability formula if necessary.
   C.   When editing for mechanics and format, check for errors in grammar, spelling, and punctuation, and make sure the proper format has been followed consistently.

II.   The best words to use are those that are both correct and effective.
   A.   _____ (p. 151) words (conjunctions, prepositions, articles, and pronouns) are used to express relationships; _____ (p. 151) words (nouns, verbs, adjectives, and adverbs) — whether connotative or denotative, concrete or abstract—carry content.
   B.   In business writing, the best words to use are those that are strong (meaning _____) and _____ (pp. 152-153), familiar, short, and uncamouflaged by unneeded suffixes.
   C.   Avoid biased language that might offend the audience.

III.   Words do not achieve their full meaning until they are assembled into sentences, which must have a least a subject (noun or pronoun) and a _____ (p. 157).
   A.   Effective writing mixes the three types of sentences: simple, consisting of one subject-predicate set; _____ (p. 158), consisting of two or more independent clauses joined by such words as *and, but,* or *or;* and complex, consisting of one main independent clause and a _____ (p. 158) clause, which cannot stand alone.
   B.   The most readable writing has many short sentences, is in the active voice, has no unnecessary words or phrases, avoids _____ (p. 161) and pompous language, takes a moderate tone, and does not string together sentences that should be separate. It makes firm statements whenever possible instead of hedging, minimizes indefinite _____ (p. 162) starters, expresses parallel ideas in parallel form, reduces awkward pointers to a minimum, eliminates dangling _____ (p. 163),

44

avoids long sequences of nouns, keeps subject and predicate close together, and emphasizes key thoughts.

IV. A paragraph is a series of sentences related to a single thought.
    A. The typical paragraph consists of a _____ (p. 165) sentence, related sentences that develop the topic, and _____ (p. 166) words and phrases.
    B. Of the many ways paragraphs can be developed, these five are most common: by _____ (p. 166), by comparison or contrast, by discussion of cause and effect, by _____ (p. 167), and by discussion of problem and solution.
    C. Paragraphs are most effective when they stick to one point, are relatively short (about 100 words), and are varied in structure and length.

V. When producing documents, follow basic design principles to help readers comprehend your message.
    A. Use _____ (p. 169) to provide contrast and give readers a resting point. Other design elements that deserve attention are margins and line justification, headings and captions, typeface, and type style, such as boldface or italics.
    B. For effective design, pay attention to consistency, balance, restraint, and detail.
    C. The final stage in producing your document is _____ (p. 173), ensuring that it is letter perfect.

Check your answers at the end of this chapter.

Quiz Yourself

1. What is the Fog Index, and how is it calculated?

2. What is the difference between a word's connotative meaning and its denotative meaning?

3. What is a camouflaged verb?

4. What types of biased language should writers be on the lookout for?

5. Explain what active voice is.

6. What is a hedging sentence?

7. Give an example of a dangling modifier.

8. What is a paragraph?

9. Identify five of the most common ways that paragraphs can be developed.

10. List five design elements you should pay attention to when producing longer documents.

Check your answers at the end of this chapter.

Build Your Skills: Eliminate The Legalese, Please

The following excerpt from a standard contract issued by a moving and storage company is replete with legal terms. Try your hand at rewriting this passage in plain English:

No liability shall be provided for the mechanical or electrical derangements of pianos, radios, phonographs, clocks, refrigerators, television sets, automatic washers, or other instruments or appliances unless evidence is provided of external damage to such equipment, or unless said articles or appliances are serviced as provided in subparagraph (1) below. The carrier reserves the right to inspect these articles or appliances to determine whether they are in good working order before accepting them for shipment. Carrier assumes no liability whatsoever for returning, refocusing, or other adjustments of television sets unless such services were made necessary due to carrier's negligence.

1. Upon request of shipper, owner, or consignee of the goods, carrier will, subject to the provisions of subparagraph (2) below, service and unservice such articles as stoves, automatic washers, and dryers at origin and destination. Such servicing does not include removal or installation of articles secured to the premises or plumbing, electrical, or carpentry services necessary to disconnect, remove, connect, and install such articles and appliances.

2. If carrier does not possess the qualified personnel to properly service and unservice such articles or appliances, carrier, upon request of shipper or consignee or as agent for them, shall engage third persons to perform the servicing and unservicing. When third persons are engaged by the carrier to perform any service, the carrier will not assume responsibility for their activities or conduct; amount of their charges; nor the quality or quantity of service furnished.

Build Your Skills: Can This Letter Be Improved?

This letter from a bank manager is designed to interest customers in opening an Registered Retirement Savings Plan (RRSP) with the bank. Rewrite the letter so that it has stronger words, more effective sentences, and more coherent paragraphs.

Dear Valued Customer:

As a highly esteemed and valued customer of this financial establishment, I know that you appreciate it whenever we are able to offer you an opportunity to earn a higher return on your financial investments. For this reason, I would like to inform you of the benefits that can be obtained by making an investment in an Registered Retirement Savings Plan (RRSP) with Canada Trust.

It is possible to move closer to achieving your financial goals by opening an RRSP, which enables you to obtain the protection of your income dollars from taxes, while at the same time giving you earnings growth and a cushion of financial comfort for impending retirement years.

The mechanism that affords you this valuable opportunity is simple. The full amount of your financial contribution to your RRSP in a given tax year can be deducted from your taxable income in that year. In addition, the interest earned on your investment accumulates on a tax-exempt basis until such time as you withdraw it after your retirement. At the time of your retirement, most people who rely on earnings for the bulk of their working years are in a lower tax bracket. Hence, the interest earned on the RRSP, as well as the principal withdrawn, are taxed at a lower rate than they would have been had they been declared as income during the wage-earning years.

We at Canada Trust are able to offer your RRSP terms that are attractive. For example, did you know that you are allowed to invest up to 18 percent of your annual earned income to a maximum of $13,500, whichever is higher, in an RRSP? However, if you belong to a company pension plan or a defered profit sharing plan, your maximum will be lower.

Opening an RRSP at Canada Trust is truly easy. If you must make a withdrawal before retirement, the amount you withdraw will be subject to income tax; however, this does not apply if the withdrawal of funds is necessitated by death or by permanent disability.

Just complete the enclosed document at your earliest convenience and return it to me, the undersigned. By taking a few moments to complete the enclosure at this time, you will make your retirement appreciably more secure and vastly more comfortable in the long run. Isn't it worth it?

Do not delay! Act now!

Very truly yours,

Jocelyn Burkhardt

Develop Your Word Power

Spelling Challenge Identify the misspelled word in each of the following sentences, and spell it correctly in the space provided. If all the words in a sentence are spelled correctly, write *C* in the space.

_____   1.   How many commitee members are from Purchasing?

_____   2.   Add the colum of figures twice to make sure the total is right.

_____   3.   Mr. Nguyen's choise is the brown chair.

_____   4.   All your purchases are chargible when you have King credit.

_____   5.   He is certanly going to ask for a raise.

_____   6.   I would put it in the business category.

_____   7.   Current conditions are very changable.

_____   8.   Quality products are not cheep!

_____   9. A new office manager has already been choisen.

_____   10. I turned over all my comercial accounts to Suzanne.

Vocabulary Challenge Match the words in the first column with the definitions in the second column.

_____   11. conviction A. believability

_____   12. credence   B. formal introduction

_____   13. credential   C. standard of judgment

_____   14. criterion   D. evidence of authority

_____   15. debut   E. fixed belief

Circle the best definition of the highlighted word in each of the following sentences.

16. Melissa **contends** that none of the sites is acceptable.

    A. believes   B. asserts   C. suggests

17. See whether you can hold your **contentious** staff together long enough to finish the project.

    A. quarrelsome   B. prize-winning   C. unmotivated

18. Paul's conclusions were **contradictory**.

    A. stubborn   B. inconsistent   C. unacceptable

19. The jute pad was installed **contrary** to our wishes.

    A. in accordance with   B. beyond   C. against

20. You have bought a **counterfeit** microchip that we did not produce.

    A. ready-made   B. fake   C. printed

Select one of these words to complete each of the following sentences, and write the word in the space provided.

    continual   **continuous**   **credible**   **creditable**   **cursory**

21. The _____ roar of the air conditioners drowns out casual conversations.

22. The district attorney cannot prosecute unless a _____ witness is found.

23. A _____ reading of the letter yielded no new information, so she reread it.

24. The team's fans formed a _____ line in front of the stadium, forcing delivery crews to detour.

25. Considering your lack of experience, you have done a _____ job.

Follow-up Word Study Check your answers at the end of this chapter. In the spaces below, write the words that you spelled or used incorrectly. (Use a separate piece of paper if you missed more than five words.) Then use your dictionary to carefully study the spelling, pronunciation, definition, and history (etymology) of each word. Finally, to help fix the word in your memory, write it in a sentence.

Word   Sentence

_____   _____

_____   _____

_____   _____

_____   _____

_____   _____

Check Your Answers

Master Key Concepts

I. A. beginning, ending

II. A. functional, content
    B. nouns, verbs

III. predicate
    A. compound, dependent
    B. obsolete, pronoun, modifiers

IV. A. topic, transitional
    B. illustration, classification

V. A. white space
    C. proofreading

Quiz Yourself

1. The Fog Index measures the readability of a document. To calculate the Fog Index, choose several 100-word writing samples. For each sample, count the number of words in each sentence, the number of sentences, and the number of words with three or more syllables. Calculate the average number of words per sentence and the percentage of words with three or more syllables. Add these two numbers, and then multiply by 0.4. The resulting number is the Fog Index. For a general business audience, a level of 8 to 11 is about right. (p. 149)

2. The denotative meaning of a word is its dictionary definition; the connotative meaning includes the associations and feelings evoked by the word. (p. 152)

3. A camouflaged verb is a verb that has been changed into a noun or adjective by adding suffixes such as -*ion, -tion, -lng, -ment, -ence,* and so on. (p. 153)

4. Writers should look for potential cultural bias, gender bias, racial and ethnic bias, age bias, and disability bias. (pp. 154-156)

5. The active voice places the subject of a sentence before the verb, and the object of the sentence follows it. Active voice produces shorter, stronger sentences than passive voice. (pp. 159-160)

6. A hedging sentence is one that tries too hard to avoid stating a judgment as a fact. Hedging sentences frequently include words like *may* and *seem.* (p. 162)

7. Here are some examples of dangling modifiers-phrases with no real connection to the subject of the sentence:
    *   Walking to the office, a red sports car passed him.
    *   Going down in the elevator, the office seemed to be in a different world.
    *   Working as fast as possible, the budget soon was ready. (pp. 163-164)

8. A paragraph is a cluster of sentences all related to the same general topic. It is a unit of thought. (p. 165)

9. Five of the most common ways to develop a paragraph are
    *   Illustration
    *   Comparison or contrast
    *   Cause and effect
    *   Classification
    *   Problem and solution (pp. 166-168)

10. Design elements you should pay attention to when producing longer documents include
    *   White space
    *   Margins and line justification
    *   Headings and captions
    *   Typefaces
    *   Type styles (pp. 170-171)

Build Your Skills: Eliminate the Legalese, Please!

Here is one possible revision of the contract. Other alternatives might be equally acceptable. The important thing is to simplify the language.

We are not legally responsible for mechanical or electrical adjustments that your electrical appliances or musical instruments might require after the move. For example, you will bear the cost of retuning your piano or readjusting your television set, unless there is clear physical evidence that the item was damaged during the move because of negligence on our part. To avoid potential misunderstandings, we may inspect your appliances before the move to see whether they are working properly. Items that may be inspected include pianos, radios, phonographs, clocks, refrigerators, television sets, automatic washers, and other instruments and appliances.

The company does accept financial responsibility for problems that may result when we disconnect and reconnect appliances at the old and new locations, provided that you or your legal representative has authorized us to handle the procedure. If our employees are unable to connect or disconnect your appliances, we will—at your request—employ someone qualified to do this work; however, we will not assume legal responsibility for his or her actions. In addition, we will not undertake, or be responsible for, any permanent alterations involving carpentry, plumbing, or electrical work that may be required to accommodate your appliances.

Build Your Skills: Can This Letter Be Improved?

This letter can be improved in many ways. Here is one version that eliminates some of the obvious flaws:

Dear Friend:

If you are looking for an opportunity to make your money work harder, consider opening an Registered Retirement Savings Plan (RRSP) with Canada Trust.

An RRSP allows you to achieve two important goals: sheltering current income from taxes and building a nest egg for retirement. Every year, you can deduct the full amount of your RRSP contribution from your taxable income. You also pay no taxes on the interest earned until you withdraw your funds after retirement— when you'll probably be in a lower tax bracket.

With an Canada Trust RRSP, you can invest up to 18 percent to your annual earned income or a maximum of $13,500. However, if you belong to a company pension plan or a deferred profit sharing plan, your maximum will be lower.

"But," you may be wondering, "what if I need the money for an emergency before I retire? Can I get my money out?" The answer is yes. But if you make a withdrawal before you retire, the amount you withdraw is subject to an income tax. No tax is applied, however, if the withdrawal follows the death or permanent disability of the depositor.

Opening an RRSP with Canada Trust is easy! Just complete the enclosed document, and mail it to me in the postage-paid envelope. A few seconds spent now will reduce your current tax burden and make your retirement more secure.

Sincerely,

Jocelyn Burkhardt

Develop Your Word Power

1. committee	6. *C*	11. E	16. B	21. continual
2. column	7. changeable	12. A	17. A	22. credible
3. choice	8. cheap	13. D	18. B	23. cursory
4. chargeable	9. chosen	14. C	19. C	24. continuous
5. certainly	10. commercial	15. B	20. B	25. creditable

PART THREE
LETTERS, MEMOS, AND OTHER BRIEF MESSAGES

Chapter 8
Writing Direct Requests

The main point of Chapter 6 is that direct requests are most likely to yield the desired result and to leave the desired impression on the audience when they are organized according to the direct plan. As you read the chapter, observe how a single pattern—main idea, explanation, courteous close—can effectively be applied to many situations. When you finish reading, try to apply the direct plan to some of the direct requests that you make.

Master Key Concepts

Use the following terms to fill in the blanks in the outline. All terms are used, but none is used more than once.

adjustment	confident	middle	relevant
advertisement	credit	order	routine
appreciation	direct	purchase	
compensation	memo	recommendation	

I. _____ (p. 181) requests are meant to elicit some action or information from an interested and willing audience.
   A. Begin with a clear statement of the most important question or idea, specifyng the exact nature and scope of your request.
   B. Use the _____ (p. 182) section to explain why you are making the request, couching your explanation in terms that show how the audience will benefit by complying.
   C. Conclude with a courteous expression of _____ (p. 182) and a specific request for action, complete with any time limits that apply.

II. For placing orders, the direct plan takes on many of the characteristics of a well designed order form: an offer to _____ (pp. 184-185) the goods, a complete description of the goods being ordered, a delivery and billing address, payment details, and a courteous close that suggests some future reader benefit.

III. Even a request for _____ (p. 186) information or action may have a significant effect on an organization's relationship with customers, clients, suppliers, and shareholders.
   A. Requests for action from someone within the organization may be written in _____ (p. 186) format but should still make the desired action clear, appealing, and easy.
   B. Requests to other businesses may be in response to an _____ (pp. 189-190) or may simply be inquiries about products.

C. People outside the organization are often asked to do something—attend a meeting, return an information card, endorse a document, confirm an address, supplement information on an order. A brief form letter is sometimes adequate for this purpose.

IV. A request for a minor, matter-of-course claim or _____ (p. 192) may follow the direct plan as long as the tone is positive and unemotional and sufficient detail is provided.
  A. When filing for an adjustment, you must be prepared to back up your request with _____ (p. 192) documents.
  B. If you make a request for an adjustment, you should suggest specific and fair _____ (p. 192).

V. The direct approach is used for routine _____ (pp. 192-193) requests, although a standardized application form is sometimes used by the creditor; in addition, businesses applying for credit should supply a financial statement and perhaps a balance sheet.
  A. A request to buy on credit is sometimes included with a company's first-time _____ (p. 194) for goods.
  B. Adopting a _____ (p. 194) tone and mentioning the probability of future business are good tactics to use when requesting credit in a first-time order.

VI. When requesting a _____ (p. 194) for a job, promotion, scholarship, club membership, or credit card you may also follow the direct plan.

Check your answers at the end of this chapter.

Quiz Yourself

1. When is it most appropriate to use the direct plan for a request?

2. Briefly explain the organizational plan for a direct request.

3. What type of information should be included in the middle section of a direct request?

4. In placing an order for goods, what basic facts should you include?

5. When an inquiry is written in memo format to employees of the company, how should it be organized?

6. List some of the reasons a business might request routine action from customers or other people outside the company.

7.   What type of information could you include to document a claim or a request for adjustment?

8.   What information do businesses supply when applying for credit?

9.   How should a company seeking credit along with its first-time order for goods organize its letter of request?

10.   When writing letters of inquiry about people, what approach should you take?

Check your answers at the end of this chapter.

Build Your Skills: What's Wrong With This Direct Request?

Someone representing the publisher of a free monthly bulletin for educators has drafted this letter. What could he do to make it more effective as a direct request?

May 7, 2001
Mr. Padman Jayaratne
17 Meadow Lane
Bridgewater, NS B4V 7T3

Dear Mr. Jayaratne:

As a reader of *Know-It-Now,* you can take advantage of varied articles on current trends and events in education. Right now we are updating our mailing list; we hope that you'll be able to take time to help us in this important endeavor. It should not be too time consuming.

If we are to keep sending you our publication each month, we must ask you to fill out the enclosed card. Please mail it to us relatively soon.

Sincerely

Jason Bettancourt

Circulation Department
JB/ta

Develop Your Word Power

Spelling Challenge Identify the misspelled word in each of the following sentences, and spell it correctly in the space provided. If all the words in a sentence are spelled correctly, write *C* in the space.

_____   1.   A compitent administrative assistant is an asset to any company.

_____   2.   I cannot conceive of any product that everyone would buy.

_____   3.   Be slow to condem and quick to praise.

_____   4.   Is he concious of how poorly educated he sounds?

_____   5.   Enthusiasm is contageous.

_____   6.   I brought in a sample of their lotion for comparisen.

_____   7.   We are compleatly out of that model but can get another one soon.

_____   8.   How can you concentrate with all this construction going on?

_____   9.   My consciense will not allow me to quit without two weeks' notice.

_____   10. Her work is consistant although not outstanding.

Vocabulary Challenge Match the words in the first column with the definitions in the second column.

_____   11. defer   A. to put off

_____   12. deplete   B. to scatter

_____   13. deride   C. to misrepresent

_____   14. dispel   D. to scoff at

_____   15. distort   E. to decrease

Circle the best definition of the highlighted word in each of the following sentences.
16. Jack is **deft** at data entry.

   A. hard of hearing   B. daffy   C. skillful

17. It is time to edit all the **defunct** policies out of the employee manual.

   A. awkward   B. sanitized   C. extinct

18. My position on opening a branch office is **diametrically** opposed to yours.

   A. in some measure   B. directly   C. firmly

19. It is hard to see the point in a report this **diffuse**.

    A. wordy   B. mild   C. different

20. Her **disdain** for the junior accountants has created ill feeling in the office.

    A. admiration   B. extra work   C. scorn

Select one of these words to complete each of the following sentences, and write the word in the space provided.

demise   dexterity   diagnosis   dilemma   dissonance

21. She was faced with the _____ of resigning or being fired.

22. The _____ with which you closed to deal was admirable.

23. The report is based on Hawkes & Associates' _____ of the company's ills.

24. A workplace characterized by _____ creates stress.

25. The _____ of our department left 20 people scrambling for jobs.

Follow-up Word Study Check your answers at the end of this chapter. In the spaces below, write the words that you spelled or used incorrectly. (Use a separate piece of paper if you missed more than five words.) Then use your dictionary to carefully study the spelling, pronunciation, definition, and history (etymology) of each word. Finally, to help fix the word in your memory, write it in a sentence.

Word   Sentence

_____   _____

_____   _____

_____   _____

_____   _____

_____   _____

Check Your Answers

Master Key Concepts

I.   direct
     B. middle
     C. appreciation

IV. adjustment
     A. relevant
     B. compensation

II. purchase

III. routine
   A. memo
   B. advertisement

V. credit
   A. order
   B. confident

VI. recommendation

Quiz Yourself

1. The direct plan should be used for a request when you can assume that your audience will be interested in what you have to say or at least be willing to cooperate with you. (p. 181)

2. Direct requests have three basic parts:
   a) An opening that states the request or presents the main idea
   b) A middle section that explains the request or idea in more detail so the reader knows how to respond correctly
   c) A cordial closing that clearly states the desired action (p. 182)

3. The middle section of a direct request should include any information that suggests a reader benefit. In addition, this section should cover facts about the subject of your request and your reason for making it. (pp. 182-183)

4. When placing an order for goods, include:
   - The date the order is placed
   - A clear statement that you want to buy the merchandise
   - A complete description of the items you want, including catalog number, quantity, name or brand, color, size, price, and total amount due
   - The address where the goods should be shipped
   - The billing address (if different from the shipping address)
   - The method of shipment desired
   - Payment details (pp. 184-185)

5. Inquiries in memo format follow the same direct plan as a letter. They begin with a statement of the purpose of the inquiry, followed by an explanation of the request and a final reminder of the desired action. (pp. 188-189)

6. Businesses might make a routine request to customers or other outsiders for any of the following reasons:
   - To invite them to attend a meeting
   - To encourage them to return an information card
   - To ask them to endorse a document
   - To request that they confirm their address
   - To ask them to provide additional information about an order (p. 190)

7. To document your claim or request for adjustment, you could send a copy of your canceled cheque, the sales slip or receipt, dated correspondence, a description of the merchandise, and any other relevant document. (p. 192)

8. To obtain credit, businesses supply such information as the company name, the length of time in business, the name of the company's bank, and addresses of businesses where credit has already been established. (pp. 192-193)

9. Since the main idea in this situation is to get permission to buy on credit, the company's letter should open with that request. (p. 192)

10. Use the direct approach when you are writing letters of inquiry. Begin by stating your reason for writing, such as asking for a recommendation. Explain why you are making the request, and close with an expression of appreciation that includes a request for specific action. (p. 194)

Build Your Skills: What's Wrong with This Direct Request?

This request is not an effective piece of business communication because it fails to open with a direct statement. The writer also seems to assume that the reader may not bother to answer, although there is no reason to open the letter on such a negative note. Moreover, the instructions for complying with the request are unclear; a specific response date should be given. It would also be wise to explain whether the reader has to pay her own postage.

Develop Your Word Power

1. competent	6. comparison	11. A	16. C	21. dilemma
2. C	7. completely	12. E	17. C	22. dexterity
3. condemn	8. C	13. D	18. B	23. diagnosis
4. conscious	9. conscience	14. B	19. A	24. dissonance
5. contagious	10. consistent	15. C	20. C	25. demise

Chapter 9
Writing Routine, Good-News, and Goodwill Messages

The main point of Chapter 9 is that the direct plan can be used to organize routine, good-news, and goodwill messages so that you can compose them quickly and accurately. As you read the chapter, think about all the kinds of messages that fall into this category. When you finish reading, think about adding appropriate enclosures, such as resale and sales-promotion material.

Master Key Concepts

Use the following terms to fill in the blanks in the outline. All terms are used, but none is used more than once.

action	condolence	encourage	positive
adjustment	congratulations	goodwill	sales promotion
benefits	details	grudging	
claim	direct	main	

I.   Understanding how _____ (p. 207) messages are organized allows you to compose excellent examples quickly.
  A. By opening with a clear statement of the _____ (p. 208) point, you prepare the reader for the explanation that follows.
  B. The middle and longest section of the message explains the _____ (p. 209) while maintaining the supportive tone established at the beginning.
  C. The final section summarizes the main point, courteously indicates what should happen next, and highlights reader _____ (p. 210).

II. When responding positively to an inquiry, order, or request, use the _____ (p. 210) plan.
  A. When responding to a request for information or _____ (p. 210), remember that how you handle the request will influence your reader's perception of you, your company, and it's products or services.
  B. When you're answering a request and a potential sale is involved, you have an additional goal: to _____ (p. 210) the future sale.

III. When responding favorably to a request of _____ (p. 213), you have the opportunity to build customer loyalty.
  A. When responding to a claim or adjustment request, avoid a _____ (p. 213) tone, and avoid blaming any particular person or division; instead, emphasize that your organization tries to do a good job.
  B. A _____ (p. 214) letter written as a personal answer to a unique situation follows the direct approach when the company is settling the problem according to the customer's request.

IV. Letters approving credit often mark the beginning of a relationship with a customer, so they build goodwill and offer resale or _____ (p. 216) information as well as explain the terms of credit.

V.   Use the direct approach when conveying positive information about people, such as recommendation letters or good news about employment.

VI.   Because directives, instructions, and business summaries are routine messages, they should follow the direct plan.

VII.   Good-news messages about products and operations include letters to customers and press releases.

VIII. A _____ (p. 221) message is a friendly, unexpected note with no direct business purpose; it focuses on the recipient, not the sender.
   A. Letters of _____ (p. 222) tell readers you have noticed their accomplishments and are happy about their success.
   B. Letters of appreciation document the contributions of employees and other business associates.
   C. Letters of _____ (pp. 223-224) help ease the stress of someone who is suffering from health or business problems, or the loss of a loved one.

Check your answers at the end of this chapter.

Quiz Yourself

1. Describe the basic organizational plan for routine, good-news, and goodwill messages.

2. What are the three main goals in replying to a request for information if a potential sale is involved?

3. What are the two main goals in replying to routine requests if no sale is involved?

4. What general impression would you try to convey when responding to claims if your company is at fault?

5. What details should be included in the middle section of a routine approval of a request for credit?

6. What information should be included in a letter of recommendation?

7. What is the difference between directives and instructions?

8. What is the appropriate tone for a goodwill message, and what are some ways of achieving this tone?

9. Discuss what to include and what to avoid when writing letters of condolence.

10. What approach should a company with a limited budget take toward seasonal greetings to customers?

Check your answers at the end of this chapter.

Build Your Skills: What's Wrong With This Good-News Letter?

Someone representing the publisher of mass-market paperbacks has drafted this letter. What could she do to make it more effective as a good-news message?

August 16, 2001
Mr. Fernando Hidalgo
The Readers' Nook Bookstore
1172 Queen's Blvd.
Brandon, MB R7B 4E1

Dear Mr. Hidalgo:

This is in response to your query about advertising expenses and local promotion efforts. Our usual policy is to share advertising expenses on a 40-60 basis.

Our new line of Unicorn Romances debuts this month. It would be in your best interest to display the entire line in a large rack on the counter by the cash register. We believe that customers will be attracted to our books by a new display. This display features a beam of light bouncing against the ceiling on what look like clouds. It's an expensive display and hard to install, but we believe that it's worth it.

As far as your local promotion efforts go, they should get some assists from our national TV and radio campaign. That's about the best we can offer, although for a short time we will participate in the local efforts you mentioned. Making a rare exception, we will share expenses for this local campaign on a 50-50 basis.

Call us soon to set up the details for this campaign.

Sincerely,

Kathy Walker Reaban

Promotion Director
KWR/opp

Build Your Skills: What's Wrong With This Goodwill Letter?

A representative of a computer company has drafted this letter. What could he do to make it more effective as a goodwill message?

February 18, 2001
Mr. Albert Chan
Chief of Program Design
Interdata Software
1003 Derry Road
Concord, ON L4K 6Y6

Dear Mr. Chan:

This letter is to inform you that the recent reception given by you for our programmers was well received.
They liked Interdata Software and the Speedit Editor, which was developed by you.
You will, I trust, accept our appreciation for this assistance.

Cordially yours,

Gerald MacKenzie

Vice-President, Systems
GMK/bn

Develop Your Word Power

Spelling Challenge Identify the misspelled word in each of the following sentences, and spell it correctly in the space provided. If all the words in a sentence are spelled correctly, write *C* in the space.

_____   1. How well do your figures corellate with theirs?

_____   2. A curteous attitude helps maintain goodwill.

_____   3. Their debt may exceed their ability to repay.

_____   4. Do not be decieved by their expressions of friendship.

_____   5. With prior permission, you can conduct a controled burn.

_____   6. When you finish today's correspondance, file these.

_____   7. He gets angry whenever he hears any critisism.

_____   8. All final desicions on marketing are made by Beth Bryant.

_____   9. Please make an appointment for a time convenent to you.

_____   10. I will take complete responsibility for any dificiency.

Vocabulary Challenge Match the words in the first column with the definitions in the second column.

_____   11. divert   A. to trespass

_____   12. emit   B. to deflect

_____   13. emulate   C. to try to equal or excel

_____   14. encroach   D. to intensify

_____   15. enhance   E. to send forth

Circle the best definition of the highlighted word in each of the following sentences.

16. Investors and farmers should **diversify** to minimize risk.

    A. branch out   B. insure themselves   C. plan

17. The **diversity** of the audience made analysis of their needs difficult.

    A. restlessness   B. hostility   C. variety

18. First impressions are sometimes **erroneous**.

    A. stimulating   B. incorrect   C. superficial

19. Pick's **elan** is an asset to his sales career.

    A. dash   B. luxury automobile   C. good looks

20. The office staff turned out **en masse** to wish her good luck in her new job.

    A. in a party mood   B. after work   C. as a group

Select one of these words to complete each of the following sentences, and write the word in the space provided.

divisive   dogmatic   dynamic   effective   eloquent

21. Jane's _____ , energetic presentation generated enthusiasm for the new selling season.

22. The federation's _____ appeal conveyed powerful images of human suffering.

23. Try to avoid being _____ in meetings; let others share their opinions too.

24. Promoting from within is sometimes_____ but sometimes beneficial.

25. Terry Lee's group is well known for its _____ , results-oriented approach.

Follow-up Word Study Check your answers at the end of this chapter. In the spaces below, write the words that you spelled or used incorrectly. (Use a separate piece of paper if you missed more than five words.) Then use your dictionary to carefully study the spelling, pronunciation, definition, and history (etymology) of each word. Finally, to help fix the word in your memory, write it in a sentence.

Word   Sentence

_____   _____

_____   _____

_____   _____

_____   _____

_____   _____

Check Your Answers

Master Key Concepts

I.   positive
   A.   main
   B.   details
   C.   benefits

II. direct
   A.   action
   B.   encourage

III. adjustment
   A.   grudging
   B.   claim

IV. sales promotion

VIII. goodwill
   A.   congratulations
   C.   condolence

Quiz Yourself

1. The basic organizational plan for routine, good-news, and goodwill messages is to:
    a) Give a clear statement of the main idea
    b) Provide necessary details
    c) Close courteously (pp. 207-208)

2. The three main goals in replying to a request for information if a potential sale is involved are to:
    - Respond to the immediate request
    - Encourage the future sale
    - Convey a good impression of you and your firm (p. 210)

3. The two main goals in replying to a request for information if no sale is involved are to:
    - Respond to the request
    - Leave a favorable impression of your company or foster good working relationships (p. 212)

4. When replying to claims when your company is at fault, try to restore the customer's faith in the firm. Instead of shifting the blame or offering excuses, emphasize the company's efforts to do a good job and imply that the error was unusual. (p. 213)

5. The middle section of a letter approving credit should include a full statement of the credit arrangements, the upper limit of the account, dates that bills are sent, possible arrangements for partial monthly payments, discounts for prompt payments, interest charges for unpaid balances, and due dates. (p. 217)

6. A letter of recommendation should include:
    - The name of the candidate
    - The job or benefit that the candidate is seeking
    - An indication of whether the writer is answering a request or taking the initiative
    - The nature of the relationship between the writer and the candidate
    - Facts relevant to the position or benefit sought
    - The writer's overall evaluation of the candidate's suitability for the job or benefit sought (pp. 217-218)

7. Directives are memos that tell employees *what* to do. Instructions tell people inside and outside the company *how* to do something, and they may take other forms besides memos. (p. 219)

8. Goodwill messages should have a warm, sincere, and friendly tone. To achieve this tone, adopt the "you" attitude, focusing on the audience's feelings and interests rather than on your own. Generally, you should keep the message short and relatively casual. Avoid exaggeration, and back up any compliments with specific points that demonstrate your sincerity: (p. 221)

9. A letter of appreciation may become an important part of an employee's personal file. (p. 222)

10. When writing letters of condolence:
   * Keep reminiscences brief
   * Write in your own words
   * Be tactful
   * Take special care to spell names correctly and to be accurate with your facts
   * Write about special qualities of the deceased
   * Write about special qualities of the bereaved person
   * Don't let fear of saying something wrong keep you from saying anything at all. (p. 223-225)

Build Your Skills: What's Wrong with This Good-News Letter?

The tone of this letter is unfriendly and unenthusiastic. The letter does not succeed in conveying good news and in cultivating a cordial business relationship.

The first sentence is trite and neglects to immediately deliver the good news, which remains buried in later sections of the letter. Nor is the "you" attitude employed.
In the second paragraph, the writer does not show how information about the new display is related to the main point of the letter. Thus this material seems confusing and distracting; in addition, the superior attitude of the writer is annoying. Discussion of price-in this case, the 50-50 split of advertising expenses-should highlight a reader benefit.

The close is hardly courteous and fails to excite the reader about this business deal. Directions for the reader's response should be spelled out in more detail.

Build Your Skills: What's Wrong with This Goodwill Letter?

The tone of the letter tends to be pompous and distant instead of friendly and appreciative. The writer actually thanks the reader for the favor, which is only vaguely described. Nor does the letter highlight the good qualities of the reader. It would be relevant to mention the names of the programmers, if the group was small. Finally, the close should strive to maintain cordial relations by suggesting a lunch date or some other gesture of friendship.

Develop Your Word Power

1. correlate	6. correspondence	11. B	16. A	21. dynamic
2. courteous	7. criticism	12. E	17. C	22. eloquent
3. *C*	8. decisions	13. C	18. B	23. dogmatic
4. deceived	9. convenient	14. A	19. A	24. divisive
5. controlled	10. deficiency	15. D	20. C	25. effective

Chapter 10
Writing Bad-News Messages

The main point of Chapter 10 is that bad-news messages are most likely to be accepted when they follow the indirect plan. As you read the chapter, think about how embedding the bad news within positive buffers helps make it more acceptable. When you finish reading, think about the bad news you have had to convey and how using the indirect approach might have helped ease your task.

Master Key Concepts

Use the following terms to fill in the blanks in the outline. All terms are used, but none is used more than once.

accusing	diplomatic	well disposed	routine
restore	fair	promises	
buffer	indirect	reasons	

I. When presenting bad news, you have three objectives: helping your audience understand that the bad news is a firm decision, helping your audience understand that your decision is _____ (p. 236) and reasonable, and helping your audience remain _____ (p. 236) toward you and your organization.

   A. The indirect plan consists of four parts: a neutral, non-controversial opening called a _____ (p. 236); the reasons supporting the negative decision; a clear and _____ (p. 236)statement of the negative decision; and a positive close that is neither apologetic nor insincere.

   B. The direct plan, which starts with a clear statement of the bad news, may be used when the bad news is _____ (p.242), when you want to convey a forceful message, or when you know that the audience prefers candor.

II. When conveying bad news about an order, try to promote an eventual sale along the lines of the original order, keep instructions and additional information as clear as possible, and keep the customer from losing interest by maintaining a positive tone.

   A. When you must back order an item for a customer, the _____ (p. 243) approach allows you to confirm the original order and bolster the sale before explaining the problem.

III. When conveying negative answers and information, say no clearly, but be sure you fulfill any _____ (pp. 243-244) you make; for this, the indirect plan is usually most effective, although the direct plan may also be used.

   A. If bad news about products or services is routine and will not have an emotional impact on the reader, the direct approach is more efficient; but if the news will seriously affect the reader, it is better to state the _____ (p. 244) before the bad news.

   B. When declining to cooperate with routine requests, you may use either the direct plan or the indirect plan.

   C. In declining invitations and requests for favors, the indirect plan is better for communicating with acquaintances and strangers; the direct plan, for communicating with friends.

IV. When refusing adjustment of claims and complaints, your job is to avoid accepting responsibility and yet avoid blaming or _____ (p. 248) the customer.

V. Refusing to extend credit is always a sensitive matter, so the best approach is to use the indirect plan to soften the bad news. State your reasons as factually and impersonally as possible. Also explain the steps required to _____ (p. 251) credit.

VI. Use the indirect plan for conveying unfavorable news about people--such as refusals to write recommendations, rejection of job applicants, negative performance reviews, and termination notices—because the reader will almost certainly be emotionally involved.

Check your answers at the end of this chapter.

Quiz Yourself

1. What are the four parts of a bad-news letter organized according to the indirect plan?

2. What are the characteristics of an effective buffer?

3. When presenting reasons for your negative decision, what two common evasive tactics should you avoid?

4. What are some of the techniques you might use to end a bad-news letter on a positive note?

5. List your goals when conveying bad news about an order to a customer.

6. Discuss when you should use the direct versus the indirect plan in writing bad-news messages.

7. Briefly explain what your goal should be when writing a refusal to make an adjustment or to honor a complaint.

8. How would you vary a letter refusing to extend credit to two candidates—one with a long record of delinquent payment and one who is just starting out professionally and lacks a sufficient credit history to meet your requirements?

9. Why might an employer refuse to write a recommendation letter for a former employee?

10. How might you give a negative performance review in a positive manner?

Check your answers at the end of this chapter.

Build Your Skills: What's Wrong With This Bad-News Letter?

Someone representing the distributor of lawn-care equipment has drafted this letter. What could he do to make it more effective as a bad-news message?

April 28, 2001
Mr. Eugene Hnatyshen
814 River Road
Saskatoon, SK S7K 1T8

Dear Mr. Hnatyshen:

We regret to inform you that the 22-inch Kleen-Kut mower and grass catcher is unavailable at this time. However, we do expect to receive a shipment of mowers in a short time. When they arrive, we'll send one off to you.

These mowers are excellent products, and we are sorry that you are unable to buy one right away. Please accept our countless apologies for this delay.

While you're waiting for your lawn mower, you might want to flip through our catalog, available at any local hardware store. Or ask us to send you one. At any rate, nearly all of our catalog items are in stock and can usually be ordered easily.

Sincerely,

Fengshan Ma

Customer Relations
FM/eh

Develop Your Word Power

Spelling Challenge Identify the misspelled word in each of the following sentences, and spell it correctly in the space provided. If all the words in a sentence are spelled correctly; write *C* in the space.

_____   1.   The are definetly planning to attend the meeting on the 9th.

_____   2.   We are dependant on a small distributor for supplies of that item.

_____   3.   Our vacation includes a week at one of the most desireable resorts.

_____   4.   You will not be dissappointed with your purchase.

_____   5. The last quarter was disasterous, but sales are improving.

_____   6. I have no dout that Hal will do a good job.

_____   7. After deducting operating expenses, you are left with a defecit.

_____   8. Read the discription of all available modifications on page 3.

_____   9. Every office worker should have access to a dictionery.

_____   10. Our goal is to limit the number of disatisfied customers.

Vocabulary Challenge Match the words in the first column with the definitions in the second column.

_____   11. enumeration   A. front

_____   12. esprit de corps   B. copy

_____   13. extrovert   C. sense of union

_____   14. facade   D. list

_____   15. facsimile   E. outgoing person

Circle the best definition of the highlighted word in each of the following sentences.

16. The most **expedient** course is simply to repackage the unsold items.

   A. speediest   B. least expensive   C. advantageous

17. Gretchen **expended** a lot of energy putting out the first issue of the company newsletter.

   A. spent   B. wasted   C. invested

18. Can we somehow **exploit** our reputation for social responsibility?

   A. publicize   B. take advantage of   C. abuse

19. Her delivery of **extemporaneous** speeches is excellent.

   A. about current events   B. long and complicated   C. with few or no notes

20. His behavior can partially be excused on the basis of **extenuating** circumstances.

   A. a long list of   B. mitigating   C. embarrassing

Select one of these words to complete each of the following sentences, and write the word in the space provided.

equable   **equitable**   **esoteric**   **facetious**   **fallacious**

21. Peter's _____ disposition makes him a pleasure to work with.

22. The staff will prosecute because Royal's solicitors made _____ statements.

23. Leave the more _____ references out of the bibliography for general readers.

24. The attorneys will negotiate _____ solutions to these disputes.

25. A serious meeting is no place for _____ remarks!

Follow-up Word Study Check your answers at the end of this chapter. In the spaces below, write the words that you spelled or used incorrectly. (Use a separate piece of paper if you missed more than five words.) Then use your dictionary to carefully study the spelling, pronunciation, definition, and history (etymology) of each word. Finally, to help fix the word in your memory, write it in a sentence.

Word   Sentence

_____   _____

_____   _____

_____   _____

_____   _____

_____   _____

Check Your Answers

Master Key Concepts

I. fair, well disposed
    A. buffer, diplomatic
    B. routine

II. A. indirect

III. promises
     A. reasons

IV. accusing

V. restore

Quiz Yourself

1. The four parts of a bad-news letter organized according to the indirect plan are:
    a) A buffer
    b) Reasons supporting the negative decision
    c) A clear, diplomatic statement of the negative decision
    d) A helpful, friendly, positive close (p. 236)

2. An effective buffer accomplishes several things:
    *   It starts the message pleasantly with a point agreeable to the reader.
    *   It introduces the subject of the letter.
    *   It expresses neither a yes nor a no.
    *   It provides a smooth transition to the second paragraph. (p. 236)

3. When presenting reasons for your negative decision, try to avoid these evasive tactics:
   - Hiding behind company policy
   - Apologizing needlessly (p. 237)

4. To end a bad-news letter on a positive note:
   - Don't repeat, or apologize for, the bad news
   - Include off-the-subject resale information
   - Be confident about keeping this customer (p. 242)

5. Your goals when conveying bad news about an order to a customer are:
   - To work toward an eventual sale
   - To keep instructions or additional information as clear as possible
   - To maintain an optimistic, confident tone. (p. 243)

6. When composing a negative message, use the direct plan if the reader will not be emotionally involved with your response. However, follow the indirect plan if you believe the reader may react emotionally to your refusal to grant the request. (p. 243)

7. When refusing to make an adjustment or honor a complaint, your objective as a writer is to avoid accepting responsibility for the unfortunate situation and yet avoid blaming or accusing the customer. In the long run, your objective is to retain the customer's goodwill. (p. 248)

8. In refusing credit to an applicant with a record of delinquent payments, you would offer little hope for future credit approvals, whereas you could be more encouraging to someone with little credit history. (p. 250)

9. Many employers refuse to write recommendation letters out of fear of legal hazards, especially if the person's performance has not been satisfactory. (p. 251)

10. Although it is important to make certain your performance evaluation is honest, your goal is to leave the impression that you want the employee to succeed. Mentioning the employee's strong points and suggesting concrete ways for improving performance can help make the review a more positive experience. (pp. 252-253)

Build Your Skills: What's Wrong with This Bad-News Letter?

This letter could squelch the reader's enthusiasm for the product and might prompt him to cancel the order. It fails to provide any specific resale information to sustain the reader's interest, and it opens with a trite expression of bad news. Information about when the mower will be sent is vague and unhelpful. In addition, the last sentence in the third paragraph is overly apologetic. Finally, the close makes only a half-hearted attempt to interest the reader in the company's other products. The letter's overall implication is that this company is unreliable, not always equipped to fill orders.

Develop Your Word Power

1. definitely	6. doubt	11. D	16. C	21. equable
2. dependent	7. deficit	12. C	17. A	22. fallacious
3. desirable	8. description	13. E	18. B	23. esoteric
4. disappointed	9. dictionary.	14. A	19. C	24. equitable
5. disastrous	10. dissatisfied	15. B	20. B	25. facetious

Chapter 11
Writing Persuasive Messages

The main point of Chapter 11 is that persuasive messages require a special form of the indirect plan—attention, interest, desire, action (AIDA)—and particular attention to the needs of the audience. As you read the chapter, think about how reader needs, benefits, and appeals are linked in persuasive messages. When you finish reading, analyze the strengths and weaknesses of some of the persuasive messages you have received and then try improving those that are weak.

Master Key Concepts

Use the following terms to fill in the blanks in the outline. All terms are used; but none is used more than once.

AIDA	consumer	influencing	reminder
benefits	credibility	logic	selling
bounds	embarrassed	notification	ultimatum
collection	highlighting	personal	

I. Persuasion means _____ (p. 265) an audience by informing them and by aiding their understanding. The audience is free to choose.
   A. The task of persuading an audience requires you to understand people's needs, to gain _____ (p. 266), to use language skillfully, and to employ both emotions and _____ (p. 268).
   B. The _____ (p. 271) plan, used specifically for persuasive messages, begins with a statement that grabs the audience's attention, develops interest by stressing how your information benefits the audience, builds desire by providing evidence directly related to your point, and ends by urging some easy, beneficial action.

II. Because the recipient of a persuasive request may receive nothing tangible in return, these letters are particularly difficult to write. Take special care to highlight the direct and indirect _____ (p. 274) of complying with your request.

III. The most important think to remember when preparing a persuasive request for action is to keep your request within _____ (p. 276).

IV. A systematic approach is most useful in writing sales letters.
   A. The steps involved in planning a sales letter include determining the _____ (p. 277) points (most attractive features) and _____ (p. 277) benefits of your product, and planning the format and approach you should take.
   B. The best attention-getter for a sales letter is a hook that gets the reader thinking about the needs your product might be able to fill. Select your central selling point, the single point around which to build your sales message. Emphasize it by _____ (p. 279) it in your heading or opening paragraph. Use it to define benefits to potential buyers, then mention these benefits repeatedly.
   C. Most of the techniques used in writing sales letters can also be applied to fund-raising letters. Because fund-raising letters depend heavily on emotional appeals, you need to keep the message _____ (p. 283)

V. Most people are interested in settling their debts as quickly as possible, but because credit is such an emotional area, _____ (pp. 285-286) messages must be prepared with all the care lavished on other persuasive messages.

A. People who cannot pay their bills generally feel _____ (p. 286). Your job is to neutralize those feelings by using positive appeals, by accentuating the benefits of complying with your request for payment. If that approach doesn't bring results, consider a negative appeal pointing out the consequences of not acting.

B. Collection letters are sent in an escalating sequence of messages, typically beginning with a _____ (p. 287), proceeding to a routine _____ (p. 287), then a more personal inquiry, then a more demanding "urgent notice," and finally a businesslike _____ (p. 288) that avoids malicious or defamatory statements.

Check your answers at the end of this chapter.

Quiz Yourself

1. Discuss the relationship between emotions and logic in the context of a persuasive message.

2. Persuasive writers use many different plans to organize their messages, but the best known is

    the_____ plan, which stands for: _____, _____, _____, and _____.

3. Briefly discuss the contents of the final section of a persuasive message.

4. List three obstacles you must overcome when writing a persuasive request for action.

5. What are some of the legal limitations involved in writing a sales letter?

6. What is the difference between selling points and the consumer benefits?

7. If price is not a major selling point in your sales letter, how might you handle it?

8. What are some techniques that can be used in a sales letter to motivate action?

9. List three mistakes to avoid when composing fund-raising letters.

10. When a customer with an overdue account has not responded to any of the four previous type of collection letters, you may need to issue an ultimatum. What factors should you keep in mind when composing this letter?

Check your answers at the end of this chapter.

Build Your Skills: What's Wrong With This Persuasive Letter?

A business student has drafted this letter. What could she do to make it more effective as a persuasive message?

1061 Acadia Drive SE
Apartment 606
Calgary, AB T2J 0E2
January 10, 2001

Ms. Michelle Jacobs
Jacobs Consulting Agency
2366 Ballard Boulevard, Suite 208
Calgary AB, T2D 9F3

Dear Ms. Jacobs:

Could you please tell me how I might obtain a copy of the results of the study of male executives' attitudes toward female executives? In a recent talk you gave, as you'll probably remember, that study was mentioned. I need this study for a term paper I'm writing. Please send the information to the above address fairly soon. If you know of any other such pertinent data, perhaps you could enclose that as well.

By the way, I really enjoyed your talk. Thanks for all your help.

Sincerely,

Liz Raphael

Develop Your Word Power

Spelling Challenge Identify the misspelled word in each of the following sentences, and spell it correctly in the space provided. If all the words in a sentence are spelled correctly, write *C* in the space.

_____ 1. Please send either a chrome or a brass easel.

_____ 2. Dr. Mueller empasized the importance of good employee relations.

_____ 3. We are equipt to serve all your ecological needs.

_____   4. Yours is the eigth request for a commercial energy audit.

_____   5. BASIC is one of the elementery programming languages.

_____   6. How can we enhance the engineers' envirement?

_____   7. Please elemenate all references to egg salad from the new menu.

_____   8. We have just spent $1 million on new hospital equipment.

_____   9. Their goal is apparently to embarass us at the annual meeting.

_____   10. The emphisis in the brochure should be on elegance and style.

Vocabulary *Challenge* Match the words in the first column with the definitions in the second column.

_____   11. fastidious   A. unprovoked

_____   12. formidable   B. demanding

_____   13. fortuitous   C. supposed

_____   14. gratuitous   D. fortunate

_____   15. hypothetical   E. intimidating

Circle the best definition of the highlighted word in each of the following sentences.

16. The other employees resented her tendency to **flaunt** her promotion.

   A. mock   B. show off   C. be dissatisfied with

17. So far, Ken has **floundered** in his position.

   A. prospered   B. struggled   C. failed

18. If she continues to **flout** the new rules, she will be fired.

   A. openly disobey B. enforce   C. complain about

19. Our efforts to market the new product were **hampered** by a lack of funds.

   A. aided   B. complicated   C. impeded

20. I will not **hinder** your efforts to reorganize the department.

   A. make fun of   B. second-guess   C. obstruct

76 Chapter Checkups

Select one of these words to complete each of the following sentences, and write the word in the space provided.

gaffe   **gamut**   **harangue**   **hyperbole**   **hypertension**

21. The flower seeds we offer run the _____ from alyssum to zinnia.

22. We cannot afford another _____ like the one Barbara committed during the negotiations yesterday.

23. He suffers from _____ and should not work so hard.

24. Your sales letter will be much more convincing if you eliminate some of the _____.

25. The staff is demoralized and should not be subjected to another _____.

Follow-up Word Study Check your answers at the end of this chapter. In the spaces below, write the words that you spelled or used incorrectly. (Use a separate piece of paper if you missed more than five words.) Then use your dictionary to carefully study the spelling, pronunciation, definition, and history (etymology) of each word. Finally, to help fix the word in your memory, write it in a sentence.

Word   Sentence

_____   _____

_____   _____

_____   _____

_____   _____

_____   _____

Check Your Answers

Master Key Concepts

I. influencing
   A. credibility, logic
   B. AIDA

II. benefits

III. bounds

IV. A. selling, consumer
    B. highlighting
    C. personal

V. collection
   A. embarrassed
   B. notification, reminder, ultimatum

Quiz Yourself

1. Emotion works with logic in a unique way. People need to find rational support for an attitude they've already embraced emotionally. To get the best results, persuasive messages often call on both logic and emotion as motivators. (p. 269)

2. Persuasive writers use many different plans to organize their messages, but the best known is the *AIDA* plan: *attention, interest, desire,* and *action.* (p. 271)

3. The final section of a persuasive message is an appeal for a specific action. This section should remind the audience of the benefit of taking the desired action and make the action easy to take. (p. 271)

4. When writing persuasive requests for action you must overcome these obstacles:
   • Such requests reach people who are already busy and are reluctant to reply.
   • These requests usually offer nothing tangible in return.
   • These requests must complete with many others like them (p. 274).

5. Making false statements—such as misrepresenting the price, quality or performance of a product—in a sales letter is considered fraud. Using a person's name, photo, or other identity in a sales letter without permission constitutes invasion of privacy. (pp. 276-277)

6. Selling points are the most attractive features of a product or service. Consumer benefits are the particular advantages that buyers realize from those features. (pp. 279-280)

7. If price is not a major selling point, you might:
   • Leave out the price altogether
   • Only mention the price in the accompanying brochure
   • Bury the price in a paragraph near the end of the letter, after discussing benefits and selling points
   • Break a quantity price into smaller units
   • Compare your product's price with that of some other product or activity. (pp. 281-282)

8. To motivate action in a sales letter, offer an incentive for making an immediate decision. For example, you might guarantee delivery by a certain date or offer a discount for orders received within a certain time period. If there is no particular reason to act quickly, you might provide other incentives:
   • Prizes or special offers for early responses
   • Convenient payment terms
   • Free trial periods
   • Product guarantees
   • Convenient, no-strings request cards for additional information. (p. 282)

9. Mistakes to avoid when composing fund-raising letters include:
   • Letting your letter sound like business communication of any kind
   • Wasting space on warm-up
   • Assuming that your organization's goals are more important than the reader's own concerns (p. 283)

10. Points to remember when you have to compose an ultimatum to a customer:
   • Don't issue an ultimatum unless you intend to back it up, and are well supported by company policy
   • Maintain a polite, businesslike manner, and don't defame harass the creditor
   • Itemize the precise consequences of not paying to encourage debtors to re-evaluate their priorities. (pp. 288-289)

Build Your Skills: What's Wrong With This Persuasive Letter?

This letter asks for a favour, but offers no reason for the recipient to grant it. The writer has not followed the AIDA plan. The letter should begin with a hook—an attention-grabber. There is nothing to arouse the recipient's interest or to inspire a desire to act. The closing comment is trite, and may well be perceived as insincere. The letter fails to use "you" focus, and thus appears to place the writer's priorities ahead of the recipient's.

Develop Your Word Power

1. *C*	6. environment	11. B	16. B	21. gamut
2. emphasized	7. eliminate	12. E	17. B	22. gaffe
3. equipped	8. *C*	13. D	18. A	23. hypertension
4. eighth	9. embarrass	14. A	19. C	24. hyperbole
5. elementary	10. emphasis	15. C	20. C	25. harangue

PART FOUR
REPORTS AND PROPOSALS

Chapter 12
Writing Short Reports

The main point of Chapter 12 is that businesses use many types of short reports and proposals, the purpose of which is reflected in their organization and format. As you read the chapter, think about the way that function influences format. When you finish reading, look for examples of business reports and proposals and try to classify them in the categories outlined in the chapter.

Master Key Concepts

Use the following terms to fill in the blanks in the outline. All terms are used, but none is used more than once.

direct	memo	previews	tailored
indirect	parallel	purpose	transitions
informal	periodic	receptive	
justification	personal activity	resist	

I. Business reports are used for a variety of reasons and travel both up and down an organization's chain of command.
   A. The goal in developing a report is to make the information as clear and convenient as possible.
   B. A report can be _____ (p. 304) according to who originates it, what subject it covers, when it is prepared, where it is sent, why it is prepared, and how _____ (p. 305) the audience is.

II. Your audience, purpose, and subject matter influence the format, length, and basic structure of your report.
   A. A report may be formatted as a preprinted form, a letter, a _____ (p. 308), or a manuscript; the length depends on the subject and purpose and on your relationship with the reader.
   B. When planning the basic structure for your report, you must decide what to include and exclude, whether to introduce ideas in direct or _____ (pp. 308-310) order, and how to subdivide and develop ideas.

III. Choosing an organizational plan for your short report depends on the _____ (p. 310) of the report.
   A. The purpose of informational reports is to explain something in straightforward terms; generally the _____ (p. 310) order is appropriate because the readers are open minded and receptive; the most natural structure is based on subtopics related to the subject matter. Examples include the _____ (p.311) report, which describes what has been accomplished during a particular period, and the _____ (pp. 312-313) report, which describes what occurred during a conference, convention, or trip.

B. The purpose of analytical reports is to convince the reader to accept certain conclusions and recommendations; if the reader will be receptive, the reports are organized to follow the direct plan and focus on conclusions and recommendations. But if the reader will be skeptical or inclined to _____ (p. 314), the reports use an indirect approach that highlights the reasons behind your position. Examples of analytical reports include _____ (p. 314) reports, which are internal proposals used to persuade upper management to approve a project; business plans; and troubleshooting reports.

IV. In addition to deciding on the length, format, and organization of the report, you need to consider a number of other facts.
   A. For brief reports to someone you know well, you can use a relatively _____ (p. 321) style; in formal reports, you should avoid all references to I and *you* and any other language that is individualistic, personal, or "unbusinesslike."
   B. Five tools to help readers navigate longer reports are:
      1. The opening which introduces the subject, explains why it is important, and _____ (p. 323) the main ideas and the order in which they will be covered
      2. Headings and lists help readers scan the report and recognize the relationship among ideas (they should be phrased in _____ (p.324) form)
      3. _____ (pp. 326-327) tie ideas together and keep readers moving along the right track
      4. Previews of complex information, and reviews of important sections
      5. The ending, which ties up all the pieces, reminds readers how they fit together, and (in analytical reports) explicitly states the conclusions and recommendations

Check your answers at the end of this chapter.

Quiz Yourself

1. What should be your main goal in developing a report?

2. What is the main difference between voluntary reports and authorized reports?

3. What are the main advantages of electronic reports over traditional paper reports? What are the disadvantages?

4. What four issues should you consider when establishing the basic structure of a report?

5. Should informational reports be organized in direct or indirect order? Why?

6. What are the two basic ways analytical reports can be organized? When should you use each?

7. What is a business plan, and how is it used?

8. What is the difference between a formal and an informal tone, and when is each appropriate?

9. What three things should the opening of a report accomplish?

10. What functions do headings serve in a report?

Check your answers at the end of this chapter.

Build Your Skills: Can You Analyze These Reports?

Take a look at the four reports outlined below, and then analyze each in terms of these six factors:

a. Who (initiated the report)?
b. What (subject does it cover)?
c. When (is it being prepared)?
d. Where (is it being sent)?
e. Why (is it being prepared)?
f. How (receptive is the reader)?

If the outline does not provide enough information to enable you to make a decision, use your best judgment and common sense to deduce the answer.

Report 1: Instrument Division—Monthly Update

I.   Summary of monthly activities
     A. New orders
     B. Shipments
     C. Profits

II. Sales by produce line
     A. Analytical instruments
        1. New orders
        2. Shipments
     B. Industrial monitoring equipment
        1. New orders
        2. Shipments

C. Audiometers
   1. New orders
   2. Shipments

III. Problems
   A. Design problems with the Omega system
   B. Production delays in liquid scintillation system

IV. Next month's forecast

Report 2: Observations on the Tire Industry in Canada

I. Basic supply-demand characteristics
   A. Dependence on motor vehicle industry
   B. Competition from foreign suppliers
   C. Increasing importance of long-life radials

II. The outlook for tire rubber
   A. Original equipment
   B. Replacement market

III. The outlook for nontire rubber
   A. Basic segments
   B. Five-year forecast
   C. Long-term outlook

IV. Growth opportunities for innovators
   A. Run-flat tires
   B. One-piece integral tires and rims
   C. Twin-tire concept
   D. Liquid-injection molded tires

Report 3: Optimizing the Organization Structure

I. Statement of the problem
   A. Changes in the nature of the company
   B. Need for changes in the company's structure

II. Scope of work
   A. Design of the ideal organizational structure
   B. Implementation of structure over time

III. Issues for analysis
   A. Strengths and weaknesses of current structure
      1. What functions must be performed?
      2. How well does the present organization accommodate these functions?
   B. Centralization versus decentralization

C. Organizational alternatives
    1. Line/staff structure
    2. Functional organization
    3. Project-management organization
    4. Matrix organization
D. Informal organization and corporate "culture"

IV. Methods and procedures
    A. Review of company operations
    B. Interviews with company managers and employees

V. Work plan and schedule
    A. Phase I: Define requirements
    B. Phase II: Analyze alternatives and select optimum structure
    C. Phase III: Implement new structure

V. Qualifications
A. Related experience
B. Staff qualifications

VI. Projected costs

Report 4: Illegal and Improper Activities

Purpose of *policy*

I. Prohibited transactions
    A. Illegal political contributions
    B. Bribes, payoffs, and kickbacks
    C. Violations of customs law
    D. Violation of tax law
    E. Violations of laws of business conduct
        1. Monopolies or unfair competition
        2. Registration of securities
        3. Labor negotiations
    F. Payment of excessive fees or commissions

II. Actions that require approval from top management
    A. Legal political contributions
    B. Payment of extortion
    C. Any action of questionable legality

III. Compliance and enforcement
    A. Disclosure of matters set forth above
    B. Disciplinary actions
        1. Demotion
        2. Termination
        3. Legal action

Build Your Skills: You Be The Editor

The following pages are taken from a report on the international market for home health care. The report was prepared by Jack Williams, a former hospital administrator who is starting a company to provide home-health-care supplies through retail outlets. Williams prepared this report as a means of attracting potential financial backers. He has asked you to critique the report for him and to make any necessary improvements. Here is the introduction of the report, which is intended to give the reader an overview of the market and the role of Jack's proposed company.

The Market for Home Health Care

This is a report on the market for home health care, which is a large and growing market. The world's population is aging. Older people tend to be big healthcare consumers. In fact, people over 65 require twice as much health care as the rest of us.

Western governments, in their divine wisdom, have committed us to paying the medical bills of these old people. But the fact is, we can't really afford to pay the price. National health programs in many countries are rapidly growing broke.

The solution to this problem is to encourage these old folks to stay out of hospitals and nursing homes and get the care they need at home. The cost of caring for a person at home is a fraction of the cost of caring for a person in a nursing home or hospital. For this reason, governments will probably pass laws offering to reimburse people for their home-health-care expenses.

In 1998 the market was $25.2 billion, and I figure that the current market for home-health-care services is a whopping $60 billion. As more and more old folks get their health care at home, they will need equipment such as hospital beds, wheelchairs, walkers, traction devices, pads and cushions, toilet devices, and other nondisposables. Disposable supplies are another big segment, including such items as tapes, dressings, disinfectants, antiseptics, splints, restraints, curettes, adult diapers, diagnostic kits, and the like. A smaller segment of the market consists of sales of nutritional items for people who are unable to eat in the normal way. Finally, the home-health-care services market consists of services such as chemotherapy, kidney dialysis, and respiratory therapy. Each of these segments should keep this market expanding well beyond the turn of the century.

My proposed company would initially be involved in segments I and II above (durable equipment and disposable supplies). I plan to open retail stores that will sell and rent these supplies. The stores will be located in areas with a high concentration of old people, preferably next door to clinics or medical buildings.

The rest of this report explains the need for a company like mine, the strategy I would use to make my operation successful, and the way you can participate in the great home-health-care boom by investing with me.

Develop Your Word Power

Spelling Challenge Identify the misspelled word in each of the following sentences, and spell it correctly in the space provided. If all the words in a sentence are spelled correctly, write *C* in the space.

_____	1. Her poor vocabulary is a hinderance to her career.
_____	2. Those figures are not immedeately available.
_____	3. We could look for someone who is inexperienced but intelegent.
_____	4. Your service will be interrupted on September 7.
_____	5. Can you judge how well we are doing?
_____	6. He is quite knowledgible about data communications.
_____	7. We like to educate ignorant consumers.
_____	8. Since we can choose only two, some disappointment is inevitible.
_____	9. I will try not to interfear with your decisions.
_____	10. At this point, last year's sales figures are irrevelant.

Vocabulary Challenge Match the words in the first column with the definitions in the second column.

_____	11. inveterate	A.	praising
_____	12. judicious	B.	chronic
_____	13. laudable	C.	clear
_____	14. laudatory	D.	praiseworthy
_____	15. lucid	E.	prudent

Circle the best definition of the highlighted word in each of the following sentences.

16. Ms. Jaskowitz refused to **intervene** in the dispute between the two employees.
    A. keep score   B. ignore   C. interfere

17. The television state was **inundated** with letters protesting one of its documentaries.
    A. flooded   B. sued   C. perversely pleased

18. The temporary loss of a liquor license **jeopardizes** the financial health of restaurants.
    A. increases   B. explains   C. imperils

19. Robin thinks the ideal relationship between government and business is **laissez faire**.
    A. noninterference   B. all's fair   C. let the buyer beware

20. You will receive a refund in **lieu** of tickets for Saturday's performance.
    A. payment   B. view   C. place

Select one of these words to complete each of the following sentences, and write the word in the space provided.

interval   **intrigue**   **introvert**   **inverse**   **liaison**

21. The tone will sound after a ten-second _____.

22. 4/3 is the_____ of 3/4.

23. No _____ would eagerly volunteer to host a hospitality suite.

24. Their efforts to take over the company were characterized by much _____.

25. Phil will be the _____ between Marketing and Production.

Follow-up Word Study Check your answers at the end of this chapter. In the spaces below, write the words that you spelled or used incorrectly. (Use a separate piece of paper if you missed more than five words.) Then use your dictionary to carefully study the spelling, pronunciation, definition, and history (etymology) of each word. Finally, to help fix the word in your memory, write it in a sentence.

Word   Sentence

_____   _____

_____   _____

_____   _____

_____   _____

_____   _____

Check Your Answers

Master Key Concepts

I. B. tailored, receptive
II. A. memo
    B. indirect

III. purpose
    A. direct, periodic, personal activity.
    B. resist, justification

IV. A. informal
    B. previews, parallel, transitions

Quiz Yourself

1. Your main goal in developing a report is to make the information as clear and as convenient as possible. (p.304)

2. Voluntary reports, prepared on your own initiative, require more detail and support than authorized reports, which are prepared at the request of another person. (p. 304)

3. The main advantages of electronic reports over paper reports include:
    a) Cost savings
    b) Space savings
    c) Faster distribution
    d) Ability to include multimedia
    e) Easier maintenance

    The disadvantages include:
    a) Hardware and software costs
    b) System compatibility problems
    c) Training needed for readers
    d) Data security and integrity issues (pp. 305-307)

4. Deciding on the structure of a report involves asking yourself four questions:
    a) What basic format and length will the report require?
    b) What information should you include?
    c) Which approach—direct or indirect order—is better?
    d) Which method of organization will make the material both clear and convincing? (pp. 307-310)

5. Informational reports, which are designed to explain something in straightforward terms, are generally presented in direct order. Because informational reports do not attempt to persuade readers of anything, most readers react to informational reports in an unemotional way. For this reason, you do not have to worry about introducing ideas gradually to overcome resistance. (pp. 310-311)

6. Analytical reports can be organized in direct or indirect order. Use the direct order if your reader is likely to agree with you; use the indirect order if your reader is likely to resist. (p. 314)

7. A business plan is an analytical report that documents an organization's overall goals and the methods it will use to achieve those goals. It is used internally to guide operations and provide benchmarks for progress toward goals. It can also be sent to external audiences to gain support and funding for an idea, a project, or a business. (pp. 314-316)

8. An informal tone presumes a closer relationship with the reader than a formal tone does. Reports with an informal tone use personal pronouns (*I* and *you)* and employ conversational language; reports written in a formal tone avoid the use of personal pronouns and of colorful language. They attempt to establish a businesslike, unemotional, objective relationship between the writer and the reader.
An informal tone is generally appropriate for brief, internal documents. A formal tone is often adopted for longer reports dealing with controversial or complex information, particularly if the audience consists of outsiders. (pp. 321-322)

9. The opening of a report should accomplish these three things:
   a) Introduce the subject of the report
   b) Indicate why the subject is important
   c) Give the reader a preview of the main ideas and their sequence (p. 323)

10. Headings help clarify the framework of a report. Headings also show shifts from one idea to the next, and they help readers see the relationship between man and subordinate ideas. Finally, busy readers can quickly grasp the gist of a report by scanning the headings. (pp. 324-325)

Build Your Skills: Can You Analyze These Reports?

The correct classification for the four reports is as follows:

Report 1: Instrument Division-Monthly Update
      Who: Authorized
      What: Periodic report on monthly activities
      When: Routine, recurring
      Where: Internal, upward
      Why: Informational
      How: Receptive reader, direct order

Report 2: Observations on the Tire Industry in Canada
      Who: Authorized (probably)
      What: Decision-oriented industry analysis
      When: Special, nonrecurring
      Where: Internal, upward
      Why: Analytical
      How: Receptive reader, direct order

Report 3: Optimizing the Organizational Structure
      Who: Authorized (probably)
      What: Proposal on how to restructure the organization
      When: Special, nonrecurring
      Where: External
      Why: Analytical
      How: Receptive reader, direct order

Report 4:   Illegal and Improper Activities
           Who: Authorized
           What: Policy on corporate ethics
           When: Special, nonrecurring (may be updated)
           Where: Internal, downward
           Why: Informational
           How: Receptive reader, direct order

Build Your Skills: You Be the Editor

This excerpt can be improved in terms of format, style, tone, and organization. The present version is both too formal and too rambling for the intended readers.

Williams's audience, although probably open-minded, must be persuaded that this is a sound business proposition and that Williams is a capable professional manager. His report must present a convincing case for investing in the home-health-care field in general and in Williams's business in particular.

The audience will consist of sophisticated investors, accustomed to evaluating business propositions and the recipients of many competing prospectuses. If the introduction of the report does not impress them, these readers may not bother to review the rest of the report. They therefore need a quick overview of Williams's proposal and the points that make it a good idea. They will respond best to well-reasoned, factual material presented in an impersonal, businesslike tone.

Although it might be possible to salvage Williams's version through line-by-line editing, probably the best course is to start again with a fresh approach. At a minimum, the new version should eliminate some of Williams's insensitive references to "old people" and his sarcastic comment about the "divine wisdom" of government. The language should be tightened up so that unnecessary words are deleted. Transitions should be developed more carefully so that ideas flow more smoothly. In addition, Williams should clarify the purpose of the report earlier. He might also consider using headings to highlight key ideas, as well as a table or chart to call attention to important information. He might also want to add some more facts about his plans or about the market or the competition.

Here is one way to improve the introduction to Williams's report:

The Home-Health-Care Market: A High-Growth Investment Opportunity

The costs of medical care are high and rising throughout North America, and much of Europe. Although there is no simple solution to this problem, one promising approach is to encourage a greater reliance on home health care as opposed to hospitals and nursing homes. According to some estimates, a patient can be cared for at home for half the cost that would be incurred in a medical facility.

Given the cost advantage of home health care, many national governments are actively considering legislation that would provide reimbursement for home health care. In countries where such legislation passes, the need for retail access to home-health-care supplies will increase dramatically.

To meet this need, I propose to establish an international chain of stores carrying home-health-care supplies. They will be located in geographical areas with a high concentration of elderly people, who are heavy consumers of health care. These stores will provide both disposable items and durable equipment for purchase or rental. I believe I have the background necessary to make this venture a success: 15 years of experience as a hospital administrator. As later sections of this report indicate, an investment in this chain should provide an attractive return.

Why Home Health Care Will Increase

Two major factors suggest that home health care will capture an increasing share of total health- care expenditures:

- The population of people in the 65+ age group has increased over the past 15 years and continues to increase at a rapid rate. This age group spends twice as much per capita on health care as does the rest of the population.
- To help control the ever-increasing costs of health care,many governments will enact reimbursement programs that encourage home health care. As these programs take effect, the market for home health care will expand beyond the private paying patient.

What the Home Patient Will Require

As health care moves into the home, patients will require a wide variety of supplies, equipment, services, and support systems:
1. *Disposable supplies:* Tapes, dressings, disinfectants, antiseptics, splints, restraints, curettes, adult diapers, diagnostic kits, and other disposable supplies
2. *Durable equipment:* Wheel chairs, hospital beds, walkers, traction devices, pads and cushions, toilet devices, and other durable items
3. *Services:* Respiratory care, kidney dialysis, chemotherapy, and other therapeutic services
4. *Nutritional support systems:* Systems for delivering nutritional solutions intravenously.

How Demand Will Be Met

Meeting the demand for these products will require changes in the current distribution system. At present, there are relatively few retail home-health-care supply stores. Patients who require supplies or equipment have very little access to such products; when outlets do exist, they are often inconveniently located, making shopping difficult for the patient/shopper, who is typically in poor health.

The lack of competition at the retail level tends to create a "seller's" market, characterized by high prices, limited advertising, and relatively unresponsive service.

As the market expands and competitors are attracted to the business, this climate will begin to change. It is reasonable to expect that over the next five to ten years, the number of retail outlets will increase dramatically, price competition and advertising will increase, and sellers will become far more responsive to the needs of their customers.

As the dynamics of the business shift and profit margins decline, large-scale suppliers will have a competitive advantage. Because they deal in large quantities, they will be able to negotiate favorable wholesale prices. In addition, they will be able to spread their advertising costs over a broader sales base.

The best strategy for capitalizing on the dynamics of this business is to establish a high-volume, multi-national retail chain with a reputation for low prices, wide selection, consistent quality, and responsive service.

How the Report Is Organized

The remaining sections of this report provide a detailed look at the growing markets for home health care, the various segments of the business, and the strategy my company would pursue to respond to this opportunity. Detailed financial projections appear in Appendix A.

Develop Your Word Power

1. hindrance	6. knowledgeable	11. B	16. C	21. interval
2. immediately	7. C	12. E	17. A	22. inverse
3. intelligent	8. inevitable	13. D	18. C	23. introvert
4. C	9. interfere	14. A	19. A	24. intrigue
5. C	10. irrelevant	15. C	20. C	25. liaison

Chapter 13
Planning Long Reports

The main point of Chapter 13 is that careful research is a necessary foundation of any report. As you read the chapter, think about how researching a business report differs from—and resembles—researching a report for school. When you finish reading, plan the research for a business report that you might be required to write sometime during your career.

Master Key Concepts

Use the following terms to fill in the blanks in the outline. All terms are used, but none is used more than once.

accomplish	factoring	manipulate	secondary
analytical	infinitive	objective	suggestions
decimal	informational	problem	visual aids
experiments	interpretations	purpose	work plan

I. The first step in planning a long report is to define the _____ (p.337) your report will cover.
   A. Before beginning a study, be sure that you and the person who authorized the report agree on the _____ (p.338) of the assignment: what needs to be determined, why the issue is important, who is involved in the situation, where the trouble is located, when it started, how the situation originated.
   B. In contrast to the problem statement, which defines what you are going to investigate, the statement of _____ (p. 339) defines what the report will _____ (p. 339). The most useful way to phrase your statement of purpose is to begin with an _____ (p. 339) phrase.

II. Once you have defined the problem, you have to develop a logical structure for investigation, identifying the questions that you will ask and answer during the course of the study.
   A. _____ (p. 339) the problem means breaking the central problem into a hierarchy of narrower and narrower questions; _____ (p. 340) reports, which offer little analysis or interpretation, are factored into specific subtopics of the main topic, whereas _____ (p. 340) reports are factored into categories based on problem-solving methods.
   B. Any given problem may be subdivided in many different ways, as long as all the important questions are asked. To help ensure the logic of your breakdown:
      1. Choose a significant, useful basis or guiding principle for the division
      2. Limit yourself to one basis at a time in subdividing a whole into its parts
      3. Make sure that each group is separate and distinct
      4. Take care to list all the parts of a whole.
   C. To guide your analysis, you should represent your breakdown of the problem in outline form; to indicate levels of thought, you may use either alphanumeric format (combining roman numerals, letters, and Arabic numerals) or _____ (p. 343) format, and for each item you may use either descriptive labels or more informative headings.

III. Once the outline is ready, you should establish a _____ (pp. 345-346) that identifies the tasks you will perform in your research, the end products of the research, and a review of schedules and budgets.

IV. The research phase is the most important part of the investigation, because the value of the report depends on the qualify of the research.

    A. Indispensable _____ (p.348) sources of information that have already been collected include general reference works, periodicals, government documents, and internal reports and publications.

    B. Four main ways to collect primary data are to examine documents, observe people, conduct surveys, and perform _____ (p. 356).

V. As you collect information, you constantly sift and analyze what you learn in order to draw conclusions and make recommendations.

    A. When data you have collected is in numerical form, you must _____ (p. 357) the numbers—calculate averages, analyze trends, and find correlations—to interpret their significance.

    B. Analytical reports draw conclusions, which are opinions or _____ (p. 358) based on the information you have obtained.

    C. Analytical reports may also provide recommendations, _____ (p. 359) about what should be done based on the information you have obtained.

VI. Once you have finished your research and analysis, you can prepare the final outline for your report. It may be the same as your preliminary outline or changed to better suit your purpose. Once this final outline is prepared, you can identify which points should be supported with _____ (p. 361).

Check your answers at the end of this chapter.

Quiz Yourself

1. What do you accomplish by defining the problem to be investigated during your research?

2. Briefly discuss the differences in identifying key issues for investigation in informational reports versus analytical reports.

3. When wording an outline, what decision must you make about the kind of headings to use? What is the difference between the types of headings?

4. List the five basic rules of division for creating outlines.

5. What elements should be included in an informal work plan prepared for your own purposes? What elements would you have to add to make a formal work plan for a lengths, formal study?

6. List the four main ways for collecting primary data.

7. A survey should be both "reliable" and "valid". What is the difference?

8. What eight general guidelines should you follow in developing a questionnaire?

9. Calculate the mean, median, and mode for the following annual salaries:

$26,000
$26,500
$26,500
$27,000
$28,000
$29,000
$32,000
$32,500
$33,000
$36,000
$39,000

10. What is the difference between a conclusion and a recommendation?

Check your answers at the end of this chapter.

Build Your Skills: How Would You Attack The Problem?

You attend a town council meeting with a friend, where a delegation of teenagers complains about a lack of activities. Several adults voice their concerns about loitering, rowdiness, and vandalism. The council offers to provide time at the town's recreation centre, but stipulates that adult supervision is required. They challenge the young people to come up with a list of activities, and local adult volunteers willing to lead them.
Because you are taking a business communication course, you get drafted to help the teenagers write a report. Council wants to see a list of possible activities, potential leaders, and a recommendation of one activity as a pilot project.

Your specific tasks are:
- Write a clear problem statement
- Write a clear statement of the purpose of this report
- Briefly describe to the students the steps in planning a report. Explain problem factoring, and how it relates to determining issues and preparing an outline.

Build Your Skills: What's Wrong With This Outline?
You have recently been hired by a bank as the administrative assistant to the Vice President of Commercial Loans. Your boss, the vice president, has asked you to prepare a 10- to 15-page report on the life insurance industry as background information for the bank's board of directors. Your report is intended to give the board

members an overview of the life insurance business so that they will be better able to evaluate a loan to finance the start-up of a new insurance company.

Here is your preliminary outline for the report. Take a close look at it and make any necessary changes before showing it to your boss.

Overview of the Life Insurance Industry

I. Introduction
A. History of the industry
1. In Europe
2. In Canada
3. Role of minority-owned companies
B. Size of the industry
1. Assets
2. Employees
3. Income
4. Number of companies
II. Structure of the industry
A. Companies demutualize in attempt to dominate the industry
1. Control 70 percent of assets
2. Generate the bulk of premium income
B. Stock companies outnumber demutualized companies but are less influential
1. Generate only 20 percent of premium income
2. Account for less than half the insurance in force
C. Some life insurance companies carry health insurance too
1. Life insurance accounts for 71 percent of premium income
a. Ordinary accounts for 43 percent
b. Group accounts for 13 percent
c. Annuities accounts for 12 percent
d. Industrial accounts for 3 percent
2. Health insurance accounts for 29 percent of premium income a. Hospital/medical accounts for 21 percent
b. Disability accounts for 8 percent
D. Distribution channels
1. Ordinary agents
2. Combination agents
3. Independent agents
4. Mail order (small share)
E. High degree of government regulation
1. Restrictions on investment portfolios
2. Selling expenses
3. Varies from province to province
III. Industry growth
A. Ten-year statistics
1. New business issued
2. Premium income
3. Assets
4. Insurance in force
B. Profit growth
C. Future outlook is good
1. Growth of 25- to 34-year-old age group
2. Higher incomes

IV. Industry outlook
A. Negative factors
1. Price competition
2. National health insurance
3. Social Insurance benefits
4. Decline in interest rates
5. Increasing overhead expenses
B. However, companies have good opportunities
1. New products
2. New markets
3. New sales approaches
4. More aggressive investing
V. Profit economics
A. Industry has three ways to improve profits
1. Higher premium prices
2. Changes in mix and volume of sales
3. Better return on investment of surplus funds.

Develop Your Word Power

Spelling Challenge Identify the misspelled word in each of the following sentences, and spell it correctly in the space provided. If all the words in a sentence are spelled correctly, write *C* in the space.

_____   1. Make sure that your address and phone number are legible.

_____   2. Sheila will go to almost any lenths to get a promotion.

_____   3. Tracy is a likeable, energetic young woman.

_____   4. What is the likelyhood of getting delivery by midweek?

_____   5. Please send some literture on your new laser printers.

_____   6. We don't have the luxery of waiting for third-quarter figures.

_____   7. Gardening-what a wonderful way to spend your leesure time!

_____   8. All our technicians are fully licenced.

_____   9. Listen before you jump to conclusions about his limitations.

_____   10. We have steadily been loosing market share.

Vocabulary Challenge Match the words in the first column with the definitions in the second column.

_____   11. malign   A. to show plainly

_____   12. mandate   B. to keep to oneself

_____   13. maneuver   C. to slander

_____ 14. manifest   D. to manipulate

_____ 15. monopolize   E. to authorize

Circle the best definition of the highlighted word in each of the following sentences.

16. His **Machiavellian** nature gives him the edge over many opponents.

   A. masculine   B. cunning   C. ambitious

17. We cannot afford to include any **mavericks** on this project.

   A. cowboys   B. incompetents   C. unorthodox people

18. My **mentor** was a woman with a reputation for covering her iron fist with a velvet glove.

   A. boss   B. confidant   C. adviser

19. Judy has undergone a **metamorphosis** since taking the Dale Carnegie course.

   A. period of self-doubt   B. attitude adjustment   C. complete change

20. With a **modicum** of training, Andy could become a good manager.

   A. little bit   B. great deal   C. modem type

Select one of these words to complete each of the following sentences, and write the word in the space provided.

malleable   mercurial   meticulous   moot   moribund

21. Since we no longer have that option, its cost is a _____ point.

22. His _____ mood changes, unsettle the staff.

23. Tom's _____ nature helps him adjust to many different situations.

24. The employee relations committee has been _____ during the strike.

25. The best accountants are _____ in handling complicated financial reports.

Follow-up Word Study Check your answers at the end of this chapter. In the spaces below, write the words that you spelled or used incorrectly. (Use a separate piece of paper if you missed more than five words.) Then use your dictionary to carefully study the spelling, pronunciation, definition, and history (etymology) of each word. Finally, to help fix the word in your memory, write it in a sentence.

Word   *Sentence*

_____   _____

_____   _____

_____   _____

_____   _____

_____   _____

Check Your Answers

Master Key Concepts

I. problem
    A. objective
    B. purpose, accomplish, infinitive

II. A. factoring, informational, analytical
    B. decimal

III. work plan

IV. A. secondary
    B. experiments

V. A. manipulate
    B. interpretations
    C. suggestions

VI. visual aids

Quiz Yourself

1. By defining the problem to be investigated, you narrow the focus of your investigation and establish its framework. Your definition of the problem helps you decide what information you need to complete your report. (p. 338)

2. Informational reports are generally broken down into subtopics dealing with specific subjects. These subtopics might be arranged in order of importance, sequentially, chronologically, spatially, geographically, or categorically.
    Analytical reports are generally broken down into categories based on problem-solving methods. The two most common methods are hypotheses and relative merits. (p. 341)

3. When wording an outline, you must choose between descriptive (topical) and informative (talking) headings. Descriptive headings label the subject that will be discussed, whereas informative headings suggest more about the meaning of the issues. (p. 343)

4. The five basic rules of division are:
    - Divide a topic into at least two parts.
    - Choose a significant, useful basis or guiding principle for division.
    - When subdividing a whole into parts, restrict yourself to one category at a time.
    - Make sure each group is separate and distinct.
    - Be thorough when listing all the components of a whole. (pp. 344-345)

5. A simple, informal work plan should include a list of steps that will be taken, an estimate of their sequence and timing, and a list of sources of information.

A formal work plan should include:
   a) A statement of the problem
   b) A statement of the purpose and scope of the investigation
   c) A discussion of the sequence of tasks to be accomplished, together with an indication of sources, research methods, and limitations
   d) A description of end products, such as reports, plans operating improvements, or tangible products
   e) A review of project assignments, schedules, and resource requirements (pp. 345-346)

6. The four main ways of collecting primary data are:
   - Examining documents
   - Making observations
   - Conducting surveys
   - Performing experiments (p. 353)

7. A survey is considered "reliable" when the same results would be obtained if the research were repeated at a later date. A survey is considered "valid" if it measures what it was intended to measure and gives a true reflection of the sample group's opinions on a subject. (p. 354)

8. The following guidelines should be applied in developing a questionnaire:
   - Provide clear instructions so that respondents will know how to fill it out.
   - Keep it short and easy to answer.
   - Use questions that are easily tabulated.
   - Avoid questions that lead to a particular answer.
   - Ask only one thing at a time.
   - Avoid questions with vague or abstract words.
   - Pretest the questionnaire with a sample group.
   - Include a few questions that rephrase earlier questions. (p. 354)

9. The mean is $30,500; the median is $29,000; the mode is $26,500. (p. 357)

10. A conclusion is an opinion or an interpretation of what the facts mean; a recommendation suggests what ought to be done about the facts. (p. 358-359)

Build Your Skills: How Would You Attack the Problem?

The teenagers who approached Council want to be involved in more interesting activities; the adults want something to draw all teens away from undesirable activities. The problem statement might be:

This town needs more interesting activities with broad appeal to teenagers.

Council can't solve the whole problem, but will help by providing time at the recreation centre, under adult supervision. They have asked for a report that includes a list of activities and adult leaders, and a recommendation of one to be used in a pilot project. The purpose statement should look something like this:

To compile a list of activities appealing to teenagers, with an adult willing to lead each one, and to recommend one activitity for use in a pilot project.

The five steps in planning reports are:
1. Define the problem and purpose
2. Outline the issues for investigation
3. Prepare a work plan
4. Conduct research
5. Analyze the data, draw conclusions, and make recommendations

Problem factoring is the process of breaking the main problem into a series of connected questions that try to identify causes and effects. In this case, the teenagers might ask, "how do we find both an activity and a volunteer to lead it?" They might decide to have one group gather a list of activities while another group looks for volunteers. Then they can try to match leaders with activities. Breaking the problem into smaller, easier pieces also helps to determine where to start. Factoring the problem thoroughly will produce a preliminary outline.

Build Your Skills: What's Wrong with This Outline?

This outline has a number of problems:

1. This is a decision-oriented report for a receptive audience. The most efficient approach is to organize it around conclusions as opposed to subtopics (as it currently is organized). The shift from subtopics to conclusions may be made by rewording the main points (except for the introduction) to give them a conclusion-oriented focus. For example, point II might be "Industry Is Dominated by Large Demutualized Companies."

2. Because the readers will be receptive, the report should be in direct order. This means that the introduction should summarize the main points of the report in the order in which they will appear. In addition, since the report is relatively brief, a discussion of the history; of the industry is probably undesirable. Points I-A-1 and I-A-3 should definitely be omitted, and I-A-2 should include no more than a sentence or two, if it is mentioned at all.

3. Item II-B might be more useful if subpoints 1 and 2 were parallel to subpoints 1 and 2 under item II-A.

4. Item II-C should be rephrased to emphasize life insurance as opposed to health insurance.

5. Items II-D and II-E should be reworded as informative captions, parallel in grammatical structure to the other points in section II.

6. Somewhere in section II, it might be useful to identify the top five or ten companies and describe their market share. This could be included as point II-A-3, for example, assuming that the largest companies are mutual companies.

7. Under section III, all the subpoints should be rephrased as informative captions that give the reader the gist of what will be covered. For example, point III-A might be "Industry' Experienced Steady Growth for Ten Years."

8. Item III-B is probably a "ten-year statistic" and should be repositioned as item III-A-5.

9. Item III-C seems to be in the wrong place. It should be moved to section IV-B, since the points appear to be favorable factors (increase in the insurance-buying age and income group).

10. Subpoints under section IV should be rephrased as informative captions; points IV-A and IV-B should be in parallel grammatical form.

11. Section V seems to be in the wrong place. It should come before the discussion of the outlook for the industry, which provides a natural transition into the final summary, section. Therefore, section V should be placed after section III. It would fit well there, providing a natural bridge between the discussions of historical performance and of future prospects.

12. Because of the conventions of outlining, it is undesirable to have a point V-A without a corresponding point V-B. The best way to solve this problem is to change points V-A-l, V-A-2, and V-A-3 into points V-A, V-B, and V-C.

13. The report should have a final summary section, which can be shown on the outline as "Summary." The subpoints should briefly restate the four main findings/conclusions represented by sections II, III, IV, and V.

Develop Your Word Power

1. *C*	6. luxury	11. C	16. B	21. moot
2. lengths	7. leisure	12. E	17. C	22. mercurial
3. likable	8. licensed	13. D	18. C	23. malleable
4. likelihood	9. *C*	14. A	19. C	24. moribund
5. literature	10. losing	15. B	20. A	25. meticulous

Chapter 14
Completing Formal Reports and Proposals

The main point of Chapter 14 is that producing the final polished version of a formal report or proposal requires following an accepted format and sequence of parts. As you read the chapter, think about how the parts correspond to the parts for reports you have written for school. When you finish reading, check the guidelines in this chapter against a few formal business reports.

Master Key Concepts

Use the following terms to fill in the blanks in the outline. All terms are used, but none is used more than once.

acceptance	costs	recommendations	tables
appendices	information	RFP	time
bar	longer	scope	tone
charts	prefatory	synopsis	whole

I. The production of a final version of a report may involve the interaction of a number of people and may make use of sophisticated computer equipment; whatever method is used, set aside enough _____ (p. 371) for a thorough job.

II. The _____ (p. 371) and more formal a report, the more components you'll need to include.
   A. The _____ (p. 371) parts, which precede the text of the report, consist of a cover, an optional title fly, a title page, possibly a letter of authorization and a letter _____ (pp. 371-372), a letter of transmittal, a table of contents, a list of illustrations (if needed), and a _____ (p. 374) or executive summary.
   B. The text of the report consists of three basic parts: the introduction, which establishes the purpose, _____ (p. 376), background, and organization of the report; the body, which presents the detailed _____ (p. 377) obtained during the study; and the final section, which contains the summary, conclusions, and any _____ (pp. 377-378), plus source notes.
   C. When using visual aids, it is important to choose the form that best suits your message. Use _____ (p. 381) to present large quantities of detailed, specific information; line and surface _____ (pp. 382-383) to show changes over time or the interaction of two variables; _____ (p. 383) charts to compare the size of several items at one time or the composition of several items over time; pie charts to show the relative sizes of parts of a _____ (p. 384); flow charts and organization charts to illustrate physical or conceptual relationships; maps to show geographic information; and drawings, diagrams, and photographs to show how something looks or how it is used.
   D. The supplementary parts at the end of the report may include _____ (p. 387) containing additional related material, a bibliography, and an index.

III. Formal proposals contain many of the same components as formal reports.
   A. In addition to the cover, title fly, title page, contents, and list of illustrations, the prefatory section of a proposal usually contains a copy of the _____ (p. 389) issued by the client and a letter of transmittal. A synopsis or executive summary is not usually needed.
   B. The text of a proposal follows a prescribed format. The introduction usually includes subheadings for background or statement of the problem, overview of approach, _____ (p. 409), and report

organization. The body usually includes the proposed approach, the work plan, a statement of qualifications, and a breakdown of _____ (pp. 411-412). There may be a brief summary, but there are rarely supplemental materials.

Check your answers at the end of this chapter.

Quiz Yourself

1. What are the three basic divisions of a formal report?

2. List all the elements that might be included in the prefatory section of a formal report.

3. What differentiates a letter of authorization, a letter of acceptance, and a letter of transmittal?

4. What is the difference between an informative synopsis and a descriptive synopsis?

5. What is the difference between an executive summary and a synopsis?

6. What topics might you cover in the introduction of a long formal report?

7. How do summaries, conclusions, and recommendations vary in purpose?

8. Where should you put a visual aid in relation to its reference in the text?

9. What types of information might be included in an appendix?

10. What main element, often found in the prefatory section of a proposal, is not included in the prefactory section of a formal report?

Check your answers at the end of this chapter.

Build Your Skills: Organize These Report Elements

You are leader of a team that, over the past eight months, has been researching opportunities in the airline industry. Now it's time to put together your report.

Marie Villeneuve gives you a stack of papers that include:
- A six-page section about government regulation of the airline industry
- A ten-page table that lists every major piece of government legislation affecting the airlines, along with a description of each law
- The conclusions section of the report

Jim Scofield gives you:
- A two-page overview of the airline industry
- A ten-page section on the economic characteristics of airlines
- A five-page section on labor relations in the airline industry
- A seven-page computer printout that provides statistics on all current airlines, both national and commuter
- The bibliography for the report

Garet Bedrosian gives you:
- A nine-page section describing the marketing aspects of the airline industry
- A six-page section that forecasts future trends in the airline industry

Joe MacDonald gives you:
- A twelve-page section on types of aircraft being used
- A ten-page section on schedules for aircraft maintenance
- Sample aircraft maintenance schedules from United and Air Canada

Dorothy Huang gives you:
- A nine-page section on methods of financing in the aircraft industry
- A seven-page section on flight scheduling and airport availability

You have in your files:
- The letter of authorization for the research
- The letter of acceptance

You need to prepare:
- The other prefatory parts of the report
- The introduction
- The recommendations

To simplify the task of putting all these elements together, prepare an outline that includes all the prefatory and supplementary parts for the report, as well as a final outline for the text of the report. Indicate where each existing element has come from and which elements still need to be prepared.

Build Your Skills: Choose The Right Visual Aid For The Situation

You are preparing a report on the mail-order market for books. Which visual aid would you use to portray each of the following points?

1. You want to show that mail-order purchases accounted for 13 percent of all books purchased this year.
2. You want to show that the mail-order book market consists of two segments: book clubs and other forms of mail order. You want to show the relative size of the two segments over the past five years, as well as the size of the total book market.
3. You want to show statistics on the people who buy mail-order books. You have data on their gender, age, education, and annual income, which you want to display for both book-club purchases and other mail-order purchases.
4. You want to show that of all the books bought this year, 27 percent were purchased at a discount. You want to contrast this with the fact that 49 percent of all book-club books were purchased at a discount, whereas 40 percent of all other mail-order books were discounted.
5. You want to contrast the types of books purchased through retail outlets, book clubs, and other mail-order sources. You have compiled data on the source of purchases for various categories of fiction (mystery, romance, western, science fiction, adventure, the classics, and so on), as well as various nonfiction categories (reference, history, health/diet, religion, home and garden, cooking, finance and investment, biography, art, and so on).

Develop Your Word Power

Spelling Challenge Identify the misspelled word in each of the following sentences, and spell it correctly in the space provided. If all the words in a sentence are spelled correctly, write *C* in the space.

_____   1.   We carry greeting cards for any ocassion.

_____   2.   When did the accident ocurr?

_____   3.   FastFood, Inc., is the offcal caterer to the Canadian team.

_____   4.   How often will I be required to travel out of town?

_____   5.   The enclosed pamplet will tell you more about our line of shoes.

_____   6.   Please send at least partial payment for the items you ordered.

_____   7.   She has made numrous mistakes during her first week.

_____   8.   Has it ever occurred to you that you might have hurt his feelings?

_____   9.   The section on personal telephone calls has been ommitted from the employee manual.

_____   10. He had an oppertunity to apply for the position, but he didn't.

Vocabulary Challenge Match the words in the first column with the definitions in the second column.

_____ 11. precaution   A. bias

_____ 12. precedent   B. harbinger

_____ 13. precursor   C. safeguard

_____ 14. predecessor   D. forerunner

_____ 15. predilection   E. model

Circle the best definition of the highlighted word in each of the following sentences.

16. Give me a week to **ponder** your proposal.

    A. research   B. criticize   C. consider

17. Their good sales figures for the past quarter should **precipitate** a major acquisition.

    A. dampen   B. hasten   C. precede

18. Accounting experience does not **preclude** management experience as well.

    A. come before   B. make impossible   C. coincide with

19. Chen works for the most **prestigious** law firm in the city.

    A. esteemed   B. tricky   C. wealthy

20. Alan has a **prodigious** capacity for work.

    A. professional   B. modest   C. immense

Select one of these words to complete each of the following sentences, and write the word in the space provided.

portfolio   **premise**   **proficiency**   **profusion**   **prognosis**

21. Past and present customers have supplied a _____ of suggestions, and we are working overtime to evaluate them all.

22. Larry's _____ in computing is what got him the job.

23. What is your _____ for the outcome of the new advertising campaign?

24. Mary's conclusion seemed reasonable, even though it was based on a faulty _____.

25. Ask all those interviewing for the graphic design position to bring a _____ containing samples of their most recent work.

Follow-up Word Study Check your answers at the end of this chapter. In the spaces below, write the words that you spelled or used incorrectly. (Use a separate piece of paper if you missed more than five words.) Then use your dictionary to carefully study the spelling, pronunciation, definition, and history (etymology) of each word. Finally, to help fix the word in your memory, write it in a sentence.

Word   Sentence

_____   _____

_____   _____

_____   _____

_____   _____

_____   _____

Check Your Answers

Master Key Concepts

I.   time

II. longer
   A. prefatory, acceptance, synopsis
   B. tone, information, recommendations
   C. tables, charts, bar, whole
   D. appendices

III. A. RFP
     B. scope, costs

Quiz Yourself

1.   The three basic divisions of a formal report are the prefatory parts, the text, and the supplementary parts. (p. 371)

2.   The prefatory section of a formal report may include these parts:
   • Cover
   • Title fly
   • Title page
   • Letter of authorization
   • Letter of acceptance
   • Letter of transmittal
   • Table of contents
   • List of illustrations
   • Synopsis or executive summary (pp. 372-375)

3.   A letter of authorization is written by the person who requests the *report.* It generally discusses the problem, scope, time and money limitations, special instructions, and due date for the report. A letter of acceptance is a reply to the letter authorization, written by the person who is in charge of doing the study. It confirms the arrangements for doing the work. A letter of transmittal conveys the report from the writer to the reader. This letter is often merely a brief *statement* that effectively says, "Here is the report you

asked for." However, in some situations, the letter of transmittal might be used to make certain comments "off the record" to some, but not all, of the audience. Or it might call attention to important points, make comments on side issues, suggest follow-up work, or convey helpful information about the background of the report. If the report does not have a synopsis, the transmittal letter might summarize the major findings, conclusions, and recommendations. (p. 373)

4. An informative synopsis presents the main points of the report in the order in which they appear in the text. A descriptive synopsis states what the report is about and leaves out the actual findings of the report. (p. 375)

5. An executive summary is more comprehensive than a synopsis. It may contain headings, well-developed transitions, and visual aids, and it is generally about 10 percent as long as the overall document. (p. 375)

6. The introduction of a long formal report might cover these eight topics:
    *   Authorization: who asked for the report and who prepared it
    *   Problem/purpose: what the report is supposed to accomplish
    *   Scope: what is and is not covered in the report
    *   Backgrounds: conditions leading up to the report
    *   Sources and methods: how the research was conducted
    *   Definitions: explanations of unfamiliar terms
    *   Limitations: factors affecting the quality of the report
    *   Report organization: sequence of topics to be covered (pp. 376-377)

7. The purpose of a summary is to present the key findings of a report. The purpose of the conclusions section is to analyze the meaning of the findings. The purpose of the recommendations section is to outline a course of action that should be taken based on the conclusions. (pp. 377-378)

8. Put a visual aid as close as possible to its first reference in the text to help readers understand the illustration's relevance. (p. 381)

9. An appendix contains related material not included in the report because it is too lengthy or bulky or lacks direct relevance. Some typical items that might be placed in an appendix are sample questionnaires and cover letters, sample forms, computer printouts, statistical formulas, and a glossary of terms. (pp. 387-388)

10. The main element found in the prefatory material for a proposal that is not found in a formal report is the RFP (request for proposal). (p. 389)

Build Your Skills: Organize These Report Elements

Your outline should include the following elements (the topics in the main body can be ordered in a variety, of ways, but the order should be logical):
Prefatory parts
    Cover (to be prepared)
    Title fly (to be prepared)
    Title page (to be prepared)
    Letter of authorization (from files)
    Letter of acceptance (from files)
    Table of contents (to be prepared)
    List of illustrations (if needed)
    Synopsis or executive summary (to be prepared)

Text
    Introduction (to be prepared)
    Overview of the Airline Industry (from Jim)
    Economic Characteristics of the Industry (from Jim)
    Government Regulation of the Industry (from Marie)
    Types of Aircraft Being Used (from Joe)
    Flight Scheduling and Airport Availability (from Dorothy)
    Aircraft Maintenance (from Joe)
    Marketing Aspects of the Airline Industry (from Garet)
    Financing in the Airline Industry (from Dorothy)
    Labor Relations in the Airline Industry (from Jim)
    Future Trends in the Airline Industry (from Garet)
    Conclusions (from Marie)
    Recommendations (to be prepared)
    Notes (to be prepared)

Supplementary parts
    Appendices
        Table of government legislation (from Marie)
        Computer printout of airline statistics (from Jim)
        Sample aircraft maintenance schedules (from Joe)
    Bibliography (from Jim)
    Index (to be prepared, if needed)

Build Your Skills: Choose the Right Visual Aid for the Situation

The recommended visual aid for each situation is as follows:
1. Pie chart or divided bar chart
2. Line or surface chart
3. Detailed table
4. Bar chart
5. Detailed table

Develop Your Word Power

1. occasion
2. occur
3. official
4. often
5. pamphlet
6. *C*
7. numerous
8. *C*
9. omitted
10. opportunity
11. C
12. E
13. B
14. D
15. A
16. C
17. B
18. B
19. A
20. C
21. profusion
22. proficiency
23. prognosis0
24. premise
25. portfolio

Chapter 15
Writing Résumés and Application Letters

The main point of Chapter 15 is that a properly prepared résumé and application letter are essential to your search for a job. As you read the chapter, think about how both the résumé and the application letter are constructed to "sell" you to potential employers. When you finish reading, analyze your own career preferences and then write a résumé and a model application letter that can help you get the job you want.

Master Key Concepts

Use the following terms to fill in the blanks in the outline. All terms are used, but none is used more than once.

accurate	environment	objective	solicited
application	job-inquiry	personal	targeted
attention-getter	key words	résumé	updates
education	midsection	selling	values

I. Before you apply for a job, you should think about the career you want.
   A. Begin by analyzing what you have to offer—your marketable skills, educational background, work experience, and personal characteristics.
   B. The second step is to determine what you want to do, without losing sight of your _____ (p. 424). Decide what you'd like to do every day, establish some specific compensation targets, and consider the type of work _____ (p.424) you'd prefer (the kind of company, industry, and geographical area you want to work in).
   C. The next step is to make a list of companies that might be interested in your qualifications and that would enable you to accomplish your goals.

II. A _____ (p. 428) is a brief account of your qualifications in a special format; its purpose is to interest employers in giving you a personal interview.
   A. The opening section summarizes your identity, your job or career _____ (p. 430), and your qualifications and date of availability.
   B. The body of the résumé describes your _____ (p. 430), work experience, relevant skills, activities and achievements, and _____ (p. 432) data. In selecting and organizing this information, your goal is to emphasize your strongest qualifications.
   C. The organization of a résumé depends on your background and goals; it could be chronological, functional, or _____ (p. 432).
   D. When adapting your traditional paper résumé to an electronic format, you should (1) save it as a plain ASCII text file; (2) provide a list of _____ (pp. 438-439); and (3) balance common language with current jargon.

E. The "perfect" résumé is the one that convinces the employer to grant you a personal interview.

III. Your _____ (p. 441) letter tells what you can do for the company and why you believe you are qualified for the job.
  A. If your application letter has been _____ (p. 442) (if you are sending it in response to an announced job opening), begin with a simple statement of how you know about the job and why you qualify for the position; if you are sending an unsolicited letter (one to a company that has not announced an opening), you should open with an _____ (p. 443) of some sort, as in a sales letter, and a statement of your reason for writing.
  B. The _____ (p. 444) of your application letter should highlight your strongest selling points and indicate how they can benefit the potential employer.
  C. In the final paragraph, request an interview and make it easy to arrange; close by referring to your strongest _____ (p. 445) point.
  D. The "perfect" application letter achieves the simple purpose of getting you a personal interview.

IV. A job search may require three other types of written messages.
  A. A _____ (p. 448) letter—a direct request for an application form—should include enough information to show that you are a reasonable candidate.
  B. If you are asked to fill out a standard application form, be complete, _____ (p. 448), and neat.
  If you have not received a response to your application letter within a month or so, follow up with another letter that _____ (pp. 449-450) your application with any recent job-related information and ask the organization to keep your name in its active file.

Check your answers at the end of this chapter.

Quiz Yourself

1. What is the difference between a "work-content" and a "performance" goal?

2. What are some sources you might use to locate employment opportunities?

3. What six general types of information should you present after the opening section of your résumé?

4. When writing your résumé should you present your educational qualifications or your work experience first? Discuss.

5. What are some of the most common criticisms expressed by people who read résumés?

6. What organization plan would you use for an application letter?

7. What is the main difference between a solicited and an unsolicited application letter?

8. What does the midsection of an application letter accomplish?

9. What would you try to accomplish in the closing paragraph of an application letter?

10. What is the purpose of a job-inquiry letter?

Check your answers at the end of this chapter.

Build Your Skills: How Can This Résumé Be Improved?

A college student has drafted this résumé. What could she do to make it more effective?

Résumé

Alicia Suarez
2348 Main Street West
Ancaster, Ontario L9Z 5T2
Telephone (905) 376-3636

Career Objective: I have always aspired to a management position in a growing firm because I'm good with numbers and love to sell just about any product.

SALARY RANGE: $25,000 plus with good benefits, preferably a company car.

Education
Right now I'm working on a bachelor's degree in business administration. My courses are wide-ranging and include Western Civ., Speech, and various courses in finance and marketing. I expect to graduate next spring, from the McMaster University. I also attended Mohawk College for one year.

Experience
JUNIOR ACCOUNTANT. In this position I prepared and processed important financial documents for Pan American Importers, Inc. In addition, my job included running the computers. (No secretarial work was involved, although I can type 40 wpm.) Part-time, while in school.

Sales Rep. For MCI, Inc. I handled a large territory and scored many successes with a range of clients. The dollar volume of my territory climbed considerably while I was there. 1992.
Volunteer Work at Chedoke Hospital.

Activities
Treasurer for Delta Gamma Sorority at McMaster University.
Volleyball Team
Involved in Campus Entrepreneurs Society.

Workshops—This fall I attended a workshop on "Honing Your Persuasive Speaking Skills." It was sponsored by the Hamilton Chapter of IABC.

Achievements

Bilingual

Rotary Club Scholarship

Personal Data: 5'2", 140 lbs., recently married

Hobbies—Water Skiing and volleyball

Build Your Skills: What's Wrong With This Résumé?

Suppose that you are a career counselor and that Caleb Green is your client. How would you advise him to modify his résumé?

CALEB M. GREEN

2632 Hesby Avenue
New Westminster, BC   V7C 2W4
Phone: (604) 990-6110

Age: 30
Married
2 children

EXPERIENCE

Product Manager, Health Systems. Inc., Vancouver, BC, 1994-1998
I am in charge of a line of respiratory-care products that are sold to hospitals. My job is to plan the production, pricing, and marketing strategy for this line, which is sold by our sales force.

Design Engineer, Health Systems, Inc., Vancouver, BC. 1989-1994
As an engineer, I was involved in designing respiratory-care products, such as inhalation machines and nebulizers.

Associate Engineer. Vortex, Vancouver, BC 1983-1989
At Vortex, I worked on designing all sorts of plastic devices for use with hospital products. Most of these items used tubing, valves, and connectors that had to meet high heat *tolerances,* since they were usually sterilized repeatedly by hospitals.

EDUCATION

Simon Fraser University 1989-1992
I got an M.B.A. at night school while I was working full time for Health Systems. I graduated with a B average and a major in Marketing.

<u>California Institute of Technology-. Pasadena. Calif.. 1985-1989</u>
I have a B.S. degree in mechanical engineering. My grades were excellent. I was on the dean's list six semesters, and Cal Tech is a tough school, as perhaps you know. I lived in the dorm and worked part time in the school cafeteria. I was also on the swim team.

PERSONAL BACKGROUND

I was born and raised in California, but my parents moved to Vancouver when I was in high school, and I've been hear ever since. I don't ever want to leave, because my hobby is sailing.

Build Your Skills: What's Wrong With This Application Letter?

A young career woman has drafted this application letter. What could she do to make it more effective?
208 Warden Street
Etobecoke. ON M3V 2E3
March 20, 2001

Mr. Alan Frankel, President
Frankel Merchandising, Inc.
15-163 Bathurst Street
Toronto, ON M4W 4B6

Dear Mr. Frankel:

Please consider me for the position in your accounting department that was recently advertised in a trade journal.

I am hardworking, enthusiastic, and have a lot of experience in this field. My co-workers have always said that I was a star-quality team player. Just take a look at my résumé and you'll see exactly what I mean. My education also provides valuable preparation for employment in your company.

I hope that we can have an interview soon, although you should keep in mind that Thursday afternoon is the only time I'm available to discuss future employment at this point. Never-the less, after we speak, I think you'll be convinced that I'm the best applicant for the job!!

Sincerely,

Vanessa Rossetti

Develop Your Word Power

Spelling Challenge Identify the misspelled word in each of the following sentences, and spell it correctly in the space provided. If all the words in a sentence are spelled correctly, write *C* in the space.

_____ 1. Amy excells at writing collection letters.

_____ 2. We are extremally grateful for all your help.

_____ 3. A fascinating program has been scheduled for Febuary.

_____ 4. Ye Olde Pet Shoppe is no longer in existance.

_____   5.   Before you incur any additional expence, talk to us.

_____   6.   Yes, I am familar with your financial services.

_____   7.   A full-fledged investigation is feasable but unnecessary.

_____   8.   I am especialy pleased with your latest recruiting trip.

_____   9.   The cost of supplies for the Boise office should not exceed $900.

_____   10.   With your expiriense, you should do well here.

Vocabulary Challenge Match the words in the first column with the definitions in the second column.

_____   11.   incessant   A.   rambling

_____   12.   incipient   B.   beginning

_____   13.   incoherent   C.   not noticeable

_____   14.   incongruous   D.   not harmonious

_____   15.   inconspicuous   E.   without interruption

Circle the best definition of the highlighted word in each of the following sentences.

16. Even after a day of work, his desk was **immaculate**.

   A.   spotless   B.   buried   C.   polished

17. His talent as a supervisor is to **impel** people to do their best.

   A.   allow   B.   urge   C.   shame

18. In a crowded office, it is all too easy to **impinge** on another's right to privacy.

   A.   encroach   B.   presume upon   C.   take advantage of

19. From the **inception** of this program, Pat has taken an active role.

   A.   formulation   B.   outcome   C.   beginning

20. You will **incur** Mr. Crane's displeasure if you lobby too hard for your own ideas.

   A.   bring about   B.   increase   C.   face

Select one of these words to complete each of the following sentences, and write the word in the space provided.

impending   impenetrable   impertinent   impervious   impulsive

21. She has a strong ego that is _____ to their insults.

22. With Ms. Cartwright guarding the door, Dr. Hruska's office is _____.

23. Would it be _____ of me to suggest that you try a larger size?

24. The point of using this appeal is to motivate _____ buying on the part of those standing in line.

25. Candidates for the graphic design position should bring a _____ of their work.

Follow-up Word Study Check your answers at the end of this chapter. In the spaces below, write the words that you spelled or used incorrectly. (Use a separate piece of paper if you missed more than five words.) Then use your dictionary to carefully study the spelling, pronunciation, definition, and history (etymology) of each word. Finally, to help fix the word in your memory, write it in a sentence.

Word   Sentence

_____   _____

_____   _____

_____   _____

_____   _____

_____   _____

Check your Answers

Master Key Concepts

I. B. values, environment

II. résumé
    A. objective
    B. education, personal
    C. targeted
    D. key words

III. application
    A. solicited, attention-getter
    B. midsection
    C. selling

IV. A. job-inquiry
    B. accurate
    C. updates

Quiz Yourself

1. When thinking about a career, ask yourself about what you'd like to do every day. Talk to people in various occupations, and read about a wide variety of jobs. Think about your long- and short-term earnings goals. What level of compensation will satisfy you? Finally, think about the type of work environment you prefer. Think in broad terms about the size and type of company you would feel comfortable in; consider location; and most important, think about corporate culture. (pp. 424-425)

2. The best way to look for a job is to explore as many pathways as possible, taking advantage of the normal recruiting process and looking for opportunities on your own. Sources to explore include:
    • Business journals and newspapers
    • Government and private publications that focus on employment opportunities in various occupations.

- Professional and trade journals in specific career fields
- Directories of employers
- Classified ads in local and major newspapers
- Web sites of interest (p. 426)

3. The main body of your résumé should present six key elements:
   - Career objective or summary of qualifications
   - Education
   - Work experience
   - Relevant skills
   - Activities and achievements
   - Personal data (pp. 430-432)

4. Your résumé should present your strongest qualifications first. If you are still in school and have held only part-time or summer jobs, your educational qualifications will probably be your best selling point and should be given prominence. If you have been out of school for several years and have held responsible, full-time jobs related to the position you seek, you should discuss your work experience before describing your education. (pp. 430-431)

5. People who read résumés complain about these common faults in the résumés they receive:
   - Too long
   - Too short or sketchy
   - Hard to read
   - Wordy
   - Too slick
   - Amateurish
   - Poorly reproduced
   - Misspelled and ungrammatical throughout
   - Lacking a career objective
   - Boastful
   - Dishonest
   - Gimmicky (p. 440-441)

6. Application letters are persuasive sales messages. They are organized according to the direct plan-more specifically, the AIDA plan, to develop attention, interest, desire, and action. (p. 442)

7. A solicited application letter is one sent in regard to an announced job opening. An unsolicited, or "prospecting," letter is one sent to a company that has not announced an opening. (p. 442)

8. The midsection of an application letter should
   - Summarize your qualifications that are directly related to the job (or mentioned in an employment ad)
   - Show how you have put your qualifications to use
   - Provide evidence of desirable personal qualifications
   - Tie salary requirements (if requested) to the benefits of hiring you
   - Refer to your résumé (p. 444)

9. In the closing paragraph of an application letter, ask for an interview and make the interview easy to arrange. (p. 445)

10. The purpose of a job-inquiry letter is to request an application form. (p. 448)

Build Your Skills: How Can This Résumé Be Improved?

Although this student has valuable qualifications, they are so poorly presented that she is not likely to be asked for an interview, much less offered a position. First, the résumé is plagued by copious typographical errors. Second, the headings are presented in an inconsistent format; to solve the problem, all headings at the level of "Education" and "Experience" should be either underscored or typed in capital letters, depending on Alicia's preference. Third, the résumé is wordy and conveys little concrete information. In addition, the use of the first-person pronoun should be avoided.

The career objective should emphasize Alicia's desire to use her skills in marketing and finance. Mentioning a salary range and desired benefits on a résumé is presumptuous; these matters are best discussed during the interview itself.

When discussing education, Alicia should clearly indicate the name of each institution and then concisely state her major and minor, her grade point average (if over 3.0), and any courses related to her career goals. The course in Western civilization, however valuable personally, is not directly relevant. A better choice would be to list specific courses in finance and marketing. Alicia should state the date she expects to graduate and the type of degree she is pursuing.

Alicia's wordy job descriptions bury the names of the employers, which should be prominently listed. For the first position, Alicia should explain her duties in more detail, noting what kinds of financial documents she can prepare. If programming or using particular software was part of the job, this should be made clear. There is no reason, however, to explain what the job did not involve. Typing speed is irrelevant, given Alicia's aspirations. For the second position, she should indicate the size of the sales territory and the exact volume of increase she produced. The responsibilities of the job could also be further delineated. For example, did Alicia deal with both corporate and consumer clients? Also, when discussing volunteer work, Alicia should indicate how the experience was relevant. For example, did she answer phones during a fundraising drive, do bookkeeping, or work as a summer intern in the marketing department? For all positions, specific dates should be supplied.

The discussion of Alicia's activities might also be amplified with concrete details. As sorority treasurer, what size budget did she oversee? What did she do for the Campus Entrepreneurs Society? Arrange for guest speakers? Organize workshops? Conduct membership drives? Handle club finances? The reader might not recognize such abbreviations as IABC, so Alicia should use the full name.

The personal data Alicia provides is irrelevant and could be held against her. It should be eliminated. Since her hobbies—water skiing and volleyball—are not especially distinctive or related to her goals, they could also be eliminated.

In this case, space is needed to list references, which have not been given. Or Alicia may prefer to state that references are available on request.

Build Your Skills: What's Wrong with This Résumé?

You might tell Caleb Green several things:
1. Begin with a statement of your career objectives.
2. Use the past tense consistently when describing all experiences and education.

3. If you are still employed, change the date of your current job from "1994-1998" to "1994-present"; add months to the dates for all jobs and education.

4. Omit the personal pronouns, and begin each item of experience or education with an active verb. For example, you might begin describing your work as a manager as follows: "Coordinated production, pricing, and marketing strategy for a line of respiratory-care products."

5. Offer specific evidence of your accomplishments. For each main item in the resumé, you should state two or three outstanding accomplishments, again using action verbs and setting the accomplishments off in list format. For example, you could round out the description of your work as a product manager with something of this sort:
    *   Increased sales for the entire line from $2.3 million to $5.6 million in three years
    *   Launched three new products within a two-year period
    *   Eliminated a chronic six-month backlog for nebulizers

6. Correct typographical errors and misspellings (strategy, health, engineer, hear).

7. Revise the section on your education. Give more details about your MBA from Simon Fraser, and make the section on Cal Tech (California Institute of Technology) more objective. Mention any specific academic honors or courses that are relevant to your career goal. Omit the reference to living in the dorm; this is irrelevant.

8. Either eliminate or revise the personal background section. Omit the fact that you are a sailor who is unwilling to relocate.

Build Your Skills: What's Wrong with This Application Letter?

This letter would fail to impress a prospective employer. First, Vanessa does not state which position interests her, and the reference to the trade journal does not give its title and date. Throughout the letter are several statements about Vanessa's accomplishments, yet none is supported with specific details regarding education, experience, and relevant outside activities. Although Vanessa asks the reader to look at the enclosed resumé, her request is flippant and demands that the reader hunt for pertinent facts. Such data should instead be emphasized in the letter. In the close, Vanessa does not give her daytime phone number and seems unconcerned about scheduling an interview at the reader's convenience.

Develop Your Word Power

1. excels	6. familiar	11. E	16. A	21. impervious
2. extremely	7. feasible	12. B	17. B	22. impenetrable
3. February	8. especially	13. A	18. A	23. impertinent
4. existence	9. *C*	14. D	19. C	24. impulsive
5. expense	10. experience	15. C	20. A	25. impending

Chapter 16
Interviewing for Employment and Following Up

The main point of Chapter 16 is that a job interview gives the company a chance to evaluate you and gives you a chance to evaluate the company. As you read the chapter, think about the attitudes and preparation that contribute to a successful interview. When you finish reading, rehearse a job interview, either mentally or with a friend, until you feel that you can handle any type of interview you may encounter.

Master Key Concepts

Use the following terms to fill in the blanks in the outline. All terms are used, but none is used more than once.

acceptance	compatible	resignation	thank-you
bad-news	directed	screening	two
capabilities	questions	stress	warm-up

I. A good job interview enables the interviewer to find the best person for the job and helps the applicant find the job best suited to her or his _____ (pp. 458-459).
    A. Most employers conduct two or three interviews before making a job offer. The typical sequence includes: a preliminary _____ (p. 459) to eliminate unqualified applicants, an initial evaluation by a personnel or recruiting employee, and a final interview by the supervisor or department manager. An applicant may encounter interviews that are _____ (p. 459) (structured by a checklist or series of prepared questions), unstructured (involving broad, open-ended questions), or designed to produce _____ (p. 459) (as a test of the applicant's ability to cope with pointed questions, hostility, and criticism).
    B. Employers want to hire people who are suitable for the job and who will fit into the organization.
    C. An interview gives the applicant a chance to find out whether the people, the organization, and the work itself are _____ (p. 461) with his or her skills, interests, and goals.
    D. To reduce the natural tension that accompanies a job interview, take steps in advance to handle it successfully: investigate the company and the job, evaluate what you have to offer, develop answers to likely questions, think ahead about _____ (pp. 462-463) to ask, bolster your confidence for the interview, polish your interview style, plan to look good, and be ready when you arrive.
    E. The way you handle an interview depends on whether it is at the screening, selection, or final stage; nevertheless, all interviews have three stages: the _____ (p. 468), the question-and-answer stage, and the close.

II. Your job search may require you to write other kinds of messages to employers.
    A. Within two days of each interview, send a _____ (p. 471) note that expresses appreciation, conveys your continuing interest, and asks for a decision.
    B. If you have not heard from the interviewer within _____ (p. 473) weeks, send a letter of inquiry based on the assumption that the delay doesn't imply an outright rejection.
    C. If you receive a job offer while you still have interviews scheduled with other companies, write an enthusiastic note requesting more time to make your decision.
    D. Within five days of a job offer that you want to take, send a letter of _____ (p. 474); bear in mind that such a letter is a legally binding contract.

E. If you receive a job offer that you do not want to accept, send a tactful and sincere letter following the _____ (p. 474) plan; try to leave the door open for future contact in case the job you do accept doesn't work out.

F. If you must quit one job in order to take another, send a letter of _____ (p. 475) that follows the bad-news plan; try to sound positive so that your former employer will willingly supply recommendations in the future.

Check your answers at the end of this chapter.

Quiz Yourself

1. Briefly describe the sequence in the typical interview process.

2. Interviews take various forms, depending on what the recruiter is attempting to discover about the applicant. Explain the differences between directed and open-ended interviews, and name one advantage of each.

3. What two things are employers looking for in potential employees?

4. How can you find out whether you are likely to be compatible with your employers?

5. List six things you should do in preparing for an interview.

6. Before you go to an interview, what facts should you try to find out about the prospective employer and job?

7. Give some general pointers on how to discuss salary during a job interview.

8. What organizational plan should you use in writing a thank-you note to a job interviewer?

9. What should you do if, after the interview, you are not advised of the decision by the promised date or within two weeks?

10. How should you organization a letter of acceptance?

Check your answers at the end of this chapter.

Build Your Skills: Are Your Questions Ready?

When interviewing for a job, you have two objectives: to create a good impression and to determine whether the job and the organization are right for you. The questions you ask help you achieve both objectives. To prepare yourself, make a list of 15 or 20 questions that you would like answered during a typical job interview.

Build Your Skills: What's Wrong With This Follow-Up Letter?

A job applicant has drafted this follow-up letter. What could he do to make it more effective?

1906 Bentley Avenue
Monkton, NB
June 12, 2001

Ms. Elizabeth Monroe
Director of Human Resources
Monkton Transit Authority
600 Claremont Boulevard
Monkton, NB

Dear Ms. Monroe:

Talking with you was a real pleasure. It's exciting to know that even people in large corporations have outside interests like scuba diving and backpacking. If I'm hired, I look forward to joining you on some of the Explorer's Club outings we chatted about.

Please keep me in mind for the position we discussed. Hope to hear from you soon.

Sincerely yours,

Al Giordano

Develop Your Word Power

Spelling Challenge Identify the misspelled word in each of the following sentences, and spell it correctly in the space provided. If all the words in a sentence are spelled correctly, write *C* in the space.

_____   1. We communicate with our foriegn offices via the intranet.

_____   2. Sandra Hayes is the fourth factory representative we have had.

_____   3. Take a vacation that fulfils all your dreams!

_____   4. In the annual report, you can generalise about our problems.

_____   5. Can you garantee delivery by May 1?

_____   6. This photograph was taken from a heighth of 200 feet.

_____   7. Over fourty people have applied for the clerical position.

_____   8. Your new camera is frajel, so treat it gently.

_____   9. The federal goverment requires us to subject several reports.

_____   10. Guard against auto theft with a Lookout alarm.

Vocabulary Challenge Match the words in the first column with the definitions in the second column.

_____   11. induce   A. to provoke

_____   12. infuse   B. to mediate

_____   13. instigate   C. to insert

_____   14. intercede   D. to cause

_____   15. interject   E. to instill

Circle the best definition of the highlighted word in each of the following sentences.

16. When I think of summer, I have an **indelible** image of blue and white.

   A. strong   B. inappropriate   C. unerasable

17. We might be able to stop the **innuendo** by making a public statement.

   A. indirect criticism   B. competition   C. investigation process

18. Mr. Billings spends an **inordinate** amount of time on the telephone.

   A. excessive   B. unmeasurable   C. unauthorized

19. Can **insipid** conclusions support strong recommendations?

   A. faulty   B. bland   C. brilliant

20. We are **insolvent** and cannot meet our obligations.

   A. inebriated   B. puzzled   C. bankrupt

Select one of these words to complete each of the following sentences, and write the word in the space provided.

ingenious   ingenuous   insatiable   interminable   intermittent

21. Because she is so sincere and _____, she is able to calm angry people.

22. An _____ beep is probably more effective than a steady tone.

23. New DinnerTime frozen entrees are big enough for even _____ appetites.

24. She came up with an. _____ solution to the problem that I had never thought of.

25. His _____ quest for a "hot deal" is finally beginning to irritate me.

Follow-up Word Study Check your answers at the end of this chapter. In the spaces below, write the words that you spelled or used incorrectly. (Use a separate piece of paper if you missed more than five words.) Then use your dictionary to carefully study the spelling, pronunciation, definition, and history (etymology) of each word. Finally, to help fix the word in your memory, write it in a sentence.

Word   Sentence

_____   _____

_____   _____

_____   _____

_____   _____

_____   _____

Check Your Answers

Master Key Concepts

I.   capabilities
   A. screening, directed, stress
   C. compatible
   D. questions
   E. warm-up

II. A. thank-you
   B. two
   D. acceptance
   E. bad-news
   F   resignation

Quiz Yourself

1. The typical interview sequence consists of three steps:
   a) A preliminary screening (often held on campus) that enables the company to eliminate unqualified applicants
   b) An initial visit to the company, designed to give the personnel officer or department manager an opportunity to narrow the field a little further
   c) A final interview that gives the supervisor a chance to decide whether a particular candidate is the right person for the job (p. 459)

2. The directed interview is planned from start to finish by the interviewer. He or she poses a series of prepared questions within a specific time period and makes note of the interviewee's responses. An open-ended interview has a less structured and more relaxed format. The interviewer poses broad, general

questions and encourages the interviewee to talk freely. Directed interviews are useful for gathering facts; open-ended interviews are useful for bringing out the interviewee's personality. (p. 461)

3. Employers are looking for:
    *   Evidence that the person can handle the job (suitability)
    *   Evidence that the person will fit in with the organization (pp. 460—461)

4. To find out whether you are likely to be compatible with potential employers, do some research about the company and its personnel. Arrange to talk with an employee if you can. Analyze the people you meet during your interviews to determine whether you have similar values, interests, and backgrounds. (p. 461)

5. To prepare for a job interview:
    a) Do some basic research about the organization and the job.
    b) Think ahead about what questions you might be asked and what questions you should ask.
    c) Build your confidence.
    d) Polish your interview style.
    e) Plan to look good.
    f) Be ready when you arrive. (pp. 461-466)

6. Before going to a job interview, try to find out these facts about the employer:
    *   Company name
    *   Location(s)
    *   Company age
    *   Products and services
    *   Position in the industry
    *   Earnings
    *   Growth
    *   Organization

    Try to find out these facts about the job:
    *   Job title
    *   Job functions
    *   Job qualifications
    *   Career path
    *   Salary range
    *   Travel opportunities
    *   Relocation opportunities (p. 462)

7. Don't make money a major point of discussion. Try to avoid the subject until late in the interview, and let the company representative bring up the topic. If you are asked directly about your salary expectations, say that you would expect to receive the standard salary for the job. If the interviewer doesn't mention salary, you can simply ask what the position pays, but do not inquire about fringe benefits until you have a firm job offer. (p. 469)

8. A thank-you note to a job interviewer should be organized like a routine message, using the direct plan. The main idea (your gratitude for the interview) should come first. (p. 471)

9. If, after the interview, you are not advised of the decision by the promised date or within two weeks, you might send a letter of inquiry. (p. 473)

10. A letter of acceptance should follow the good-news plan. Begin by accepting the position and expressing thanks. Identify the job you are accepting. Cover any necessary details in the middle section of the letter, and then conclude by saying that you look forward to reporting for work. (p. 474)

Build Your Skills: Are Your Questions Ready?

Although various students want to ask job interviewers different things, their questions should deal with these basic issues:

- Are these my kind of people?
- Can I do this work?
- Will I enjoy the work?
- Is the job what I want and what I'm worth?
- What is the status of the person I'd work for?
- What sort of future can I expect with this organization?

Build Your Skills: What's Wrong with This Follow-Up Letter?

This letter would not impress a prospective employer. By mentioning only the hobbies that he shares with the interviewer, Al fails to convey a serious, professional approach to his career. Instead, he should immediately express thanks for the interview and specify exactly which position was discussed. He should also express enthusiasm for the company. Finally, he should make the rather casual close more formal and focused. It should convey an offer to submit more information and briefly reiterate how Al can contribute to the company's goals.

Develop Your Word Power

I. foreign	6. height	11. D	16. C	21. ingenuous
2. *C*	7. forty	12. F	17. A	22. intermittent
3. fulfills	8. fragile	13. A	18. A	23. insatiable
4. generalize	9. government	14. B	19. B	24. ingenious
5. guarantee	10. *C*	15. C	20. C	25. interminable

PART SIX
ORAL COMMUNICATION

Chapter 17
Listening, Interviewing, and Conducting Meetings

The main point of Chapter 17 is that the success of interviews and meetings relies greatly on the participants' listening and planning skills. As you read the chapter, think about how the "you" attitude and self-confidence might also help someone participate successfully in interviews and meetings. When you finish reading, categorize the problems that came up in an interview or meeting in which you participated, and speculate on the actions or attitudes that could have solved those problems.

Master Key Concepts

Use the following terms to fill in the blanks in the outline. All terms are used, but none is used more than once.

agenda   evaluation   listening   nonverbal
conversation   feedback   minutes   open-ended
disciplinary   group dynamics

I. Oral communication—speaking and listening—saves time, provides opportunities for _____ (p. 484) and social interaction, and conveys nonverbal information, but it also limits the ability to edit one's thoughts, requires close attention, and is influenced by the speaker's appearance and delivery style.
    A. In business, you need to think before you speak, to adjust your speaking style to fit the situation, to be sure that your _____ (p. 485) signals are consistent with your words, and to use the "you" attitude.
    B. _____ (p. 486) is a process of five related activities: sensing, interpreting, evaluating, remembering, and responding; there are three types of listening, which differ in their purpose and in the amount of feedback that occurs: content listening, critical listening, and active or empathic listening.

II. A business interview is a planned _____ (p. 488) with a predetermined purpose that involves asking and answering questions.
    A. Interviews can be categorized as job interviews, information interviews, persuasive interviews, exit interviews, _____ (p. 489) interviews, counseling interviews, conflict-resolution interviews, _____ (p. 489) interviews, and termination interviews.
    B. When planning an interview, you need to think about the kinds of questions you will ask and the structure of the interview. The four basic types of interview questions are:
    *   _____ (pp. 490-491), questions that invite the interviewee to offer an opinion
    *   Direct open-ended questions
    *   Closed-ended questions
    *   Restatement questions

C. The sequence of questions depends on the purpose of the interview, but the interview should always have an opening, a body, and a close.

III. Meetings are called to solve problems or share information.
   A. A meeting's success depends in great part on the _____ (p. 494), the various interactions and processes:
     • Appropriate role-playing
     • Development of good group norms
     • Effective decision making
   B. The key to productive meetings is careful planning of purpose, participants, _____ (p. 497), and location.
   C. The meeting leader's duties include pacing the meeting, appointing a note taker, following the agenda, stimulating participation and discussion, summarizing the debate, reviewing recommendations, and circulating copies of the _____ (pp. 497-498).

Check your answers at the end of this chapter.

Quiz Yourself

1. Describe the process you should use for effective oral communication.

2. List and briefly describe the five stages of the listening process.

3. List three types of listening, and indicate the goals of each.

4. What are five traits that distinguish good listeners from bad ones?

5. Define the term "business interview."

6. What is a persuasive interview?

7. Briefly describe four basic types of interview questions.

8. Briefly describe the three types of roles that people play in meetings.

9. What are the four phases of the group decision-making process?

10. List four main steps that meeting leaders can take during the planning stage to ensure that meetings will be productive.

Check your answers at the end of this chapter.

Build Your Skills: Plan Your High-Stakes Interview

To develop your ability to handle challenging interviews, try your hand at planning your strategy for asking for a raise. Use a current or past job as a frame of reference, or invent a job. Write down your plan for conducting the conversation with your boss. Include a list of questions you should ask, points you want to make, and responses you can give to your boss's possible objections.

Develop Your Word Power

Spelling Challenge Identify the misspelled word in each of the following sentences, and spell it correctly in the space provided. If all the words in a sentence are spelled correctly, write *C* in the space.

_____   1. Do you preceive any differences between this loaf and that one?

_____   2. Julie is persistant and should eventually find a job she wants.

_____   3. Try to persuade Mr. Mitchell to send full payment tomorrow.

_____   4. Do you have any phisical problems that may affect your work?

_____   5. Greg's preferrence is the oak finish.

_____   6. The urge to avoid all taxes is quite prevalent.

_____   7. I would have preferred to discuss this matter in private.

_____   8. In about a week, we will install the permenent awning.

_____   9. Your visit Monday was a pleasant surprise.

_____   10. Having some of the new models is preferrable to having none.

Vocabulary Challenge Match the words in the first column with the definitions in the second column.

_____   11. prohibitive   A. exciting

_____   12. provisional   B. repetitive

_____   13. provocative   C. forbidding

_____   14. redundant   D. negligent

_____   15. remiss   E. temporary

Circle the best definition of the highlighted word in each of the following sentences.

16. Dr. Jepson has been a **prolific** writer.

    A. productive   B. antiabortion   C. wordy

17. The new lobby will **protrude** into the courtyard.

    A. meld   B. project   C. flow

18. We have completed this project **pursuant** to the terms of our contract .

    A. in spite of   B. confoming to   C. because of

19. Jeff's career has been his **raison d'être**.

    A. constant problem   B. means of support   C. reason for being

20. Remember to **recapitulate** at the end of your presentation.

    A. summarize   B. surrender   C. retrench

Select one of these words to complete each of the following sentences, and write the word in the space provided.

propensity   **protégé**   **proxy**   **rendezvous**   **repertoire**

21. Sylvia has a _____ for accepting more work than she can handle.

22. What other skills do you have in your _____?

23. You will be my _____ during my absence.

24. Ms. Xu's _____ is being groomed to take over when she retires.

25. They have scheduled a _____ for discussing the details.

Follow-up Word Study Check your answers at the end of this chapter. In the spaces below, write the words that you spelled or used incorrectly. (Use a separate piece of paper if you missed more than five words.) Then use your dictionary to carefully study the spelling, pronunciation, definition, and history (etymology) of each word. Finally, to help fix the word in your memory, write it in a sentence.

Word   Sentence

_____   _____

_____   _____

_____   _____

_____   _____

_____   _____

Check Your Answers

Master Key Concepts

I.   feedback
    A. nonverbal
    B. listening

II. conversation
    A. evaluation, disciplinary
    B. open-ended

III. A. group dynamics
    B. agenda
    C. minutes

Quiz Yourself

1. To communicate effectively, you should apply the same process to oral communication as you use in written communication. Before you speak, think about your purpose, your main idea, and your audience. Organize your thoughts in a logical way; decide on a style that suits the occasion; then edit your remarks mentally. Revise your message if it does not appear to be having the desired effect on your listeners. (p. 485)

2. The five stages of the listening process are:
    a) Sensing—physically hearing the message and taking note of it
    b) Interpreting—decoding and absorbing the message
    c) Evaluating—forming an opinion about the message
    d) Remembering—storing a message for future reference
    e) Responding—acknowledging the message by reacting to the speaker in some fashion (pp. 486-487)

3. Three types of listening are:
    • Content listening, in which the goal is to understand and retain information imparted by a speaker
    • Critical listening, in which the goal is to evaluate the message
    • Active or empathic listening, in which the goal is to understand the speaker's feelings, needs, and wants in order to solve a problem (p. 487)

4. Unlike bad listeners, good listeners:
    • Judge content, not delivery
    • Listen for ideas
    • Are flexible
    • Resist distractions
    • Keep an open mind (pp. 487-488)

5. A business interview is a planned conversation with a predetermined purpose that involve asking and answering questions. (p. 488)

6. A persuasive interview is one in which you try to convince the other person of something. Persuasive interviews are often associated with selling. You discuss the other person's needs and show how your product or concept is able to fulfill those needs. (p. 489)

7. The four basic types of interview questions are:
   - Open-ended questions, which invite the interviewee to offer an opinion as opposed to a yes-or-no or one-word answer
   - Direct open-ended questions, which suggest a specific response
   - Closed-ended questions, which require a yes-or-no or one-word answer
   - Restatement questions, which restate an interviewee's answer in order to invite a more detailed response (pp. 490-491)

8. The three main types of roles that people play in meetings are:
   - Self-oriented roles-motivated primarily to fulfill personal needs
   - Group maintenance roles-help members work well together
   - Task-facilitating roles-help members sold the problem or make the decision

9. The four stages in group decision making are:
   a) Orientation phase
   b) Conflict phase
   c) Emergency phase
   d) Reinforcement phase (p. 495)

10. Meeting planners need to:
    a) Determine the purpose-is the meeting really needed?
    b) Select the participants, inviting only those whose presence is essential.
    c) Set the agenda and distribute it so participants will be prepared.
    d) Prepare the location, recognizing that setting and facilities can have a significant impact on the meeting. (p. 497)

Build Your Skills: Plan Your High-Stakes Interview

Because the purpose of this interview is to persuade the boss to grant the raise, the interview should focus on the presentation of information as opposed to the asking of questions. The choice of a strategy for the interview depends on the relationship between the student and the boss. If the you have a good, close relationship with your boss and expect a sympathetic and favorable reaction, the interview may be conducted in a direct fashion. You may begin with a direct request for a raise and give three or four reasons to justify the request.

If the response is likely to be negative, however, you may want to lead up to the request more gradually through a series of questions that will pave the way for an objective appraisal.
In either case, the plan should cover the three basic parts of the interview: (1) an opening gambit that will introduce the request, (2) a presentation of evidence that supports the request, and (3) a closing statement that motivates the boss to reach a positive decision. The heart of the interview plan should be a list of points you will introduce, as well as a list of questions that you might ask. These questions should include a mix of open-end, direct open-end, closed-end, and restatement questions.

In addition, the interview plan should include a list of the boss's possible reactions, together with guidelines for responding to various points that might be raised.

Develop Your Word Power

1.	perceive	6.	*C*	11. C	16. A	21.	propensity
2.	persistent	7.	*C*	12. E	17. B	22.	repertoire
3.	*C*	8.	permanent	13. A	18. C	23.	proxy
4.	physical	9.	pleasant	14. B	19. C	24.	protégé
5.	preference	10.	preferable	15. D	20. A	25.	rendezvous

Chapter 18
Giving Speeches and Oral Presentations

The main point of Chapter 18 is that speeches and oral presentations require just as much preparation and skillful execution as a formal report does. As you read the chapter, think about the parallels between these "oral reports" and their written cousins. When you finish reading, analyze the strengths and weaknesses of someone else's speech or oral presentation; then list ways that the weaknesses could have been overcome.

Master Key Concepts

Use the following terms to fill in the blanks in the outline. All terms are used, but none is used more than once.

audience	interest	positive`	stage fright
handouts	location	presentations	transitions
idea	notes	purpose	visual aids

I. Although they resemble any other message, speeches and oral _____ (p. 506) are delivered under relatively public circumstances, so they require a few special communication techniques.
   A. The first step in preparing for a speech or presentation is to define the _____ (p. 506), which helps determine content, style, and amount of audience interaction.
   B. The second step in preparing to speak is to analyze the _____ (p. 506), including its size, composition, and attitude.
   C. The third step in preparing to speak is to plan your strategy: developing the main _____ (p.508), developing an outline, estimating length, and deciding on the style.

II. A carefully prepared outline can also become the script for your speech. Many speakers include notes to indicate where _____ (pp. 509) will be used.
   A. In the introduction of your speech you need to arouse the audience's _____ (p. 512), build credibility, and preview the topics to be covered.
   B. In the body of your speech, you can help the audience understand by emphasizing structure, that is, by summarizing your remarks as you go along and by providing _____ (p. 514) from one idea to the next; you also need to make a special effort to keep the audience's attention.
   C. In your close you should restate the main points, outline any specific actions that should be taken, and end on a _____ (p. 516) note.
   D. Give people an opportunity to ask questions either during or after the talk.
   E. When preparing visual aids for your talk, make sure they are necessary and useful; among media to choose from are _____ (p. 518) for members of the audience, chalkboards, flip charts, overheads, and slides.

III. You have a variety of methods to choose from when delivering your talk, including memorizing the speech, reading it, speaking from _____ (p. 520), and impromptu speaking.
   A. Before you speak, you should practice your presentation and try to check out the _____ (p. 521) in advance.
   B. When delivering the speech, you can use a number of techniques to overcome _____ (p.522) and to keep the attention and interest of the audience.
   C. Prepare in advance for questions that may arise during the question-and-answer period; give short, direct, unemotional answers to questions.

Check your answers at the end of this chapter.

Quiz Yourself

1. What are the four main purposes for speeches and presentations?

2. What are the main things you should learn about your audience when preparing for a speech or presentation?

3. How should a short (ten minutes or less) speech be organized? How should a longer speech be organized?

4. What is involved in estimating the length of a speech or presentation?

5. In general, when would you use a casual, informal style in a presentation, and when would you use a more formal approach?

6. What are the three main tasks to be accomplished in the introduction to a speech or presentation?

7. List three things you can do to hold audience attention during a speech.

8. Briefly describe some of the most commonly used visual aids for speeches and oral presentations.

9. Briefly describe the four speech delivery modes. When might you use each approach?

10. List at least five things you could do to overcome stage fright.

Check your answers at the end of this chapter.

Build Your Skills: Plan Your Five-Minute Speech

You have been asked to prepare a five-minute speech about your school to present to a group of high school seniors who are deciding which college to attend. You don't know any of the students, but you have been told that they are 25 high achievers from Northern Ontario who are visiting your campus and others. Write out a plan for this speech.

Develop Your Word Power

Spelling Challenge Identify the misspelled word in each of the following sentences, and spell it correctly in the space provided. If all the words in a sentence are spelled correctly, write *C* in the space.

_____ 1. We should establish a prosedure for handling returns.

_____ 2. Dr. Stein is a promenent psychologist.

_____ 3. At the next meeting, let's persue the idea of reorganizing.

_____ 4. Your losses in the second quarter may be bigger than you realise.

_____ 5. How many responses did we receive?

_____ 6. Try to avoid a recurence of that unfortunate episode.

_____ 7. All moving parts are replacible within 30 days of purchase.

_____ 8. It is my priviledge to recommend Samuel Sharpe for the award.

_____ 9. The questionnaire has 50 items on two pages.

_____ 10. I didn't reconnize any of the names on the list.

Vocabulary Challenge Match the words in the first column with the definitions in the second column.

_____ 11. repugnant   A. firm

_____ 12. resilient   B. severe

_____ 13. rigorous   C. doubtful

_____ 14. skeptical   D. offensive

_____ 15. steadfast   E. buoyant

Circle the best definition of the highlighted word in each of the following sentences.

16. We recommend **retention** of all register receipts for at least five years.

   A. analysis   B. keeping   C. memorization

17. A new vacation policy is **retroactive** to January 1.

    A. effective to a past date   B. scheduled for review   C. effective to a future date

18. In **retrospect**, we can be proud of our modest gains during that period.

    A. looking back   B. all due modesty   C. conclusion

19. He has **reverted** to his old habit of smoking.

    A. referred   B. returned   C. become hostile

20. Her **savoir faire** is an asset in dealing with clients.

    A. nice appearance   B. bubbly personality   C. diplomacy and tact

Select one of these words to complete each of the following sentences, and write the word in the space provided.

reprimand   **reproach**   **respite**   **stalemate**   **stigma**

21. Christmas Day is only a brief _____ in the hectic Christmas shopping season.

22. With time, you will overcome the _____ of bankruptcy.

23. Until we resolve this _____, we cannot negotiate further.

24. Robert's handling of the situation is beyond _____.

25. A formal _____ should make our extreme displeasure clear.

Follow-up Word Study Check your answers at the end of this chapter. In the spaces below, write the words that you spelled or used incorrectly. (Use a separate piece of paper if you missed more than five words.) Then use your dictionary to carefully study the spelling, pronunciation, definition, and history (etymology) of each word. Finally, to help fix the word in your memory, write it in a sentence.

Word   *Sentence*

_____   _____

_____   _____

_____   _____

_____   _____

_____   _____

Check Your Answers

Master Key Concepts

I. presentations
    A. purpose
    B. audience
    C. idea

II. visual aids
    A. interest
    B. transitions
    C. positive
    E. handouts

III. notes
    A. location
    B. stage fright

Quiz Yourself

1. The four main purposes of speeches and oral presentations are:
    - To inform
    - To explain
    - To persuade
    - To entertain (p. 507)

2. When analyzing the audience for a speech or presentation, you should find out its size, its composition, people's likely reaction to what you have to say, their level of understanding, and their relationship with you. (p. 508)

3. A short speech should be organized like a letter or brief memo, using the direct approach if the subject involves routine information or good news, and using the indirect approach if the subject involves bad news or persuasion.
    A longer speech should be organized like a formal report, using a direct approach if the purpose is to entertain, motivate, or inform, and using conclusions/recommendations or a logical argument if the purpose is to analyze, persuade, or collaborate. (p. 509)

4. When estimating the length of a speech or presentation, you should keep in mind that the average speaker talks at the rate 125 to 150 words a minute, which is approximately one paragraph. You need to allot a reasonable amount of time for your introduction, your conclusion, and the question-and-answer session. If you deduct this time from the overall time allotted, you will know the number of minutes remaining for the body of your speech. (p. 510-511)

5. You would use a casual, informal style for a relatively small group, especially if you want audience participation. You would use a formal tone if you are addressing a large audience or if it is an important occasion. (p. 512)

6. The three main tasks to be accomplished in the introduction of a talk are arousing audience interest, building credibility, and previewing the presentation. (pp. 512-514)

7. Ways to hold audience attention during a speech include:
    - Relating your subject to the audience's needs
    - Using clear, vivid language
    - Explaining the relationship between your subject and familiar ideas (p. 515)

8. The most commonly used visual aids are:
    *   Handouts—papers that the audience can refer to after the presentation to remind themselves of important ideas. Handouts may be given to the audience before or after the presentation.
    *   Chalkboards and whiteboards—useful in illustrating points during a presentation.
    *   Flip charts—large sheets of paper, attached at the top like a tablet and propped against an easel. The speaker can either prepare the charts in advance or create them on the spot as the presentation progresses.
    *   Overheads—transparent sheets of film, with information written or drawn on them, that can be projected on a screen in full daylight, or images of any regular typed or printed material that can be cast on a screen with the use of a special projector.
    *   Slides—mounted pieces of film showing either text or visual material that are projected on a screen in a darkened room. Slides must be prepared in advance; showing slides tends to limit audience interaction.
    *   Computers—when attached to special projectors, this technology, allows you to create and modify your visual aids as the presentation unfolds. (p. 518)

9. The four delivery modes and their characteristics are as follows:
    *   Memorizing—committing all or part of the speech to memory, word for word. This is not generally a good way to deliver an entire speech or presentation, but it is often an effective technique for the introduction, the conclusion, or special quotations or stories.
    *   Reading—delivering a prepared script by reading it verbatim. Reading is an appropriate approach when precise wording is necessary and is often used for delivering policy statements and technical papers. Reading has the disadvantage of limiting eye contact and interaction with the audience.
    *   Speaking from notes—speaking in a conversational way with the help of notes, transparencies, or an outline. This method permits eye contact and audience interaction and gives the speaker flexibility to deviate from the planned material. Notes are used for most decision-making presentations and for many brief speeches.
    *   Impromptu speaking—delivering remarks spontaneously, without any advance preparation. Impromptu speaking is not recommended for long, formal presentations, but it is appropriate for responding to questions during a meeting. (pp. 519-520)

10. Things you can do to overcome stage fright include:
    *   Prepare more material than necessary.
    *   Think positively about your audience, yourself, and what you have to say.
    *   Be realistic about stage fright.
    *   Before going on tell yourself that you're ready.
    *   Have your first sentence memorized.
    *   If your throat is dry, drink some water.
    *   Don't panic.
    *   Use visual aids to maintain audience interest.
    *   Keep going.
    *   Concentrate on your message and audience, not on yourself. (p. 522)

Build Your Skills: Plan Your Five-Minute Speech

When planning this brief informative speech, you should develop an outline that begins with an attention-getter and preview, proceed to make three or four basic points, and closes with a review and a memorable statement.

The outline should reflect a clear understanding of the purpose of the speech and its main theme or central idea, which should be established at the outset of the talk. In addition, the outline should give an indication of the style you will use to reach the audience.

Because the speech can be no more than the equivalent of five paragraphs, the three or four main points must be relatively straightforward.

Visual aids are probably unnecessary in this situation, although you might want to give the audience some handouts that provide additional information about the school.

Develop Your Word Power

1. procedure
2. prominent
3. pursue
4. realize
5. *C*

6. recurrence
7. replaceable
8. privilege
9. *C*
10. recognize

11. D
12. E
13. B
14. C
15. A

16. B
17. A
18. A
19. B
20. C

21. respite
22. stigma
23. stalemate
24. reproach
25. reprimand

APPENDICES

Appendix A
Format and Layout of Business Documents

The main point of Appendix A is that conscientious attention to format and layout makes business documents more effective by helping them get to the right person, makes an impression of professionalism, and tells the recipient who wrote them and when. As you read the chapter, think about how the various elements of format and layout contribute to these goals. When you finish reading, study some business documents that you have received for real-life variations on the patterns recommended in this chapter.

Master Key Concepts

Use the following terms to fill in the blanks in the outline. All terms are used, but none is used more than once.

agendas	distribution	mailing	paper
attention	documents	memo-letters	reference
block	internationally	salutation	simplified
centered	letterhead	minutes	thirds
complimentary			

I. Readers unconsciously judge business _____ (p. 531) on the basis of appearance: neatness, professionalism, and reading ease.
   A. High-quality _____ (p. 531) of a standard size and color is especially important in letters and other correspondence directed to outsiders.
   B. Letters to outsiders are commonly written on _____ (p. 532) stationery, which has the company name and address and other information printed at the top; internal documents, such as memos and standardized reports, are often typed on printed forms designed to highlight the required information in minimal space.
   C. To make the best impression, letters are _____ (p. 532) on the page with good-size margins all around; the proper spacing should be used after all punctuation; and the typing should appear clean, dark, and neat.

II. Regardless of their content, letters have certain standard parts and optional additional parts and are generally arranged in one of three basic letter styles.
   A. Business letters typically have seven standard parts:
   - heading, usually in the form of a letterhead
   - date
   - inside address identifying the recipient of the letter
   - _____ (p. 537), a greeting to the recipient
   - body, or main message
   - _____ (p. 537) close, a word or two of courtesy to conclude the letter
   - a signature block.

B. Depending on the requirements of the letter, any combination of these additional letter parts may also be used:
*   Addressee notations indicating special handling required for delivering the letter
*   _____ (p. 538) line identifying the recipient when the inside address does not include the name of a specific person
*   Subject line telling the recipient what the letter is about
*   Second-page heading for long letters
*   Company name in the signature block if it does not appear in the letterhead
*   _____ (p. 540) initials indicating who prepared and who composed the letter
*   Enclosure notation indicating the inclusion of additional materials
*   Copy notation indicating the names of those who are receiving copies of the letter, preferably in order of rank or in alphabetical order
*   _____ (p. 540) notation indicating special mailing procedures
*   Postscript, which is an afterthought or a message requiring special emphasis

C. The three most common formats for business letters are:
*   The _____ (p. 540) format, in which each part of the letter begins at the left margin
*   The modified block format, in which all items begin at the left except for the date, complimentary close, and typewritten name, which start in the center of the page
*   The _____ (p. 541) format, in which the salutation and complimentary close are eliminated.

III. Envelopes should match the company letterhead and are sized to accommodate the stationery.
A. Envelopes contain two blocks of copy-the sender's name and address and the recipient's name and address—both of which should conform to Canada Post standards.
B. An 8-1/2-by-11-inch piece of paper can be folded in _____ (p. 545) lengthwise to fit in a standard No. 10 envelope; if it must be sent in a smaller envelope, it should first be folded in half and then in thirds.

IV. When sending _____ (pp. 545-546) mail, remember that postal service differs from country to country.

V. Clarity, careful arrangement, and neatness are important in internal memos, whether they are typed on preprinted forms or on plain paper; the heading identifies the date, writer, recipient, and subject; the complimentary close is eliminated.

VI. The format for e-mail messages depends on your audience and purpose. The two major elements of e-mail messages are the header and the body. You can send your message to several people by creating a _____ (p. 547) list.

VII. Special time-saving message formats reduce the amount of time spent typing and writing messages: _____ (p. 549) are printed like memos but provide space for an inside address so the message can be folded and sent in a window envelope; short-note replies are responses written at the bottom of original documents instead of on a new piece of paper; letterhead postcards bear the organization's name and address and may also be preprinted with a list of responses that the *"writer"* can check off.

VIII. When laying out reports, pay special attention to margins, headings, spacing, indents, and page numbers.

IX. Two types of documents are used in connection with meetings: _____(p. 552) are outlines of the topics that will be covered in a meeting, and _____ (p. 552) are the official notes of what has occurred during the meeting.

Check your answers at the end of this appendix.

Quiz Yourself

1. What items of information are frequently provided in a company's letterhead? Why might a company decide to limit the number of items included in the letterhead?

2. What are the seven standard parts of a letter?

3. Give two examples of an acceptable complimentary close.

4. In what cases might you use an attention line?

5. What do these notations mean?

    a. cc   _____   d. bc   _____

    b. pc   _____   e. bcc   _____

    c. c   _____   f. bpd   _____

6. What is the difference between standard (mixed) punctuation and open punctuation?

7. What format is used for typing an envelope?

8. What are the basic elements of an e-mail address?

9. What are the basic guidelines for page numbering in reports?

10. What are the items that typically appear on an agenda?

Check your answers at the end of this appendix.

Build Your Skills: Fix The Format

Your assistant is on vacation, and a student is filling in. You assumed that everyone knows how to format a business letter, but you were wrong. The student presented the following letter for your signature. Using arrows to show where things should be moved and little boxes to show where blank lines should be left (one for each line), mark the letter for retyping.

Eco-Care Disposal Services, Inc.
2572 North Pine
Brandon, MN R7N 2G3 204/287-3892

June 21, 2001

Ms. Marybeth Cosentino

Subject: Dumpsters for new apartment buildings

Hagedorn Property Services, Inc.

2809 Fair Avenue, Suite 101

Brandon, MN R8N 1A5

Dear Ms. Cosentino:

Congratulations on finishing the new Davenport Gardens complex. We look forward to helping you keep it clean and tidy.

Your dumpsters have been ordered from the factory and should arrive sometime next week. As soon as the dumpsters arrive, I will call you to set up delivery to Davenport Gardens. Keep us in mind as you put the finishing touches on the complex. We'd be pleased to send over one of our experienced cleanup crews if you find the scheduled completion date approaching too quickly.

Sincerely,

Lou Shafer, Manager Residential Services

gw

PS: After only a little negotiation, the factory agreed to use the custom paint color you asked for. The plant manager liked it so much that he supposedly has repainted his office Davenport Beige!

pc: Dana Evans, Traffic Department

Develop Your Word Power

Use the spelling and vocabulary words from previous chapters to complete the crossword puzzle.

Across

1. administration
5. something outdated
11. breakable
14. to invalidate
16. being
17. person under the care of someone
22. discontented
23. pause
24. predicament
26. to spend
31. directing
33. brings about
35. dull
37. beat
40. obvious
41. skillful
42. place
43. trite saying
44. right away
45. to deal in broad concepts

Down

1. to promise
2. wavering
3. in position number 9
4. effectiveness
5. to prevent
6. to publicize
7. obstacle
8. unconcerned
9. diplomacy and tact
10. one or the other
12. keen insight
13. primary
15. debatable
17. outmoded
18. social blunder
19. contact person
20. succinct
21. 4 times 10
25. intended
27. trifling
28. uninformed guess
29. supposition
30. fault finding
32. proper to be recommended
34. cure-all
36. shortage
38. pertaining to everyday concerns
39. representative.

Check Your Answers

Master Key Concepts

I.   documents
  A. paper
  B. letterhead
  C. centered

II. A. salutation, complimentary
  B. attention, reference, mailing
  C. block, simplified

III. B. thirds

IV. internationally

VI. distribution

VII.   memo-letters

IX. agendas, minutes

Quiz Yourself

1. Letterhead is typically printed with the name and address of the company. It may also contain the company's telephone number, cable address, product lines, date of establishment, officers and directors, slogan, and symbol (logo). A company might decide to limit the amount of information printed on the letterhead in order to avoid a cluttered appearance, save space, and prevent the stationery from becoming outdated. (p. 532)

2. The seven standard parts of a letter are:
  a) Heading
  b) Date
  c) Inside address
  d) Salutation
  e) Body
  f) Complimentary close
  g) Signature block (p. 533)

3. The complimentary close should reflect the relationship between the writer and the reader. Currently, the trend seems to be toward using one-word closes, such as *Sincerely* or *Cordially.* (p. 537)

4. You might want to use an attention line if you know only the last name of the person you are sending the letter to or if you want to direct the letter to a position title or department. (p. 538)

5. These notations have the following meanings:
  a) cc—carbon copy
  b) pc—photocopy
  c) c—copy
  d) bc—blind copy
  e) bcc—blind courtesy copy
  f) bpc—blind photocopy (pp. 539-540)

6. Standard punctuation uses a colon after the salutation (a comma if the letter is social or personal) and a comma after the complimentary close. Open punctuation uses no colon or comma after the salutation or the complimentary close. (pp. 542-543)

7. Envelopes are typed in block form and single-spaced. If a No. 10 envelope is used, the block identifying the recipient should begin 4 inches from the left side and 2-1/2 inches from the top; if a No. 6-3/4 envelope is used, the recipient's address should begin 2-1/2 inches from the left edge and 2 inches from the top. (p. 544)

8. In an e-mail address, the user name falls to the left of the @ sign. Following the @ sign is the name of the computer where the user has an account, followed by either a country code or a code for the type of organization that operates the computer. (pp. 547-548)

9. The first page of a report (the title page) is not numbered. The other prefatory parts are numbered with lower-case roman numerals, beginning with ii. The first page of the text of the report is given an arabic numeral 1, and the rest of the report is numbered consecutively.

10. Most agendas follow this order:
    a) Call to order
    b) Roll call
    c) Approval of agenda
    d) Approval of minutes
    e) Chairperson's report
    f) Subcommittee reports
    g) Unfinished business
    h) New business
    i) Announcements
    j) Adjournment (p. 553)

Build Your Skills: Fix the Format

The format of the letter should be adjusted as follows:

June 21, 2001

Ms. Marybeth Cosentino

Subject: Dumpsters for new apartment buildings

Hagedorn Property Services, Inc.

2809 Fair Avenue, Suite 101

Brandon, MN R8N 1A5

Dear Ms. Cosentino:

Congratulations on finishing the new Davenport Gardens complex. We look forward to helping you keep it clean and tidy.

Your dumpsters have been ordered from the factory, and should arrive sometime next week. As soon as the dumpsters arrive, I will call you to set up delivery to Davenport Gardens. Keep us in mind as you put the finishing touches on the complex. We'd be pleased to send over one of our experienced cleanup crews if you find the scheduled completion date approaching too quickly.

☐
Sincerely,

☐
☐
☐

Lou Shafer, Manager

Residential Services

☐
gw

☐
PS: After only a little negotiation, the factory agreed to use the custom paint color you asked for. The plant manager liked it so much that he supposedly has repainted his office Davenport Beige!

pc: Dana Evans, Traffic Department

☐

Develop Your Word Power

```
G O V E R N M E N T . . . A N A C H R O N I S M
U . A . . I . . F . . E . V . D . I . . O . A
A . I . . N . F R A G I L E . V . R . N . C . Y
R . L . . T . I . C . T . R . E . H . C . O . I
A . L . . H . C . U . H . E . T . A . H . R
N . L . . I . I . M . E . R . I . N . N U L L I F Y . A
T . A . . E . E . E . N . . . M . S . C . . . . A . F
E . T . . . . L . N . . . M . O . . . I . . . N . T . I
E X I S T E N C E . . P R O T E G E . . . R . . . A . I
. N . . . . . Y . L . A . O . A . . . T . T . E
G . . . . E . . . D I S S A T I S F I E D
F . . . . N . . . A . . . S . . . . R
O . R E S P I T E . D I L E M M A
R . . . . A . . . S . . . E . . . E X P E N D
T . . C . R . . . Y . . . E . A . A . . . . I
Y . . O . Y . M A N A G I N G . I N C U R S
. . . N . . . . D . . . . T . . S . . A
. . . J . P . V A P I D . . . S . R H Y T H M
. . . E . A . I . . E F . A P P A R E N T . U
. . . C . N . S . P . F . . . T . . . E . D
L I E U . A . A D R O I T . C L I C H E . A
. . . R . C . B . O . I . . . O . . . . N
I M M E D I A T E L Y . T . G E N E R A L I Z E
```

Appendix B
Documentation of Report Sources

The main point of Appendix B is that documenting your work gives it credibility, gives readers the means for checking your findings and pursuing the subject further, and is the accepted way to give credit to the people whose ideas you have drawn on. As you read the chapter, think about how the recommended formats and practices would help someone trying to look up references for further information. When you finish reading, practice documenting several types of reference works.

Master Key Concepts

Use the following terms to fill in the blanks in the outline. All terms are used, but none is used more than once.

author-date	key-number	Reference
copyright	MLA	secondary
extracts	note card	source
fair use	publication	superscript

I. To consult _____ (p. 554) sources you need to make use of libraries, computerized data banks, and note cards.
   A. Libraries can be used to consult basic references, books, articles, abstracts, and government documents.
   B. Large masses of data are stored in computerized data banks; many companies have such data bases, in addition to providing access to commercial databases.
   C. When recording information from documents onto a _____ (p. 557), be sure to include all relevant data about the source.

II. Under the _____ (p. 558) laws, you must acknowledge the source of direct quotations and paraphrased passages but need not cite the source of general knowledge; the _____ (p. 558) doctrine requires you to obtain written permission from the copyright holder if, generally speaking, your use of the material would prevent the author from selling it.

III. _____ (p. 558) Lists, which can also be titled Bibliography or Works Cited, include the sources you consulted in preparing your report. Such lists are usually placed at the end of the report.
   A. When preparing a Reference List, list items alphabetically by author, listing each author's last name first. Information should be broken into three man parts: (1) information about the author, (2) information about the work, and (3) information about the _____ (p. 559).
   B. For titles, capitalize all words but prepositions, conjunctions, and articles with four or fewer letters.
   C. Use a shortened form for the names of publishers.
   D. Consult one of the standard style manuals (MLA, APA, Chicago Manual, etc.) for specifics on setting up items in Reference Lists. The style varies depending on whether the source is a book, periodical, newspaper, public document, unpublished material, or an electronic document.

IV. Several methods of in-text citation have been developed. The _____ (p. 562) system provides an end-of-report list of references and refers to them in the text by author's last name and publication date; a variation of this method, the author-page system, is used by the _____ (p. 562). The _____ (p. 562) system identifies items in the reference list by arabic numeral and then uses this number in parentheses with a colon and the page number. The _____ (p. 563) system places superscript numbers within the text that are keyed to either footnotes or endnotes. Items in such _____ (p. 563) notes generally follow the same order as bibliographic entries, except the commas are often substituted for periods, the publication information appears in parentheses, and the author's name is not in reverse order.

V. Quotations from secondary sources must always be followed by a reference mark. Brief quotations can be typed right into the main body of the text, surrounded by quotation marks. Longer excerpts must be set off as _____ (p. 563).

Check your answers at the end of this chapter.

Quiz Yourself

1. What information should be put on note cards?

2. Discuss the fair use doctrine.

3. What is an annotated bibliography?

4. For entries in a Reference List, what is the order of the three main types of information?

5. What punctuation is used to set off publication information in a source note referring to a book?

6. List five style books that provide additional information on the format for notes and bibliographies.

7. What information should be included in a reference to a letter, a speech, or an interview?

8. Describe three basic methods for handling reference citations.

9. If a book has four or more authors, how do you handle the authors' names in a Reference List?

10. In general, what is the difference between the formal and the informal style in shortened note references?

Check your answers at the end of this chapter.

Build Your Skills: Compile A Bibliography

To hone your ability to prepare a bibliography, compile one on the subject of marketing products in underdeveloped countries. Use a mix of reference types, including books, business journals, popular magazines, academic papers, and newspapers. Include at least 20 entries, presented in acceptable format and arranged in the proper order.

Develop Your Word Power

Use the spelling and vocabulary words from previous chapters to complete the crossword puzzle.

Across
1. hateful
5. genuine
8. well known
9. polite
11. directly
14. frequently
15. pertinent
16. agility
19. to leave out
20. severe
25. beneficial
26. indirect criticism
29. social blunder
30. something given stress
31. implied
34. being
35. facts behind a conclusion
38. to authorize
39. conspicuous
41. take advantage of
42. admits
43. person under the care of someone influential
44. aware

Down

1. event
2. flooded
3. skepticism
4. concise
5. pamphlet
6. to struggle
7. heterogeneity
10. severity

12. cash
13. case for samples
17. analysis
18. something outdated
21. to prevent
22. possessing understanding
23. group formed for a purpose
24. direct opposite

27. in position number 19
28. opinionated
32. in position number 9
33. pertaining to everyday concerns
36. to slander
37. pleasant
40. uninvolved

Check Your Answers

Master Key Concepts

I. secondary
    C. note card

II. copyright, fair use

III. Reference
     A. publication

IV. author-date, MLA, key-number, source

V. extracts

Quiz Yourself

1. A separate note card should be made for each fact, quotation, or general concept you want to record. In addition to this information, include the author's name, the book or article title, and other information necessary for your bibliography. (p. 557)

2. The fair use doctrine says that you cannot use other people's work without written permission if your use might unfairly prevent the author from benefiting in some way—say, by selling a copy of the work or by receiving a royalty payment for it. In such cases, even if you credit the source in your report, you must obtain written permission from the copyright holder to reprint the material. You should probably get permission to use:
   • More than 250 words from a book
   • Any piece of artwork
   • Any dialogue from a play or line from a poem or song
   • Any portion of consumable materials, such as workbooks
   • Multiple copies of copyrighted work (p. 558)

3. An *annotated* bibliography comments on the subject matter and viewpoint of the source, as well as on its usefulness to readers. (pp. 558-559)

4. In a Reference List, the order of the three main types of information for entries is
   • Information about the author
   • Information about the work
   • Information about the publication (p. 559)

5. If a book has four or more authors, the first author's name is spelled out in full (with the last name first), and the remaining authors are listed with their names first name first. The names are separated with commas, and *and* is inserted before the last name It is also acceptable to list only the first author's name, followed by *et al.* or the more informal *and.* (p. 559)

6. These references provide additional information on preparing notes and bibliographies:
    *   *The MLA Handbook for Writers of Research Papers,* by Joseph Gibaldi and Walter S. Achten
    *   *Publication Manual of the American Psychological Association*
    *   *The Chicago Manual of Style,* by The University of Chicago Press
    *   *MLA Handbook for Writers of Research Papers,* by Joseph Garibaldi
    *   *MLA Style Manual and Guide to Scholarly Publishing,* by Joseph Garibaldy
    *   *Online! A Reference Guide to Using Internet Sources,* by Harnack, et al. (pp. 559-560)

7. When referencing a letter, a speech, or an interview, begin with the name, title, and affiliation of the "author"; then describe the nature of the communication, the date, possibly the place, and (if appropriate) the location of any files containing the reference. (pp. 561-562)

8. Ways to handle reference citations include:
    *   The author-date system uses regular bibliography style for the list of references. In the text, reference to a given work is documented by noting the author, date of publication, and page number, set off in parentheses within the text.
    *   The key-number system also uses regular bibliography style for the list of references but numbers each reference in sequence in Arabic numerals, followed by a period. (Sometimes the "bibliography" is arranged in order of the appearance of each source in the text, rather than in alphabetical order.) In the text, references are documented with two numbers separated by a colon; the first is the number assigned to the source, the second is the page number.
    *   The superscript system uses superscript arabic numerals that are keyed to either footnotes or endnotes that include the source information. (p. 562-563)

9. In a source note, publication information for books is set off in parentheses. The first item following the opening parenthesis is the name of the city in which the publisher is located. A colon follows the name of the city, after which the name of the publisher appears (often in shortened form). A comma separates the publisher's name from the publication date. The closing parenthesis follows the date. (p. 563)

10. The formal style for shortened references uses the Latin abbreviations *ibid., op. cit.,* and *loc. cit.* to indicate previously cited sources. The informal style uses the author's last name, a short form of the title, and the page number where the information can be found. (p. 564)

Build Your Skills

The bibliography may be arranged either in alphabetical order according to the author's last name, by subject categories, or by type of reference.

Each entry should start at the left margin, and succeeding lines should be indented. Entries should be single-spaced, with a double space between them. The entry should include author, title, and publication information. Punctuation should conform to accepted format.

Page numbers should not be included for books but should be included for articles and chapters of books.

In addition to being presented in an acceptable format, the bibliography should reveal that you have been selective and thorough in searching for sources. The entries should be relatively recent and should provide a mix of general and specific references. A person should be able to use the bibliography to get a balanced, current, and reliable overview of the subject.

Develop Your Word Power

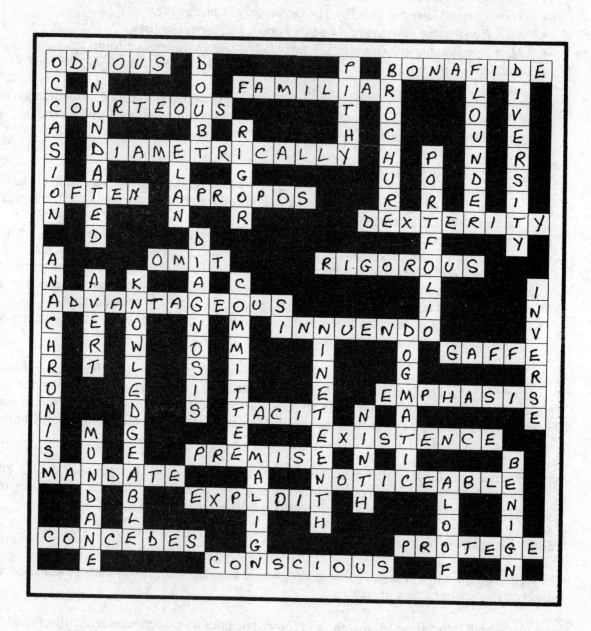

Handbook
Fundamentals of Grammar and Usage

The main point of the Handbook is that the misuse of language can impede communication. As you read the chapter, think about the ways that errors in grammar, punctuation, mechanics, and vocabulary may contribute to misunderstandings. When you finish reading and doing the exercises, analyze your weak points and work to overcome them.

Master Key Concepts

Use the following terms to fill in the blanks in the outline. All terms are used, but none is used more than once.

abbreviations	dashes	mechanics	proper
antecedents	ellipsis	mood	punctuation
capitals	grammar	possessive	semicolons
clauses	hyphens	prepositions	syllables

I. _____ (p. 567) is the way that words are combined into sentences; sentences are composed of parts of speech, the most basic of which are nouns, pronouns, verbs, adjectives, and adverbs.
   A. Nouns name a person, a place, a thing, or an idea; to use nouns correctly, learn the difference between _____ (p. 568) nouns and common nouns, the method of making a noun plural, and the method of making a noun possessive.
   B. Pronouns are words that stand for nouns; to use pronouns correctly, learn how to deal with multiple _____ (p. 571), how to avoid unclear antecedents, how to select gender-neutral pronouns, how to select the correct case for pronouns, and when to use possessive pronouns.
   C. Verbs describe an action or a state of being; to use verbs correctly, learn about verb tenses, irregular verbs, transitive and intransitive verbs, the voice of verbs, and the _____ (p. 578) of verbs.
   D. Adjectives modify (tell something about) nouns and pronouns.
   E. Adverbs modify verbs, adjectives, and other adverbs.
   F. Nouns, pronouns, verbs, adjectives, and adverbs are linked together in sentences by four other parts of speech: _____ (p. 582), conjunctions, articles, and interjections.
   G. Whole sentences contain, at minimum, a subject and a predicate; to be able to construct whole sentences, learn about commands, the difference between phrases and _____ (pp. 585-586) in longer sentences, sentence fragments, fused sentences, sentences with linking verbs, and misplaced modifiers.

II. When used properly to mark different sorts of sentences and sentence elements, _____ (p. 590) keeps readers from losing track of your meaning.
   A. Periods are used at the end of sentences that are not questions, after some _____ (p. 590), and in money expressions.
   B. Question marks are used after any direct question that requires an answer.
   C. Exclamation points are used after highly emotional sentences.
   D. _____ (p. 591) are used to separate closely related independent clauses, items in a series that already contain commas, and independent clauses when the second one begins with a transitional word or phrase.
   E. Colons are used after salutations in a letter and at the end of a sentence or phrase introducing a list, a quotation, or an idea.

F. Commas separate the items in a series, separate an opening phrase or dependent clause from an independent clause, follow an introductory statement, surround parenthetical phrases or words, separate adjectives modifying the same noun, separate some abbreviations (such as *Inc.* and *Jr.*) from the words they identify separate days from years in dates, separate quotations from the rest of the sentence, and separate words and phrases whenever needed to prevent confusion or an unintended meaning.

G. _____ (p. 593) are used around parenthetical comments that represent a sudden turn in thought, around parenthetical comments that require emphasis, and around parenthetical phrases that contain commas.

H. _____ (p. 594) are used to separate the parts of compound words, to separate the parts of compound adjectives that come before the noun (but not after the noun), and to divide words at the ends of lines.

I. Apostrophes are used in the _____ (p. 595) form of nouns and in contractions.

J. Quotation marks surround words that are repeated exactly as they were said or written, set off the titles of newspaper and magazine articles, and indicate special treatment for words and phrases.

K. Parentheses surround comments that are entirely incidental and surround dollar amounts in legal documents.

L. _____ (p. 596) points are used to indicate that material has been left out of a direct quotation.

M. Underscores and italics provide emphasis and indicate the titles of books, magazines, and the like.

III. A number of small details known as _____ (p. 597) demonstrate a writer's polish and reflect on the organization's professionalism.

A. _____ (p. 597) are used at the beginning of sentences, as the first letter of proper nouns and adjectives, for official titles, and as the first letter of salutations and complimentary closes.

B. Abbreviations are used mainly in tables, graphs, lists, and forms.

C. Numbers from one to ten are generally spelled out, and numbers over ten are generally indicated with Arabic numerals; for handling numbers in other situations, many other rules exist.

D. Dividing words at the ends of lines should be done at _____ (p. 599) or existing hyphens.

IV. Using the right word in the right place is a crucial element in business communication.

A. Frequently confused words are sets of words that sound similar but are spelled differently; be careful not to mistake one for another.

B. Frequently misused words tend to be misused for reasons other than sound.

C. Frequently misspelled words are commonly used words that are difficult to spell for a variety of reasons.

D. Transitional words and phrases are useful for showing the relationship between two sentences or clauses.

Check your answers at the end of this chapter.

Quiz Yourself

1. What is the difference between grammar and usage?

2. In general, which nouns are capitalized, and which are not?

3. Explain what an antecedent is, in grammatical terms, and name two types of antecedents that cause confusion.

4. List the six verb tenses, and briefly describe how they are regularly formed.

5. Name the two voices of verbs, and explain when each should be used.

6. What are the five most important parts of speech, and what are the four other parts of speech that link them together in sentences?

7. Explain the differences between a phrase and a clause.

8. Explain what sentence fragments and fused sentences are and why both are unacceptable.

9. How can you text the appropriateness of inserting a comma between adjectives modifying the same noun?

10. In the absence of a different company style, what is the basic rule of thumb for spelling out numbers?

Check your answers at the end of this chapter.

Build Your Skills: Can You Correct The Errors In This Memo?

The following memo contains errors in grammar, punctuation, mechanics, and spelling. Find them and correct them.

TO:All employees

FROM: Martin Smores, V.P. Administration

SUBJECT: Educational Refund Plans

It is the policy of this company to encourage employees to continue there education in fields which are related to their current work, or deemed in the companies best interests in the soul judgement of the Company.

To be eligible for the program, full-time employment is required.

Only course work taken at accredited schools and colleges by a nationally recognized accrediting agency are eligible for refunds under the plan.

An employee wishing to participate in the refund plan will obtain written approval from their supervisor prior to enrollment in courses.

All initial costs associated with taking courses will be born by the employee.

Upon completion of courses, evidence of course completion such as grades received and receipts for bills paid must be submitted to the company.

When the requirements of the refund plan having been met, costs will be reimbursed as follows:
Tuition costs and labratory fees—100% Required textbooks—50%

Build Your Skills: Writing With Style

Writing involves two kinds of style. One is a set of guidelines for handling certain grammatical elements—as in "house style" and "style manual." The other is an individualized pattern of word choice, sentence construction, and paragraph organization—a sort of personalized "signature"—that each writer develops. In most business writing, you are expected to suppress this individual style; you are, after all, representing your organization and not yourself. You can never totally eliminate your outlook from your writing, however. You can only learn to make the most of it.

Word Choice

- *Use the best word you can think of.* The word that most accurately says what you mean is probably harder for you to identify and use correctly than for a reader to recognize in context. So develop your vocabulary, and eschew only pompous words and unnecessary jargon.
- *Use figures of speech appropriately.* In one sense, your ability to come up with a clever metaphor or simile is a mark of style. This sort of style, however, is to be avoided in business writing. The same goes for slang and the breezier idioms. You can exercise plenty of creativity by selecting solid, objective words and putting them together for maximum impact.
- *Use contractions knowledgeably.* In formal writing, contractions should be avoided. But in informal writing that includes contractions, you can gain impact by sometimes using a complete phrase instead—for example, *will not* instead of *won't*.

Sentence Construction

- *Repeat words, phrases, and constructions for emphasis.* Awkward repetition is a sign of ignorance. Deft repetition is a sign of sophistication.
- *Place modifiers as close as possible to the words they modify.* In long, complicated sentences, it is easy to get lost. Help your readers by telling them the how and the why as soon as you tell them who or what. If you end up with verbal spaghetti, you probably need to rewrite—perhaps making more than one sentence out of the mess.
- *Use a variety of sentence structures.* Some sentences should be simple and short. When your ideas are a bit more complicated, you can use complex sentences. Other thoughts naturally go together, and you can use compound sentences to show that they are related.
- *Begin sentences in different ways.* Most sentences begin with the main clause, consisting of a subject and a predicate and a few modifiers. For variety, however, and to show how your ideas are related, occasionally begin sentences with more complicated modifying words, phrases, and clauses. Just don't overdo any one device.
- *Make sure that every sentence has its own logic.* If you're talking about a series of things or ideas, put them in logical order. In compound and complex sentences, give the main idea the stronger position; in other words, do not subordinate the main idea. Also, make sure that the ideas in a compound sentence are truly related.

Paragraph Organization

- *Vary the placement of your topic sentences.* Every paragraph must somewhere state exactly what its point is, but that statement does not always have to come first.
- *Use sentence structure to build a rhythm in your paragraphs.* Short, punchy sentences have impact. But they tend to become boring if used exclusively, so you should build paragraphs with sentences that are long and short, simple and complex and compound.
- *Vary the length of your paragraphs.* Paragraphs that are all about the same length also become monotonous. You can make some paragraphs short, with only three or four sentences, and add a couple of sentences to the paragraphs that require more development. Remember that although longer paragraphs may sometimes be necessary, long paragraphs tend to bore readers.

The more you write, the more you will be able to refine these and other techniques. You will eventually notice, however, that they all have one purpose: to make your ideas clear and interesting to readers.

1. Style is a mix of elements, involving choices between passive and active, formal and informal, bland and colorful language. In the following situations, what mix of elements would be appropriate?
   a) You are a newly hired researcher, with a relatively low position in the organization. You are writing your first memo to your boss.
   b) You are the vice president of a large corporation and must announce to the employees that, because of disappointing financial performance, your company will not be offering generous raises this year.
   c) You have been asked to take charge of the company picnic. You are writing a memo for general distribution announcing the time, place, and program for the event.

2. One good way to learn how to control your style is to study other writers who have a clear "voice." Analyze the writing style of these writers:
   - Hugh Garner (twentieth-century Canadian novelist)
   - Samuel Johnson (eighteenth-century English essayist)
   - An unknown reporter for *The Globe and Mail*

Develop Your Word Power

Use the spelling and vocabulary from previous chapters to complete the crossword puzzle.

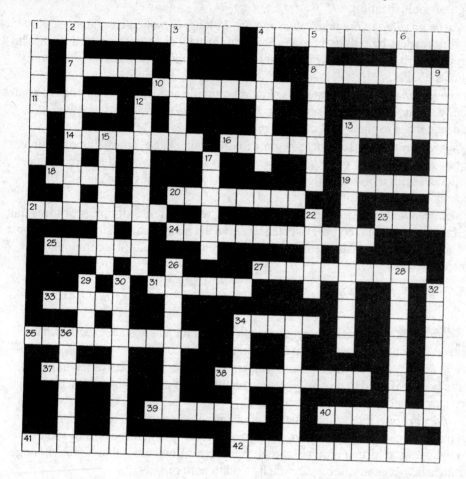

Across
1. noninterference
4. insolent
7. intended
8. trifling
10. verbal attack
11. to examine
13. adviser
14. friendly
16. to cause
18. skillful
19. option
20. opinionated
21. bodily
23. onguard
24. unending
25. yearly
27. discord
31. death
33. representative
34. frequently
35. book of words in a language
37. sincerely
38. frivolously amusing
39. shortage
40. person under the care of someone influential
41. up and down
42. not committing oneself

Down
1. praiseworthy
2. right away
3. clothing
4. indirect criticism
5. advantageous
6. to try to equal or excel
9. very
12. capable of being put on credit
13. mixed
15. plotting
17. between seventh and ninth
22. outmoded
26. arousing longing
28. discreet
29. debatable
30. equivalent
32. workable
34. event
36. habitual

Check Your Answers

Master Key Concepts

I. grammar
    A. proper
    B. antecedents
    C. mood
    F. prepositions
    G. clauses

II. punctuation
    A. capitals
    D. semicolons
    G. dashes
    H. hyphens
    I. possessive
    L. ellipsis

III. mechanics
    A. abbreviations
    D. syllables

Quiz Yourself

1. Grammar is nothing more than the way words are combined into sentences, while usage is the way language is used by a network of people. (p. 567)

2. Common nouns, which refer to general classes of things, are not capitalized; proper nouns, which refer to particular persons, places, and things, are capitalized. (p. 568)

3. An antecedent is a noun in the beginning of a sentence that corresponds to a pronoun later in the sentence. Both multiple antecedents and unclear antecedents cause confusion if not handled knowledgeably. (pp. 571-572)

4. These are the six verb tenses and how they are regularly formed:
    a) Present: the basic form
    b) Past: the basic form with an *ed* ending
    c) Future: *will* or *shall* followed by the basic form
    d) Present perfect: *have* or *has* followed by the past tense of the main verb
    e) Past perfect: *had* followed by the past tense of the main verb
    f) Future perfect: *will have* followed by the past tense of the main verb (pp. 576-577)

5. Verbs have two voices, active and passive. The active voice is preferable in most sentences, because it allows fewer words to be used and is more direct. But when the writer doesn't know (or doesn't want to say) who performed the action, the passive voice becomes necessary. (p. 579)

6. These are the five most important parts of speech:
    a) Nouns
    b) Pronouns
    c) Verbs
    d) Adjectives
    e) Adverbs

The following four parts of speech link them together in sentences:
a) Prepositions
b) Conjunctions
c) Articles
d) Interjections (pp. 582-583)

7. Because it does not have both a subject and a predicate, the group of words known as a phrase can never be written as a sentence; a group of words that does contain both a subject and a predicate, known as a clause, can be written as a sentence if it is an independent thought. (p. 586)

8. A sentence fragment is an incomplete sentence (a phrase or dependent clause) written as though it were a complete sentence. A fused sentence combines two independent thoughts without showing any point of separation. Because sentence fragments and fused sentences do not clearly express a single thought, they are easily misinterpreted by the reader (p. 586)

9. To test the appropriateness of inserting a comma between adjectives modifying the same noun, try reversing the order of the adjectives. If the order cannot be reversed, leave out the comma. A comma is also left out when one of the adjectives is part of the noun. (pp. 586-588)

10. In the absence of a different company style, generally spell out all numbers from one to ten and use Arabic numerals for the rest. (p. 599)

Build Your Skills: Can You Correct the Errors in This Memo?

The errors in the memo, together with recommended corrections, are shown below:

TO: All employees

FROM: Martin Smores, V.P. Administration

DATE: March 3, 2001

SUBJECT: Educational Refund Plans

It is the policy of this company to encourage employees to continue there education in fields which are related to their current work, or deemed in the companies best interest in the soul judgement of the company.

To be eligible for the program full-time employment is required.

Only course work taken at accredited schools and colleges by a nationally recognized accrediting agency are eligible for funds under the plan.

An employee wishing to participate in the refund plan will obtain written approval from their supervisor prior to enrollment in courses.

All initial costs associated with taking courses will be born by the employee.

Upon completion of courses, evidence of course completion such as grades received and receipts for bills paid must be submitted to the company.

When the requirements of the refund plan having been met, costs will be reimbursed as follows:

Tuition costs and laboratory fees—100%

Required books—50%

Build Your Skills: Writing with Style

1. Various styles are appropriate for these differing situations:
    a) The researcher should use a passive, formal, bland style.
    b) The vice president should use an active, formal, bland style.
    c) The person in charge of the picnic should use an active, informal, colorful style.

2. These writers have different styles:
    *   Hugh Garner uses short, simple sentences, often a series of them strung together. He prefers short, concrete words with a heavy visual impact. His writing is rich in connotative meaning.
    *   Samuel Johnson is a master of complex and compound sentences, most of which are very long by contemporary standards. His vocabulary tends to be abstract, Latinate, obscure, and very precise.
    *   *The Globe and Mail* reporter falls somewhere between Garner and Johnson in terms of sentence type and length. The reporter's vocabulary is general and familiar with a mix of abstract and concrete terms, and is relatively low in connotative impact.

Develop Your Word Power

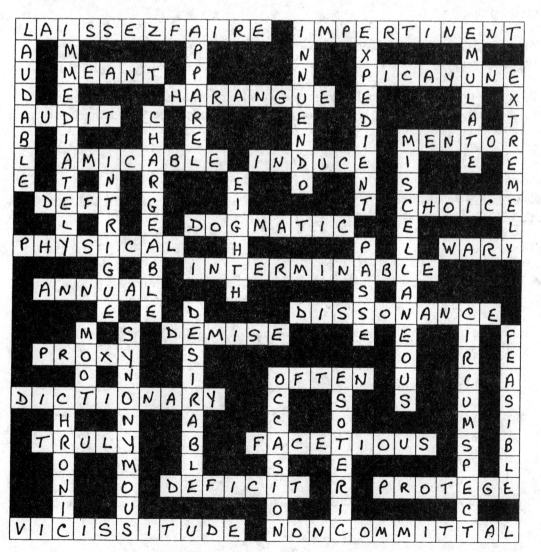

Lesson 1
Sentences

What is a sentence? Saying that it is a word or group of words that starts with a capital letter and ends with a period is only partly right. Sentences also require a subject (someone or something) and a predicate (doing or being):

Rosemarie conducts the meeting.

In this sentence, *Rosemarie* is the subject, the someone or something; *conducts the meeting* is the predicate that explains what Rosemarie does.

Subjects are usually nouns or pronouns, and predicates always include at least one verb. However, subjects and predicates may take many different forms. In the following sentences, the subject is underlined once and the predicate verb is bold and underlined:

He **quit**.
She **was** ready to start legal proceedings.
Deborah and Stephen **worked** together on the BNA account. The executive assistants **copied and collated** the report. They **are working** on a new business plan.
Has he **had** any trouble with the audit?
Give us your analysis.

In the last sentence in this list, the subject, *you,* is understood; therefore, only the predicate is present. Some sentences with an understood subject—for example, *Stop!*—contain only one word.

Some sentences use a certain type of predicate verb—usually a form of *is*—to link the subject with a word that further describes it:

The man **is** happy.

Occasionally this order is inverted, especially in questions:

Happy **is** the man.
Is the man happy?

Regardless of the order of the words, these statements are sentences—because they have both a subject and a predicate.

The most basic sentences consist of a subject and a predicate verb in a simple one-two pattern: *They paid.* But sentences are usually more complicated. Many sentences also have modifiers that further describe the subject or predicate verb; they often have an object as well, someone or something that is acted on by the subject of the sentence. For example:

In most cases, new <u>customers</u> promptly **pay** bills.

In this sentence, *bills* is the object. Customers pay what? They pay bills. In addition, *new* modifies the subject, and *promptly* and *in most cases* modify the predicate verb. If you took away all these extra words and were left with only *Customers pay,* you would still have a sentence.

In the following exercises, underline subjects once and predicate verbs twice:

1.   He found a tactful way to tell her.

2.   While adding the column, she noticed a couple of errors.

3.   The letter gave him a clue to their thinking.

4.   Her favorite activity in her new job was analysis of letters from customers.

5.   Were his methods fair?

6.   Tracy and Susanne were awarded the top positions.

7.   Take one.

8.   We are sending the replacement postpaid.

9.   Under the desk was a wastebasket.

10. Were his supplies all in order?

Some sentences contain more than one subject-predicate set:

<u>Ben</u> **discovered** the faulty VCR, and <u>he</u> **was** the one who took it to be fixed.

Notice the comma separating the two subject-predicate sets. You could split the one long sentence into two shorter sentences at this comma, and each of the new sentences would have a subject and a predicate. But be careful. Not every sentence containing a comma can be broken in two:

While looking for a replacement, <u>we</u> **found** Judy.

Only the latter part of this statement has a subject and a predicate verb and could therefore stand alone as a sentence. The same is true of the following statement:

Because she had the experience, <u>she</u> **got** the job.

Although the first part of this statement has a subject and a predicate verb (*she had*), it could not stand along; *because she had the experience* actually modifies the predicate, tells why she got the job.

In the following exercises, circle all the complete sentences.

11. Show me how to do it.

12. Writing and speaking to perfection.

13. Michael, Betty, and Tom, without whom we would not have succeeded.

14. In an emergency, use it to signal passing motorists.

15. Spending enough to make it worthwhile.

16. With everyone else on vacation, she became responsible for completing the report.

17. Since he became a supervisor.

18. Punctuate correctly, and then print the revised document.

19. When our company first got into the ice cream business, profits were spectacular, and soon we became too confident.

20. Expenses down, profits up.

Including too much in one sentence is just as serious a problem as leaving out a subject or predicate. The following sentence pastes together too many ideas:

When she was offered the job, she immediately wrote a letter accepting it and then sat down to list the things she had to do to start work the following Monday, including buying a new outfit and shoes, and then she decided to take a break so she could call some of her friends to tell them about her good fortune.

This account is easier to understand when broken into shorter sentences. For example:

When she was offered the job, she immediately wrote a letter accepting it. Then she sat down to list the things she had to do to start work the following Monday, including buying a new outfit and shoes. Then she decided to take a break so she could call some of her friends to tell them about her good fortune.

Although a sentence may contain more than one subject-predicate set, you must be careful not to use a comma to combine what should be two separate sentences:

<u>Mike</u> always **watches** the hockey playoffs, his <u>brother</u> **insists** that basketball is the real winter sport.

A solitary comma is not strong enough to link these two subject-predicate sets. A comma teamed with a linking words such as *and, but, for, nor, or, so,* or *yet* would solve the problem:

<u>Mike</u> always **watches** the hockey playoffs, **but** his <u>brother</u> **insists** that basketball is the real winter sport.

 But if you did not want to add any words, you could use stronger punctuation:

<u>Mike</u> always **watches** the hockey playoffs. **H**is <u>brother</u> **insists** that basketball is the real winter sport.

<u>Mike</u> always **watches** the hockey playoffs**;** his <u>brother</u> **insists** that basketball is the real winter sport.

If you were willing to add, take out, or rearrange words, you could find many other solutions to the problem. Correct the sentences in the following exercises by crossing out extra words and inserting only periods and capital letters—not by adding any words or other punctuation:

1. The best part of the day had gone she decided to try something less demanding.

2. Thank you for your prompt payment whenever you need cleaning services for your offices, give us a call.

3. After I thought about your performance, I decided to let you take over while I am gone, I hope everything goes well in my absence.

4. Give him the report, he will know what to do with it.

5. Jackie and Bob reported exceptional sales this past month, and they surely deserve some reward, and I know they would like a cash bonus.

If you have had trouble with the exercises in this section, you may want to consult a grammar book on the following subjects:

clauses	complex sentences	phrases	sentence fragments
comma splices	compound sentences	run-on sentences	simple sentences

You might also wish to consult Section 1.7, "Sentences," in The "Handbook, Fundamentals of Grammar and Usage," in *Excellence in Business Communication*.

Lesson 1: Check Your Answers

In the following exercises, underline subjects once and predicate verbs twice:

1. He found a tactful way to tell her.

2. While adding the column, she noticed a couple of errors.

3. The letter gave him a clue to their thinking.

4. Her favorite activity in her new job was analysis of letters from customers.

5. Were his methods fair?

6. Tracy and Susanne were awarded the top positions.

7. Take one.

8. We are sending the replacement postpaid.

9. Under the desk was a wastebasket.

10. Were his supplies all in order?

In the following exercises, circle all the complete sentences.

11. Show me how to do it.

12. Writing and speaking to perfection.

13. Michael, Betty, and Tom, without whom we would not have succeeded.

14. In an emergency, use it to signal passing motorists.

15. Spending enough to make it worthwhile.

16. With everyone else on vacation, she became responsible for completing the report.

17. Since he became a supervisor.

18. Punctuate correctly, and then print the revised document.

19. When our company first got into the ice cream business, profits were spectacular, and soon we became too confident.

20. Expenses down, profits up.

Correct the sentences in the following exercises by crossing out extra words and inserting only periods and capital letters—not by adding any words or other punctuation:

21. The best part of the day had gone she decided to try something less demanding.

22. Thank you for your prompt payment whenever you need cleaning services for your offices, give us a call.

23. After I thought about your performance, I decided to let you take over while I am gone I hope everything goes well in my absence.

24. Give him the report he will know what to do with it.

25. Jackie and Bob reported exceptional sales this past month, and they surely deserve some reward, and I know they would like a cash bonus.

or break at second comma

Lesson 2
Parts of Speech: Nouns

Words that stand for a person, a place, an idea, or a thing are called nouns. Here are some examples of common nouns:

industry   markup   compiler
fitness   administration   downtown

A word preceded by *a, an,* or *the* in a sentence is usually a noun; so is a word that ends in *ation, ism, ity, ment,* or *ness.*

Nouns may be used in sentences as subjects or objects. That is, the person, place, idea, or thing that is being or doing (subject) is represented by a noun. So is the person, place, idea, or thing that is being acted on (object). In the following sentence, the nouns are underlined:

The <u>secretary</u> keyboarded the <u>report</u>.

The secretary (subject) is acting in a way that affects the report (object).

In this more complicated sentence, *installer* is used as a subject, and *carpeting* and *customer* are used as objects:

The <u>installer</u> delivered the <u>carpeting</u> to the <u>customer</u>.

Notice that *carpeting* is the object of the main part of the sentence (is acted on by the installer), whereas *customer* is the object of the phrase *to the customer.* Nevertheless, both *carpeting* and *customer* are objects.

In the following exercises, underline the subjects and circle the objects:

1. The technician has already repaired the machine for the client.

2. An attorney will talk to the group about incorporation.

3. After her vacation, the buyer prepared a third-quarter budget.

4. The new laserwriters are serving our department very well.

5. Accuracy overrides speed in importance.

Some nouns are actually composed of two or more words. *Work load,* for example, is considered a single noun; in fact, you may see it spelled as one word in some places. Here are a few of the many other nouns that combine two or more words:

vice president   attorney general
coffee maker   administrative assistant
profit-and-loss statement hanger-on

The way to tell whether word groups like these should be considered single nouns is to try separating the parts. Can the parts be used alone, or do you need both parts to talk about the same thing? Is the word group used as a single unit to mean something distinct? For example, a coffee maker is never called just a maker, not can it correctly be called a coffee pot.

So far, all the examples have been common nouns—that is, they refer to general classes of things. In business, however, you will often need to refer to specific examples of buildings, companies, people, and so on. Thus you will often need to use proper nouns, which are always capitalized:

Confederation Life	Sky Dome
Ellen Wood	Prime Minister Wilfrid Laurier
Tuesday	Red Rose (tea)

Underline the common and proper nouns in the following exercises:

6. Perhaps the client will provide more time.

7. Has the messenger delivered a package without a label?

8. Give the balance sheet to Melissa.

9. The climate for investment might improve.

10. With a wink and a nod, the assistant ushered the visitor into the office.

11. The clerks gave up their break so they could discuss the new policies with the manager.

12. We'd like to order more satchels for Craigmont Stores.

13. Tarnower Corporation donates a portion of its profits to charity every year.

14. Which aluminum bolts are packaged?

15. Please send a dozen of the following: stopwatches, canteens, headbands, wristbands, and white shoelaces.

When you refer to more than one person, place, idea, or thing of a certain class, you must use the plural form of the noun. Most plurals are formed by adding s to the end of the singular form, as in *pencils* and *special offers*. Many nouns, however, are irregular and therefore form the plural in a different way. For example, when a word gains an extra syllable by being made plural, you should add an *es* instead of just an *s*:

boss/bosses	batch/batches	Harris/Harrises

Words ending in *ay, ey; oy,* or *uy* form the plural by adding *s,* but words ending in a consonant and a *y* form the plural by changing the *y* to *i* and adding *es*—except when the word is a proper name:

day/days	party/parties	Henry/Henry's

Similarly, nouns that end in *ao, eo, io, oo,* and *uo* form the plural by adding *s*:

Video/videos	duo/duos	tattoo/tattoos

Some nouns that end in a consonant and *o* form the plural by adding *s,* others by adding *es*:

veto/vetoes   tomato/tomatoes   memo/memos

But some words ending in a consonant and o may form the plural by adding either *s* or *es,* like *zeros* and *zeroes*. Because of all this variation, you should consult a dictionary—whenever you are in doubt about forming the plural of any word that ends in a consonant and an *o.*

Most words that end in a single f form the plural by changing the f to a v and adding *es*:

shelf/shelves   loaf/loaves   wharf/wharves

Then there are the words that form the plural by changing radically:

man/men   foot/feet   salesperson/salespeople

Some words derived from Greek and Latin roots form the plural by changing an/s ending to *es:*

analysis/analyses   crisis/crises   diagnosis/diagnoses

But other frequently used foreign plurals are treated more like English words in business writing. For example, instead of using *appendices* or *maxima,* you may use *appendixes* or *maximums.* Finally, some words are the same in both singular and plural form:

trousers   series   deer   headquarters

The only way to tell whether these words are singular or plural is *to* study the rest of the sentence.

When trying to make a plural out of a noun that is actually a combination of words, you must figure out which word in the group is most important. Then you can make a plural out of that word and leave the other in its singular form:

editors-in-chief   vice presidents   attorneys general

These are just a few examples. You can save yourself the embarrassment of using the wrong plural form by consulting a dictionary whenever you have any doubts. If it says nothing about the plural of the word, just add an s. Otherwise, use the form specified in the dictionary.

Supply the plural form of each of the nouns in the following exercises:

16. copy   _____

17. bonus   _____

18. son-in-law   _____

19. folio   _____

20. Amy   _____

21. sheaf   _____

22. child _____

23. parenthesis _____

24. supply _____

25. mess _____

If you need more help with nouns, consult a grammar book on the following subjects:

collective nouns	objects	proper nouns
common nouns	plural nouns	subjects
compound nouns		

You might also check Section 1.1, "Nouns," in The "Handbook, Fundamentals of Grammar and Usage," in *Excellence in Business Communication*.

Lesson 2: Check Your Answers

In the following exercises, underline the subjects and circle the objects:

1. The technician has already repaired the machine for the client.

2. An attorney will talk to the group about incorporation.

3. After her vacation, the buyer prepared a third-quarter budget.

4. The new laserwriters are serving our department very well.

5. Accuracy overrides speed in importance.

Underline the common and proper nouns in the following exercises:

6. Perhaps the client will provide more time.

7. Has the messenger delivered a package without a label?

8. Give the balance sheet to Melissa.

9. The climate for investment might improve.

10. With a wink and a nod, the assistant ushered the visitor into the office.

11. The clerks gave up their break so they could discuss the new policies with the manager.

12. We'd like to order more satchels for Craigmont Stores.

13. Tarnower Corporation donates a portion of its profits to charity every year.

14. Which aluminum bolts are packaged?

15. Please send a dozen of the following: stopwatches, canteens, headbands, wristbands, and white shoelaces.

Supply the plural form of each of the nouns in the following exercises:

16. copy ___*copies*___

17. bonus ___*bonuses*___

18. son-in-law ___*sons-in-law*___

19. folio ___*folios*___

20. Amy ___*Amys*___

21. sheaf ___*sheaves*___

22. child ___*children*___

23. parenthesis ___*parentheses*___

24. supply ___*supplies*___

25. mess ___*messes*___

Lesson 3
Parts of Speech: Pronouns

These are the pronouns that substitute for nouns referring to specific people or things:

	Subject	*Object*	*Possessive*
Singular	I	me	my, mine
	he, she, it	him, her, it	his, her, hers, its
Plural	we	us	our, ours
	they	them	their, theirs
Singular and Plural	you	you	your, yours
	who	whom	whose

Your choice of a pronoun from this list depends on whether the person or thing represented by the pronoun is acting, is being acted on, or possesses something. If acting, the pronoun is standing in for the subject of a sentence or phrase; if being acted on, the pronoun is standing in for the object of a sentence or phrase; if possessing something, the pronoun is showing the ownership. (Notice that none of the possessive pronouns, not even *its,* has an apostrophe.)

Study the pronouns in these sentences, noting whether they are subjects (S), objects (O), or possessives (P):

Who (S) gave the receipts to her (O)?
She (S) looked at my (P) resume.
They (S) returned the defective parts to us (O).
Our (P) major concern is your (P) satisfaction.
He (S) sent me (O) a check for $239.28.
To whom (O) will you (S) give the assignment?
I (S) will sell them (O) to you (O) at a discount.

If a noun is singular, the pronoun that stands in for it is also singular. If a noun is plural, the pronoun that stands in for it is also plural:

The ledger sat on the desk.
It sat on the desk.
The desks were delivered Tuesday.
They were delivered Tuesday.

A plural pronoun may also be used to stand in for two or more singular nouns:

Put the computer and printer into the empty office.
Put them into the empty office.

172

Complete the following exercises by replacing the underlined nouns with the correct pronouns:

1. To <u>which retailer</u> will you send your merchandise?

2. Have you given <u>John and Nancy</u> a list of parts?

3. The <u>main office</u> sent the invoice to <u>Mr. and Mrs. Lityak</u> on December 5.

4. The company settled <u>the company's</u> accounts before the end of the year.

5. <u>Which person's</u> umbrella is this?

6. <u>Peter</u> gave <u>Martin</u> a great pep talk.

7. I saw Bill at the conference, and <u>Bill</u> gave me a directory for the conference.

8. Where did Mr. Schiller get <u>Mr. Schiller's</u> new car?

9. Tell the Randolphs about <u>the Randolphs's</u> obligations.

10. When do you want Meg and Robert to take <u>Meg's and Robert's</u> break?

Replacing nouns with pronouns streamlines a sentence:

Roy gave <u>Roy's</u> pencil to Terri so <u>Terri</u> should add the figures.
Roy gave <u>his</u> pencil to Terri so <u>she</u> should add the figures.

In some sentences, however, you must sometimes reuse a noun for clarity; even though you could substitute a pronoun. For example:

Tom told Richard that <u>he</u> would be going to the meeting.

Who will be going to the meeting, Tom or Richard? Readers will be less confused if you use the appropriate noun again:

Tom told Richard that Richard would be going to the meeting.

(This problem may also be solved by rewriting the sentence.)

In the following exercises, cross out nouns and write pronouns above them wherever appropriate:

11. Customers always receive what customers expect from Sear's.

12. Janet and Anne are preparing a report for Janet and Anne's boss that tells the boss about Janet and Anne's results for the first quarter of the year.

13. Bob broke the chair, and so now Bob has to fix the chair.

14. When Mara spoke at the last gathering of the company's sales representatives, Mara gave the sales representatives a complete picture of the company's operations.

15. Tell Edward to turn in Edward's expense account before the expense account is overdue.

What pronoun should you use when referring to a group? Use a singular pronoun if the focus is on the group as a single unit, a plural pronoun if the focus is on individuals within the group:

> The staff completed its report on time.
> The staff turned in their reports at various times.

In the first sentence, the staff is working together on a report and is therefore seen as a unit, requiring a singular pronoun. In the second sentence, staff members are preparing individual reports, and thus a plural pronoun is required.

In most cases, companies are considered as units. Therefore, a singular pronoun is usually used to stand in for the name of a company:

> Starbright Enterprises has lower prices than its competitors.
> Flyway Airlines has just had its best year ever.

Another problem area for business communicators is indefinite pronouns. Words like *everyone, neither,* and *each* are singular, referring to one person or thing, and so require a singular pronoun:

> Neither Elizabeth nor Connie has reached her potential yet.
> Each display area has its limitations.

Words like *many* and *several,* however, take plural pronouns:

> Many have requested their holidays already.

Still other indefinite pronouns—such as *all, any, most,* and *some—may* be either singular or plural, depending on the context:

> Some is still left in its container.
> Some are already asking for their bonuses.

Write the correct pronouns in the following exercises:

16. The sales staff is preparing guidelines for _____ clients.

17. Few of the sales representatives turn in _____ reports on time.

18. The board of directors has chosen _____ officers.

19. Several of the account executives have told _____ clients about the new program.

20. Mondo Taco, Inc., plans to expand _____ operations dramatically over the next two years.

21. Has everyone supplied _____ Social Security number yet?

22. Give the staff _____ raises early this year.

23. All can voice _____ opinions here.

24. City Securities has just announced _____ year-end dividends.

25. Either of the new products would readily find _____ niche in the marketplace.

You can learn more about pronouns by looking in a grammar book under the following headings:

agreement with antecedents	indefinite pronouns	possessive pronouns
case of pronouns	interrogative pronouns	reciprocal pronouns
demonstrative pronouns	numeral pronouns	reflexive pronouns
gender-neutral pronouns	personal pronouns	relative pronouns

You may also want to refer to Section 1.2, "Pronouns," in The "Handbook, Fundamentals of Grammar and Usage," in *Excellence in Business Communication*.

Lesson 3: Check Your Answers

Complete the following exercises by replacing the underlined nouns with the correct pronouns:

1.   To _which retailer_ will you send your merchandise? *(whom)* *(it)*

2.   Have you given John and Nancy a list of parts? *(them)*

3.   The main office sent the invoice to Mr. and Mrs. Lityak on December 5. *(It)* *(them)*

4.   The company settled the company's accounts before the end of the year. *(its)*

5.   Which person's umbrella is this? *(Whose)*

6.   Peter gave Martin a great pep talk. *(He)* *(him)*

7.   I saw Bill at the conference, and Bill gave me a directory for the conference. *(he)* *(it)*

8.   Where did Mr. Schiller get Mr. Schiller's new car? *(his)*

9.   Tell the Randolphs about the Randolphs's obligations. *(their)*

10. When do you want Meg and Robert to take Meg's and Robert's break? *(their)*

In the following exercises, cross out nouns and write pronouns above them wherever appropriate:

11. Customers always receive what ~~customers~~ expect from Sear's. *(they)*

12. Janet and Anne are preparing a report for ~~Janet and Anne's~~ boss that tells ~~the boss~~ about ~~Janet and Anne's~~ results for the first quarter of the year. *(their)* *(him/her)* *(their)*

13. Bob broke the chair, and so now ~~Bob~~ has to fix ~~the chair~~. *(he)* *(it)*

14. When Mara spoke at the last gathering of the company's sales representatives, ~~Mara~~ gave ~~the sales representatives~~ a complete picture of the company's operations. *(she)* *(them)*

15. Tell Edward to turn in ~~Edward's~~ _his_ expense account before ~~the expense account~~ _it_ is overdue.

Write the correct pronouns in the following exercises:

16. The sales staff is preparing guidelines for ____*its*____ clients.

17. Few of the sales representatives turn in ____*their*____ reports on time.

18. The board of directors has chosen ____*its*____ officers.

19. Several of the account executives have told ____*their*____ clients about the new program.

20. Mondo Taco, Inc., plans to expand ____*its*____ operations dramatically over the next two years.

21. Has everyone supplied _his or her_ Social Security number yet?

22. Give the staff ____*their*____ raises early this year.

23. All can voice ____*their*____ opinions here.

24. City Securities has just announced ____*its*____ year-end dividends.

25. Either of the new products would readily find ____*its*____ niche in the marketplace.

Lesson 4
Parts of Speech: Verbs

Verbs are a sentence's "action" or "being" words; that is, they tell what happens or what is. Verbs may consist of one or several words—*wrote* and *would have written*, for example—and the form of a verb may change to indicate subtle meaning and to complement other words in the sentence.

Among the many action verbs used in business are *send, pay,* and *produce.* The words underlined in the following sentences are action verbs as well:

They <u>bought</u> a $15 million company and <u>turned</u> it into an even bigger company.
I have seen the proposal, but <u>I cannot remember</u> some of its specific points.
Will you <u>stock</u> item 6-2993 next quarter?
Don <u>is eating</u> lunch in the cafeteria.
Notice that some of these verbs consist of a helping verb (such as *have*) and a main verb (such as *seen*).

Among being verbs, the most common is, logically enough, *be:*

	Present	*Past*	*Other Tenses*
I	am	was	will be (future)
you	are	were	have been (present perfect)
he, she, it	is	was	had been (past perfect)
we	are	were	will have been (future perfect)
they	are	were	

But other verbs—such as *feel, seem,* and *sound*—serve the same purpose and can substitute for *be.* All being verbs link the subject of a sentence with other qualities, like an equal sign; they indicate that the word on one side is linked with the word on the other side. But they do not demonstrate any action. For example, all of the following verbs describe a state of being:

Darla <u>was</u> happy about her promotion.
The figures <u>seem</u> accurate.
Your estimate <u>sounded</u> right.
I <u>will feel</u> better tomorrow.

In the following exercises, underline all being verbs:

1. Andy feels ready to demonstrate the product.

2. Chicago Fabricating sent holiday greetings to all its major customers.

3. This procedure lasts only five minutes.

4. We were reluctant to give a refund in this case.

5. Will you be using my desk while I'm out of the office?

Verb tenses allow you to talk about things happening or existing in different time periods. For regular verbs, the present tense adds a final s to the main verb, but only when used with *he, she,* or *it;* the past tense adds *ed* to the main verb; and the future tense uses the main verb with the helping verb *will.* For example:

Present: He <u>mails</u> the letters on Tuesday.
Past: He <u>mailed</u> the letters on Tuesday.
Future: He <u>will mail</u> the letters on Tuesday.

Although these are the three tenses most frequently used, you will also have occasion to use three "perfect" tenses, which imply completed or repeated actions. The "perfect" tenses use the helping verb *have* and usually the past tense of the main verb:

Present perfect: He <u>has mailed</u> the letters every Tuesday.
Past perfect: He <u>had mailed</u> the letters on Tuesday.
Future perfect: He <u>will have mailed</u> the letters by Tuesday.

Write the verb tense called for in each of the following exercises:

6. repair (future perfect) _____

7. hire (past) _____

8. move (past perfect) _____

9. motivate (present perfect) _____

10. train (future) _____

Not all verbs are as regular as these; indeed, they are called irregular verbs because in one or more of the tenses they do not follow this pattern. The most irregular of the verbs is *be,* but many other common verbs are to some extent irregular. Here is a sample:

INFINITIVE	*go*	*begin*	*drink*	*take*
PAST	went	began	drank	took
FUTURE	will go	will begin	will drink	will take
PRESENT PERFECT	have/has gone	have/has begun	have/has drunk	have/has taken
PAST PERFECT	had gone	had begun	had drunk	had taken
FUTURE PERFECT	will have gone	will have begun	will have drunk	will have taken

Provide the irregular verb form called for in the following exercises:

11. I (present perfect, *became)* _____ the resident expert on repairing the copy machine.

12. She (past, *know)* _____ how to perform an audit when she came to work for us.

13. By the time you finish the analysis, he (future perfect, *take)* _____ his vacation.

14. Next week, call John to tell him what you (future, *do)* _____ next month's meeting.

15. By the time Susan returned to our company, she (past perfect, *rise)* _____ in rank to analyst.

Another way to distinguish among verbs is to label them either transitive or intransitive. Transitive verbs—such as *give, lay, set,* and *raise*—transfer the action from the subject to the object. For example:

He gave a refund to Nissa Nelson.

In this sentence, the verb *gave* is what he (subject) did to or with the refund (object).

On the other hand, intransitive verbs—such as *feel, lie, sit,* and *rise*—do not transfer any action:

Profits rose in the first quarter.

The verb *rose* is what profits (subject) did, but profits did not act directly on anything in this sentence.

Some verbs may be transitive or intransitive. Consider the following:

He feels uncomfortable with the proposition.
She feels the texture of the cloth before deciding to buy.

In the first sentence, *he* (subject) *feels* (predicate), but nothing in the sentence receives the direct impact of his feeling. In the second sentence, however, *she* (subject) *feels* (predicate) *texture* (object); in other words, she performs an action that has a direct impact on something.

16. In the exercises below, underline the intransitive verbs and circle the transitive verbs:

17. Ms. Detweiler sent him a reminder.

18. What is the purpose of this memo?

19. When you have heard her story, call me about it.

20. They mentioned a name yesterday.

21. He sat next to my desk and described the whole thing.

The way you use verbs can have a great deal to do with the tone of your writing. For example, verbs may be either passive or active. An active sentence uses direct, subject-verb-object order:

We will refund your money.

Notice how much more indirect this passive sentence is:

Your money will be refunded.

It is not clear who is doing the refunding in this sentence.

Active sentences are more forceful than passive sentences, which is usually desirable. However, in business communication you may sometimes want to soften a statement or to avoid assigning responsibility for an action. Then you will find passive sentences useful.

Rewrite the sentences in the following exercises so that they use active verbs instead of passive verbs:

21. The report will be written by Leslie Cartwright. _____

_____

22. The failure to record the transaction was mine. _____

_____

23. Have you been notified by the claims department of your rights? _____

_____

24. We are dependent on their services for our operation. _____

_____

25. The damaged toaster had been returned by the customer. _____

_____

If you want to learn more about verbs, look in a grammar book for information on these topics:

auxiliary verbs	mood of verbs	verb tenses
irregular verbs	subjunctive mood	voice of verbs
linking verbs	transitive and intransitive verbs	

You may also wish to consult Sections 1.3, "Verbs," and 1.7.5, "Linking Verbs," in The "Handbook, Fundamentals of Grammar and Usage," in *Excellence in Business Communication*.

Lesson 4: Check Your Answers

In the following exercises, underline all being verbs:

1.   Andy <u>feels</u> ready to demonstrate the product.

2.   Chicago Fabricating sent holiday greetings to all its major customers.

3.   This procedure lasts only five minutes.

4.   We <u>were</u> reluctant to give a refund in this case.

5.   Will you be using my desk while <u>I'm</u> out of the office?

Write the verb tense called for in each of the following exercises:

6.   repair (future perfect)   *will have repaired*

7.   hire (past)   *hired*

8. move (past perfect) *had moved*

9. motivate (present perfect) *have motivated*

10. train (future) *will train*

Provide the irregular verb form called for in the following exercises:

11. I (present perfect, *became*) *have become* the resident expert on repairing the copy machine.

12. She (past, *know*) *knew* how to perform an audit when she came to work for us.

13. By the time you finish the analysis, he (future perfect, *take*) *will have taken* his vacation.

14. Next week, call John to tell him what you (future, *do*) *will do* next month's meeting.

15. By the time Susan returned to our company, she (past perfect, *rise*) *had risen* in rank to analyst.

In the exercises below, underline the intransitive verbs and circle the transitive verbs:

16. Ms. Detweiler (sent) him a reminder.

17. What <u>is</u> the purpose of this memo?

18. When you (have heard) her story, (call) me about it.

19. They (mentioned) a name yesterday.

20. He <u>sat</u> next to my desk and (described) the whole thing.

Rewrite the sentences in the following exercises so that they use active verbs instead of passive verbs:

21. The report will be written by Leslie Cartwright. *Leslie Cartwright will write the report.*

22. The failure to record the transaction was mine. *I failed to record the transaction.*

23. Have you been notified by the claims department of your rights? *Has the claims department notified you of your rights?*

24. We are dependent on their services for our operation. _We depend on their services for our operation._

25. The damaged toaster had been returned by the customer. _The customer had returned the damaged toaster._

Lesson 5
Parts of Speech: Verb Agreement

To use verbs correctly you must make decisions about verb forms based on the number represented by the subject. Take, for example, the present tense of the verb *vote:*

Singular: I vote   *Plural:*   we vote
               you vote   you vote
               he/she/it votes   they vote

In the present tense, a regular verb like *vote* takes a final s or *es* to agree with the singular pronouns *he, she,* and *it* or with any singular noun.

Other verbs are not so easy to deal with. Consider the present tense of these irregular verbs:

be: I am, we are   *have:*   I have, we have
         you are   you have
         he/she/it is, they are   he/she/it has, they have

apply: I apply, we apply   *can:*   I can, we can
            you apply   you can
            he/she/it applies, they apply   he/she/it can, they can

In the following exercises, write in the present tense of each verb:

1. You (*be*) _____ eligible for a promotion already.

2. Dave (*have*) _____ another telephone line.

3. How (*be*) _____ supposed to know when we've reached that point?

4. She (*do*) _____ her work quickly and accurately.

5. They (*be*) _____ sometimes difficult to deal with.

Getting the verb to agree with the subject in sentences like these is relatively simple. But problems arise when the sentence is complicated.

Each sentence is made up of at least one clause, a group of words with both a subject and a predicate. Sentences may also contain phrases, which do not have a subject-predicate set. Notice the difference here:

Clause: he **sent** an invoice
Clause: because he **sent** an invoice

Phrase: with an invoice
Phrase: after sending an invoice

The clauses have subjects and predicates; the phrases do not have subjects and predicates.

183

A simple sentence has only one clause like the first clause above, but many sentences combine clauses and phrases, like this:

He **sent** an invoice, and then he **entered** the amount in the books.
Because he **sent** an invoice, he decided not to call T&T Sales.
He **presented** the client with an invoice.
After sending an invoice, he **began** another project.

Notice that all the verbs in these examples are in the past tense; in other words, they agree. Only if there were a good reason for the verbs to be in different tenses would they not agree. For example:

Yesterday she **prepared** a sales report, today she **is listing** all her potential clients, and tomorrow she **will call** them.

In some sentences with two or more verbs, the helping verbs or the main verbs are sometimes identical. In that case, the duplicated word or words can be dropped:

Consumers **have been saving** and (*have been*) **spending**.

But do not drop any part of a verb that is not an exact duplicate. For example, this sentence is wrong:

They **have not** and **will not be attending** the workshops.

It becomes correct when part of the helping verb is restored:

They **have not been** and **will not be attending** the workshops.

Here is another type of agreement problem:

The building **is** attractive, economical, and **has** beautiful surroundings.

Because *is* and *has* are different and no verb is included with *economical,* this sentence is awkward. It can be improved by adding another verb:

The building **is** attractive, **is** economical, and **has** beautiful surroundings.

An even better idea is to change one of the items in the series so that it is the same type of word as the other two:

The building **is** attractive, economical, and beautifully situated.

In the following exercises, fill in the correct verb form:

6. They identified the source of the problem, and then they (*look*) _____ for ways to solve it.

7. When success (*seem*) _____ imminent, he panics.

8. Jason Beaudry never has gone to Europe and probably never (*go*) _____.

9. Why (*do*) _____ she ignore John when he talks?

10. We (*take*) _____ that point into consideration before we decided what to do.

Another problem of verb agreement relates to the subject (noun or pronoun) of a sentence. The verb should be in the plural form when the subject is plural. Otherwise, the verb should be singular. When a phrase separates the subject and the verb, the task of deciding whether to use a singular or plural verb becomes more complicated. Look at this example:

The <u>analysis</u> of existing documents **takes** a full week.

Although *documents* is plural, the verb is in the singular form. That's because the subject of the sentence is *analysis,* a singular noun. The phrase of *existing documents* can be disregarded. Here is another example:

Their <u>answers</u> to the questions are in the minutes.

Take away the phrase *to the question* and you are left with the plural subject answers. Therefore the verb takes the plural form.

Circle the correct verb form in the following exercises:

11. Each of the managers turn/turns in a monthly report.

12. The receptionist, not the clerks, take/takes all the calls.

13. Everyone upstairs receive/receives mail before we do.

14. The reasons for her decision sound/sounds logical.

15. All the products sell/sells well.

Verb agreement is also complicated when the subject is not a specific noun or pronoun and when the subject may be considered either singular or plural. In these cases, you have to analyze the surrounding sentence to determine which verb form to use. Observe carefully which of the following sentences contain are (plural form of be) and which contain is (singular form). The noun that controls the verb form is underlined in each sentence:

The <u>staff</u> is quartered in the warehouse.
The <u>staff</u> are at their desks in the warehouse.
The <u>computers</u> and the <u>staff</u> are in the warehouse.
Neither the staff nor the <u>computers</u> are in the warehouse.
<u>Every</u> computer is in the warehouse.
<u>Many a</u> computer is in the warehouse.

Did you notice that words like every use the singular verb form? In addition, when a neither nor phrase combines singular and plural nouns, the verb takes the form that matches the noun closest to it.

Circle the correct form of the verb in the following exercises:

16. Brenda and Bill has/have responsibility for the project.

17. Neither the main office nor the branch offices is/are blameless.

18. Each programmer and analyst report/reports to Jennifer.

19. Your whole family enjoy/enjoys credit privileges at Mo's.

20. Either the secretaries or the office manager take/takes care of all inquiries about employee benefits.

In the business world, some types of subject require extra attention. Company names, for example, are considered singular and therefore take a singular verb in most cases—even if they contain plural words.

But quantities are sometimes considered singular and sometimes plural. If a quantity refers to a total amount, it takes a singular verb; if a quantity refers to individual, countable units, it takes a plural verb. For example:

> <u>Three hours</u> is a long time.
> The <u>eight dollars</u> we collected for the fund are tacked on the bulletin board.

Fractions may also be singular or plural, depending on the noun that accompanies them:

> One-third of the <u>warehouse</u> is devoted to this product line.
> One-third of the <u>products</u> are defective.

Circle the correct verb form in the following exercises:

21. C & B Sales is/are listed in the directory.

22. When measuring shelves, 7 inches is/are significant.

23. About 90 percent of the employees plan/plans to come to the company picnic.

24. Carnegie Industries make/makes bookbinding equipment.

25. Two weeks is/are all we need to complete our analysis.

To learn more about verb agreement, consult a grammar book on these topics:

agreement with *there* and *here*	compound subjects	verb agreement
collective nouns	indefinite pronouns	*who* clauses
complements	intervening elements	

You may wish to refer to Sections 1.3.2, "Irregular Verbs," and 1.7.2, "Longer Sentences," in The "Handbook, Fundamentals of Grammar and Usage," in *Excellence in Business Communication,* Fourth Edition.

Lesson 5: Check Your Answers

In the following exercises, write in the present tense of each verb:

1. You (*be*) __are__ eligible for a promotion already.

2. Dave (*have*) __has__ another telephone line.

3. How (*be*) __am I__ supposed to know when we've reached that point?

4. She (*do*) __does__ her work quickly and accurately.

5. They (*be*) __are__ sometimes difficult to deal with.

In the following exercises, fill in the correct verb form:

6. They identified the source of the problem, and then they (*look*) _looked_ for ways to solve it.

7. When success (seem) _seems_ imminent, he panics.

8. Jason Beaudry never has gone to Europe and probably never (go) _will go_ .

9. Why (*do*) _does_ she ignore John when he talks?

10. We (*take*) _took_ that point into consideration before we decided what to do.

Circle the correct verb form in the following exercises:

11. Each of the managers turn/(turns) in a monthly report.

12. The receptionist, not the clerks, take/(takes) all the calls.

13. Everyone upstairs receive/(receives) mail before we do.

14. The reasons for her decision (sound)/sounds logical.

15. All the products (sell)/sells well.

Circle the correct form of the verb in the following exercises:

16. Brenda and Bill has/(have) responsibility for the project.

17. Neither the main office nor the branch offices is/(are) blameless.

18. Each programmer and analyst report/(reports) to Jennifer.

19. Your whole family enjoy/(enjoys) credit privileges at Mo's.

20. Either the secretaries or the office manager take/(takes) care of all inquiries about employee benefits.

Circle the correct verb form in the following exercises:

21. C & B Sales (is)/are listed in the directory.

22. When measuring shelves, 7 inches (is)/are significant.

23. About 90 percent of the employees (plan)/plans to come to the company picnic.

24. Carnegie Industries make/(makes) bookbinding equipment.

25. Two weeks (is)/are all we need to complete our analysis.

Lesson 6
Parts of Speech: Adjectives and Articles

Adjectives modify (describe, explain, tell something about) nouns and pronouns. The adjectives in the following sentences do this job whether they come before or after the words they modify and whether they are truly adjectives or are nouns working as adjectives:

The <u>Burnaby</u> office has received *another* payment from <u>that</u> customer.
A <u>more attractive</u> desk is earmarked for Ms. Brophy's <u>fourth-floor</u> office.
We are <u>proud</u> of your <u>outstanding</u> performance in <u>many</u> competitions.

These sentences would be much less descriptive without adjectives telling which, what kind of, and what. (Although possessive pronouns, such as *your,* seem to function as adjectives, they are classified as pronouns.)

Observe that the adjectives in these sentences fall into three categories: purely descriptive (such as *outstanding* and *more attractive*), limiting (such as *many*), and pointing (such as *that*). Descriptive adjectives are probably the easiest to identify in any sentence; they are words like *cold, impatient, useful, good.* Limiting adjectives are a little more difficult to pick oat, but numbers and such words as *most, several,* and *no* are often used to specify quantity or amount. The pointing adjectives are *this, that, these,* and *those.* The sentences also contain articles: *a, an,* and *the.*

In the following exercises, underline all the adjectives and articles:

1. A pleasant surprise awaits you for taking advantage of our fantastic offer.

2. The newest accountant on our headquarters staff is a 1999 graduate of the most prestigious university in a neighboring province.

3. She slowly rose to speak to the assembled delegates.

4. Their approach is best described as a useful combination of grand design and careful execution.

5. The colour photographs in that brochure were expensive.

Adjectives change form when they are used to compare items:

One Item	Two Items	Three or More Items
large	larger	largest
easy	easier	easiest
far	farther	farthest
good	better	best
bad	worse	*worst*
little	less	least
some	more	most
beautiful	more beautiful	most beautiful

188

As you can see from this list, simple adjectives like *large* add the ending *er* when comparing two items and *est* when comparing three or more items. This is the normal pattern. Other *words, such* as *good,* are irregular.

And words with three or more syllables use *more* and *most,* instead of the word endings, to make comparisons.

Some adjectives cannot be used to make comparisons because they themselves indicate the extreme. For example, if something is perfect, nothing can be more perfect. If something is unique or ultimate, nothing can be more unique or more ultimate.

In the following exercises, fill in the appropriate form of the adjectives that are supplied for you:

6. Of the two products, this one has the (*great*) _____ potential.

7. The (*perfect*) _____ solution is *d*.

8. Here is the (*interesting*) _____ of all the ideas I have heard so far.

9. Our service is (*good*) _____ than theirs.

10. The (*hard*) _____ part of my job is firing people.

Many adjectives used in the business world are actually combinations of words: *up-to-date* report, *last-minute* effort, *fifth-floor* suite, *well-built* engine. As you can see, they are hyphenated when they come before the noun they modify. However, when they come after the noun they modify, they are not hyphenated: the report is *up to date,* an effort made at the *last minute,* a suite on the *fifth floor,* an engine that is *well built.*

Hyphens are not used when part of the combination is a word ending in *ly* (because the word ending in *ly* usually modifies the adjective): a rapidly *shrinking* reserve, a highly *motivated* employee.

A hyphen is also omitted from combinations of words that are used frequently: *credit card* account, *data processing* department.

In the following exercises, insert hyphens wherever required:

11. A highly placed source revealed Dotson's last ditch efforts to cover up the mistake.

12. Please send a replacement that is large enough for me.

13. A top secret document was taken from the president's office last night.

14. A 30 year old person should know better.

15. If I write a large scale report, I want to know that it will be read by upper level management.

Adjectives often pile up in front of a noun, like this:

The <u>superficial, obvious</u> answer was the one she gave.
The most valuable animal on the ranch is a <u>small black</u> horse.

The question is whether a comma should be used to separate the adjectives. The answer? Use a comma when the two adjectives independently modify the noun; do not use a comma when one of the adjectives is closely identified with the noun. In the first example above, the answer was both superficial and obvious. But in the second example, the black horse is small.

Another way for you to think about this problem is to use the word *and* as a replacement for the comma.

Here is another example for you to study:

> We recommend a diet of <u>leafy green</u> vegetables.
> We recommend a diet of <u>green</u>, <u>leafy</u> vegetables.

Because some green vegetables are not leafy (cucumbers and zucchini, for example), it is correct to leave out the comma in the first example so that you know which kind of green vegetables are being discussed. But because all leafy vegetables are also green (green and leafy), the comma must be included in the second example. Again:

> He is an <u>angry young</u> man.
> He is an <u>angry</u>, <u>dangerous</u> man.

There is a difference between a young man who is angry and a man who is angry and dangerous.

Another device for deciding whether to use a comma is to try switching the adjectives. If the order of the adjectives can be reversed without changing the meaning of the phrase, you should use a comma. If the order cannot be reversed, you should not use a comma. For example:

> Here's our <u>simplified credit</u> application.
> Here's our <u>simplified</u>, <u>easy-to-complete</u> application.
> Here's our <u>easy-to-complete</u>, <u>simplified</u> application.

A credit application may be simple or complex; at any rate, you cannot talk about a *credit, simplified application*. The application in the second and third examples, however, is both simplified and easy to complete, however you arrange the words.

In the following exercises, insert required commas between adjectives:

16. The two companies are engaged in an all-out no-holds-barred struggle for dominance.

17. A tiny metal shaving is responsible for the problem.

18. She came to the office with a bruised swollen knee.

19. A chipped cracked sheet of glass is useless to us.

20. You'll receive our usual cheerful prompt service.

In these last exercises, insert both hyphens and commas as necessary:

21. It was one of the first high tech colleges in the country.

22. Joan is the stern mother hen of a busy tightly run office.

23. Energy wasting unnecessary trips must be eliminated.

24. The new past due notices will go out with today's mail.

25. If a broken down unproductive guy like Carl can get a raise why can't a take charge guy like me get one?

If you want to learn more about adjectives and articles, consult a grammar book on the following topics:

absolute adjectives	coordinate adjectives	limiting adjectives
comparative adjectives	descriptive adjectives	pointing adjectives
compound adjectives	independent adjectives	proper adjectives

You may also wish to consult Sections 1.4, "Adjectives," and 1.6.2, "Conjunctions, Articles, and Interjections," in The "Handbook, Fundamentals of Grammar and Usage," in *Excellence in Business Communication.*

Lesson 6: Check Your Answers

In the following exercises, underline all the adjectives and articles:

1. A pleasant surprise awaits you for taking advantage of our fantastic offer.

2. The newest accountant on our headquarters staff is a 1999 graduate of the most prestigious university in a neighboring province.

3. She slowly rose to speak to the assembled delegates.

4. Their approach is best described as a useful combination of grand design and careful execution.

5. The colour photographs in that brochure were expensive.

In the following exercises, fill in the appropriate form of the adjectives that are supplied for you:

6. Of the two products, this one has the (*great*) *greater* potential.

7. The (*perfect*) *most perfect* solution is *d.*

8. Here is the (*interesting*) *most interesting* of all the ideas I have heard so far.

9. Our service is (*good*) *better* than theirs.

10. The (*hard*) *hardest* part of my job is firing people.

In the following exercises, insert hyphens wherever required:

11. A highly placed source revealed Dotson's last-ditch efforts to cover up the mistake.

12. Please send a replacement that is large enough for me.

13. A top-secret document was taken from the president's office last night.

14. A 30-year-old person should know better.

15. If I write a large-scale report, I want to know that it will be read by upper-level management.

In the following exercises, insert required commas between adjectives:

16. The two companies are engaged in an all-out no-holds-barred struggle for dominance.

17. A tiny metal shaving is responsible for the problem.

18. She came to the office with a bruised swollen knee.

19. A chipped cracked sheet of glass is useless to us.

20. You'll receive our usual cheerful prompt service.

In these last exercises, insert both hyphens and commas as necessary:

21. It was one of the first high-tech colleges in the country.

22. Joan is the stern mother hen of a busy tightly run office.

23. Energy-wasting unnecessary trips must be eliminated.

24. The new past-due notices will go out with today's mail.

25. If a broken-down unproductive guy like Carl can get a raise why can't a take-charge guy like me get one?

Lesson 7
Parts of Speech: Adverbs

Adverbs modify (describe, qualify, limit) verbs, adjectives, and other adverbs:

Verb: He sent the specifications <u>promptly</u>. (How were they sent? Promptly.)
Adjective: Their <u>grievously</u> late report will not be accepted. (How late was the report? Grievously late.)
Adverb: He ran <u>very</u> quickly. (How quickly did he run? Very quickly.)

Most adverbs are formed simply by adding *ly* to the end of an adjective (with the last letter of the adjective sometimes dropped or changed): *highly, quickly, truly, nicely, poorly,* and so on. But some familiar adverbs—such as *quite, too, very, almost, often, well, soon, so,* and *many*—do not end in *ly.*

In the following exercises, underline the adverbs:

1. An unstable person is an obviously poor choice for this difficult job.

2. They are quite certain that the spaces will fill soon.

3. She often stays late to finish her rapidly accumulating paperwork.

4. Curly hair is yours with our newly developed perms.

5. A well organized report is soon read.

6. Too many of our customers have complained vigorously about her surly manner.

7. Trapped in a slowly shrinking market, the company is certainly doomed to fail eventually.

8. The market for anatomically correct dolls is too small.

9. Give the letter a quick review before you blithely send it.

10. A correctly operating bottom-of-the-line model is much better than a malfunctioning top-of-the-line model.

Some adverbs are difficult to distinguish from adjectives. For example, in the following sentences is the underlined word an adverb or an adjective?

They worked <u>well</u>.
The baby is <u>well</u>.

In the first sentence, *well* is an adverb modifying the verb worked. In the second sentence, *well* is an adjective modifying the noun *baby.*

193

The secret to choosing correctly between adverbs and adjectives in this situation is to be able to identify such being verbs as *appear, be, become, feel, look, seem, smell, sound,* and *taste.* Being verbs link a noun to an adjective describing the noun. In contrast, an adverb is used if the verb that separates it from the noun is an action verb. Here is another example:

Adjective: This balance sheet looks <u>strange</u>. (The balance sheet does not itself use eyes to look; this sentence means that the balance sheet *is* strange.)

Adverb: She looks at us <u>strangely</u>. (Here *looks* is an action verb, and *strangely* tells how she performs that action.)

If you can tell the difference between an adjective and an adverb in situations like these, you should have no trouble deciding when to use *good, real,* and *slow* (adjectives modifying nouns) as opposed to *well, really,* and *slowly* (adverbs modifying verbs, adjectives, and adverbs). For example:

> *Adjective:* He is a <u>good</u> worker. (What kind of worker is he?)
> *Adverb:* He works <u>well</u>. (How does he work?)

> *Adjective:* It is a <u>real</u> computer. (What kind of computer is it?)
> *Adverb:* It <u>really</u> is a computer. (To what extent is it one?)

> *Adjective:* The traffic is <u>slow</u>. (What quality does the traffic have?)
> *Adverb:* The traffic moves <u>slowly</u>. (How does the traffic move ?)

In the following exercises, circle the correct choice:

11. Their performance has been good/well.

12. I sure/surely do not know how to help you.

13. He feels sick/sickly again today.

14. Customs dogs are chosen because they smell good/well.

15. The redecorated offices look good/well.

Like adjectives, adverbs can be used to compare items. Generally, the basic adverb is combined with *more* or *most,* just as long adjectives are—although some adverbs have one-word comparative forms:

One Item	Two Items	Three Items
quickly	more quickly	most quickly
sincerely	less sincerely	least sincerely
fast	faster	fastest
well	better	best

In these exercises, provide the correct form of the adverbs that are provided:

16. Which of the two programs computes (*fast*) _____?

17. Kate has 13 years of experience to draw on, but she was (*recently*) _____ employed by Graphicon.

18. Could they be (*happily*) _____ employed than they are now?

19. This is the (*well*) _____ designed model of the two we have in stock.

20. You are to be praised for presenting the (*logically*) _____ reasoned argument I have ever heard.

Negative adverbs—such as *neither, no, not, scarcely,* and *seldom*—are powerful words and therefore do not need any help in conveying a negative thought. In fact, using double negatives gives a strong impression of illiteracy, so you would be well advised to avoid sentences like these:

> I <u>don't</u> want <u>no</u> mistakes. (Correct: I don't want any mistakes. I want no mistakes.)
> They <u>scarcely</u> noticed <u>neither</u> one. (Correct: They scarcely noticed either one. They noticed neither one.)

In the following exercises, correct the double negatives by crossing out unnecessary letters and words and writing in necessary letters and words:

21. He doesn't seem to have none.

22. That machine is scarcely never used.

23. They can't get no replacement parts until Thursday.

24. It wasn't no different from the first event we promoted.

25. We've looked for it, and it doesn't seem to be no where.

If you would like to learn more about adverbs, consult a grammar book on the following topics:

> adverbs versus adjectives   double negatives
> comparative adverbs   redundant adverbs

You may also wish to refer to Section 1.5, "Adverbs," in The "Handbook, Fundamentals of Grammar and Usage," in *Excellence in Business Communication.*

Lesson 7: Check Your Answers

In the following exercises, underline the adverbs:

1. An unstable person is an <u>obviously</u> poor choice for this difficult job.

2. They are <u>quite</u> certain that the spaces will fill <u>soon</u>.

3. She <u>often</u> stays late to finish her <u>rapidly</u> accumulating paperwork.

4. Curly hair is yours with our <u>newly</u> developed perms.

5. A <u>well</u> organized report is <u>soon</u> read.

6. <u>Too</u> many of our customers have complained <u>vigorously</u> about her surly manner.

7. Trapped in a <u>slowly</u> shrinking market, the company is <u>certainly</u> doomed to fail <u>eventually</u>.

8. The market for <u>anatomically</u> correct dolls is <u>too</u> small.

9. Give the letter a quick review before you <u>blithely</u> send it.

10. A <u>correctly</u> operating bottom-of-the-line model is <u>much</u> better than a malfunctioning top-of-the-line model.

In the following exercises, circle the correct choice:

11. Their performance has been (good)/well.

12. I sure/(surely) do not know how to help you.

13. He feels (sick)/sickly again today.

14. Customs dogs are chosen because they smell good/(well).

15. The redecorated offices look (good)/well.

In these exercises, provide the correct form of the adverbs that are provided:

16. Which of the two programs computes (*fast*) **faster**?

17. Kate has 13 years of experience to draw on, but she was (*recently*) **most recently** employed by Graphicon.

18. Could they be (*happily*) **more happily** employed than they are now?

19. This is the (*well*) **better** designed model of the two we have in stock.

20. You are to be praised for presenting the (*logically*) **most logically** reasoned argument I have ever heard.

In the following exercises, correct the double negatives by crossing out unnecessary letters and words and writing in necessary letters and words:

21. He doesn't seem to have ~~none~~ any.   or   He seems to have none.

22. That machine is scarcely ~~n~~ever used.   or   That machine is never used.

23. They can't get ~~no~~ any replacement parts until Thursday.   or   They can get no replacement...

24. It wasn't ~~no~~ any different from the first event we promoted.   or   It was no different from...

25. We've looked for it, and it doesn't seem to be ~~no~~ any where.   or   ... it seems to be nowhere

Lesson 8
Parts of Speech: Verbals

Some forms of verbs take a special role in sentences. Verbals are verbs that are used as nouns, adjectives, and adverbs instead of as predicate verbs. There are three basic types of verbals.

The first type of verbal, called a gerund, is formed by adding *ing* to the end of a verb and is used as a noun:

<u>Selling</u> is an acquired skill.

Selling (a gerund) is the subject of this sentence, and *is* is the predicate verb.

Be careful not to mistake gerunds for predicate verbs that use an *ing* ending. Compare these sentences:

Predicate verb: He <u>is merchandising</u> a new product.
Gerund: He has a knack for <u>merchandising</u>.

In the second sentence, *has* is the predicate verb, and *merchandising* is the object of a phrase.

The major problem that arises with gerunds is the use of a possessive noun or pronoun with them. The following sentence is incorrect:

We appreciate <u>you</u> calling about this matter.

Because *calling* takes the place of a noun in this sentence, *you* must be changed to a possessive pronoun, like this:

We appreciate <u>your</u> calling about this matter.

Only the second sentence below is correct:

Incorrect: <u>Deborah</u> delaying will jeopardize the whole program.
Correct: <u>Deborah's</u> delaying will jeopardize the whole program.

You can decide whether to use a possessive noun or pronoun with a gerund by replacing it with another noun. For example, if you replace the word *delaying* with the word *temper,* you will find that you must use a possessive noun in order to make sense:

<u>Deborah's</u> temper will jeopardize the whole program.

In the following exercises, circle the sentences that use gerunds correctly:

1. Waiting for anything makes me impatient.

2. His handling of the irate customer was admirable.

3. You saw the result of George training.

4. Take the results to manufacturing.

5. You could attribute the difference to them cheating.

The second kind of verbal is the participle, which serves in sentences as an adjective. In the following sentences, observe how the participles formed from the verb *finish* are used to modify nouns:

> The assistant put the <u>finishing</u> touches on the letter.
> The <u>finished</u> assignment is in Ms. Boromisa's office.

In both of these sentences, a form of the verb *finish* is used to provide additional information about nouns: *touches* and *assignment*. Other *verbs—put* and *is*—work in these sentences as predicate verbs.

In the following exercises, underline the participles:

6. The established procedures are rarely followed.

7. Use a roasting bag to avoid an overdone turkey.

8. Twice-audited Hodgkins & Company has become more careful with its record keeping.

9. The closed factory will be reopening in May.

10. During the editing process, most written reports are strengthened.

The third form of verbal is the infinitive, which you have probably heard of (as in "splitting infinitives"). An infinitive, such as *to be,* may function as a noun, an adjective, or an adverb. For example, in this sentence the infinitive works as a noun—in fact, as the subject of the sentence:

> <u>To err</u> is human. (What is human?)

Here it is a noun too, but this time it's the object of the sentence:

> We hope <u>to grow</u> this year. (We hope what?)

In the following sentence, the infinitive works as an adjective:

> Their plan <u>to grow</u> was hampered by a weak economy. (What kind of plan?)

And here the infinitive works as an adverb:

> It eventually grew <u>to be</u> a very large company. (How did it grow?)

Now, about splitting infinitives: In general, you should avoid putting any word or phrase between *to* and the rest of the infinitive. But sometimes you must split an infinitive to protect your sentence's clarity or smoothness. For example, splitting the infinitive in this sentence is acceptable:

> The best policy is to regularly <u>inspect</u> and <u>service</u> all the equipment.

But this one becomes awkward when the infinitive is split:

> To predictably, promptly, and reliably <u>call</u> on customers is part of your job.

It would be better like this:

   <u>To call</u> on customers predictably, promptly, and reliably is part of your job.

In the following exercises, circle the words that split an infinitive and draw an arrow to show where they would fit in more smoothly and logically:

11. Our goal is to, with your help, track down the error.

12. Did you tell her to promptly call me?

13. To cheerfully service these accounts, you need patience.

14. We have been trying to desperately avoid bankruptcy.

15. Ms. McMichaels tends to, with her great sense of timing, know just when she should sell.

In the next set of exercises, draw circles around the verbals and draw lines to the words they modify (if they indeed modify anything):

16. Handling explosives is our main business.

17. Your plan to analyze these trends is sound.

18. The trading experts recommend patience.

19. We planned to finish by Wednesday.

20. Streamlined DiTex has more flexibility than some of its competitors.

A glaring sign of carelessness in writing is the use of different types of verbals in situations that call for parallel structure. For instance, the following sentence is hard to read:

   Your responsibilities include <u>gathering</u> sales figures, <u>analysis</u> of those figures, and <u>to report</u> them to management.

You could solve the problem by putting all the underlined verbals in the same form:

   gathering, analyzing, and reporting
   collection of, analysis of, and reporting of
   to gather, to analyze, and to report

Many other sentences can be improved by introducing parallelism:

Nonparallel:	He was an expert in <u>writing</u> and had learned well how to speak.
Parallel:	He was an expert in <u>writing</u> and <u>speaking</u>.
Parallel:	He had learned well how <u>to write</u> and <u>to speak</u>.

In the following exercises, cross out and add words to give the sentences a parallel structure:

21. These were my goals: finding suitable markets and to outline a plan for penetrating them.

22. Standing firm is more difficult than to allow an exception.

23. She has demonstrated an ability to plan and skill at organizing.

24. This remarkable new product will help you to keep your time organized and with writing your correspondence.

25. Retraining people already on the payroll is better than to hire new people.

If you would like to know more about verbals, consult a grammar book on these *topics:*

dangling modifiers	misplaced modifiers	verbal nouns
gerunds	parallelism	verbal phrases
infinitives	participles	

You may also wish to refer to Section 1.7.6, "Misplaced Modifiers," in The "Handbook, Fundamentals of Grammar and Usage," in *Excellence in Business Communication*.

Lesson 8: Check Your Answers

In the following exercises, circle the sentences that use gerunds correctly:

1. (Waiting for anything makes me impatient.)

2. (His handling of the irate customer was admirable.)

3. You saw the result of George training.

4. (Take the results to manufacturing.)

5. You could attribute the difference to them cheating.

In the following exercises, underline the participles:

6. The established procedures are rarely followed.

7. Use a roasting bag to avoid an overdone turkey.

8. Twice-audited Hodgkins & Company has become more careful with its record keeping.

9. The closed factory will be reopening in May.

10. During the editing process, most written reports are strengthened.

In the following exercises, circle the words that split an infinitive and draw an arrow to show where they would fit in more smoothly and logically:

11. Our goal is to, (with your help) track down the error.

12. Did you tell her to (promptly) call me?

13. To (cheerfully) service these accounts, you need patience.

14. We have been trying to (desperately) avoid bankruptcy.

15. Ms. McMichaels tends to, (with her great sense of timing), know just when she should sell.

In the next set of exercises, draw circles around the verbals and draw lines to the words they modify (if they indeed modify anything):

16. (Handling) explosives is our main business.

17. Your plan (to analyze) these trends is sound.

18. The (trading) experts recommend patience.

19. We planned (to finish) by Wednesday.

20. (Streamlined) DiTex has more flexibility than some of its competitors.

In the following exercises, cross out and add words to give the sentences a parallel structure:

21. These were my goals: finding suitable markets and ~~to outline~~ *outlining* a plan for penetrating them.
or to find and to outline

22. Standing firm is more difficult than ~~to allow~~ *allowing* an exception. *or to stand and to allow*

23. She has demonstrated an ability to plan and ~~skill at organizing~~ *to organize*. *or skill at planning and organizing*

24. This remarkable new product will help you ~~to keep~~ *organize* your time ~~organized~~ and ~~with writing~~ *write* your correspondence. *or with organizing your time and with writing*

25. Retraining people already on the payroll is better than ~~to hire~~ *hiring* new people. *or to retrain and to hire*

Lesson 9
Parts of Speech: Prepositions

Prepositions are little words that can add a lot of meaning to sentences. These are some of the most frequently used prepositions:

about	before	for	out
after	between	in	through
among	by	into	to
at	during	of	with

Some prepositions consist of more than one word—like these:

because of	in addition to
except for	out of

And some prepositions are closely linked with a verb. When using phrases like *look up* and *wipe out,* keep the phrase intact and do not insert anything between the verb and the preposition.

Other prepositions do not stand alone either; they signal prepositional phrases that have a noun as an object:

<u>of</u> the company	<u>in</u> other words
<u>by</u> taking part	<u>into</u> a bank

Prepositional phrases always modify another part of a sentence:

Subject (*she*):   <u>Of all our technicians,</u> she is the best trained.
Object (*merit*):   They couldn't see the merit <u>in my proposal.</u>
Predicate verb (*left*): Someone left a folder <u>on my desk.</u>

To prevent misreading, prepositional phrases should be placed near the element they modify. For example, in the first example here, the prepositional phrase modifies *she* and is therefore placed right next to it.

In the following exercises, underline the prepositional phrases:

1. The knob on your radio broke after the warranty expiration date.

2. A truckload of replacements has been sent to Kingston.

3. With her luck, she will soon be named head of the department.

4. He worked for our company about two years ago.

5. You will not be included in our benefits program during our training period.

When a pronoun is part of a prepositional phrase, it should always be in the object *form—me, you, him/her/it, us, them, whom:*

Give the documents <u>to them</u>.
They will choose <u>between Harry and me</u>.

In the following exercises, underline the correct pronoun:

6. Send the memo to Sandra and he/him.

7. The red sports car belongs to who/whom?

8. I hope they award the contract to us/we.

9. This information is just between you and I/me.

10. They asked for help from Don and her/she.

It was once considered totally unacceptable to put a preposition at the end of a sentence. Now you may:

I couldn't tell what they were interested <u>in</u>. *(better than I couldn't tell in what they were interested.)* What did she attribute it <u>to</u>? (better than *To what did she attribute it?*)

Be careful, however, not to use the wrong form of a pronoun in sentences that end in a preposition. For example, is *who* or *whom* correct in this sentence?

(Who/Whom) did you speak to?

You can figure out the answer by moving the preposition and the pronoun back together:

<u>To whom</u> did you speak?

Be sure to use only the prepositions that are necessary. In the following sentences, the prepositions in parentheses should be omitted:

All (of) the staff members were present.
I almost fell off (of) my chair with surprise.
Where was Mr. Steuben going (to)?
They couldn't help (from) wondering.

The opposite problem is not including a preposition when you should. Consider the two sentences that follows:

Sales were over $100,000 <u>for</u> Linda and Bill.
Sales were over $100,000 <u>for</u> Linda and <u>for</u> Bill.

The first sentence indicates that Linda and Bill had combined sales over $100,000; the second, that Linda and Bill each had sales over $100,000, for a combined total in excess of $200,000. The preposition *for* is crucial here.

Prepositions are also required in sentences like this one:

Which type <u>of</u> personal computer do you prefer?

Certain prepositions are used with certain words. When the same preposition can be used for two or more words in a sentence without affecting the meaning, only the last preposition is required:

We are familiar (<u>with</u>) and satisfied <u>with</u> your company's products.

But when different prepositions are normally used with the words, all the prepositions must be included:

We are familiar <u>with</u> and interested <u>in</u> your company's products.

In the following exercises, cross out unnecessary words and prepositions that are in the wrong place and insert prepositions where they are required:

11. Where was your argument leading to?

12. I wish he would get off of the phone.

13. This is a project into which you can sink your teeth.

14. The Mercantile Bank must become aware and sensitive to its customers' concerns.

15. We are responsible for aircraft safety in the air, the hangars, and the runways.

Here is an incomplete list of prepositions that are used in a particular way with particular words:

among/between: *among* is used to refer to three or more (*Circulate the memo among the office staff*); *between* is used to refer to two (*Put the copy machine between Judy and Dan*)

as if/like: *as if* is used before a clause (*It seems as if we should be doing something*); *like* is used before a noun or pronoun along (*He seems like a nice guy*)

have/of: *have*, a verb, is used in verb phrases (*They should have checked first*); *of*, a preposition, is never used in such cases

in/into: *in* is used to refer to a static position (The *file is in the cabinet*); *into* is used to refer to movement toward a position (Put the file into the cabinet)

And here is an incomplete list of some prepositions that have come to be used with certain words:

according to	different from	prior to
agree to (a proposal)	get from (receive)	reason with
agree with (a person)	get off (dismount)	responsible for
buy from	in accordance with	similar to
capable of	in search of	talk to (without interaction)
comply with	independent of	talk with (with interaction)
conform to	inferior to	wait for (person or thing)
differ from (things)	plan to	wait on (like a waiter)
differ with (person)	prefer to	

If in doubt about the preposition to use with a word, look up the word in the dictionary. In the following exercises, insert the correct words:

16. Dr. Namaguchi will be talking _____ the marketing class on Tuesday, but she won't have time to answer students' questions.

17. Matters like this are decided after thorough discussion _____ all seven department managers.

18. Do you agree _____ this proposal?

19. We can't wait _____ their decision much longer.

20. CanCorp would _____ been in a good position if it had not diversified so soon.

21. Someone should try to reason _____ him.

22. Who is responsible _____ ordering sporting goods?

23. Their computer is similar _____ ours.

24. This model is different _____ the one we ordered.

25. She got her chair _____ the person who quit.

If you want to know more about prepositions, consult a grammar book on these topics:

    idioms   like/as if   prepositional phrases

You may also wish to refer to Section 1.6.1, "Prepositions," in The "Handbook, Fundamentals of Grammar and Usage," in *Excellence in Business Communication*.

Lesson 9: Check Your Answers

In the following exercises, underline the prepositional phrases:

1. The knob on your radio broke <u>after the warranty expiration date</u>.

2. A truckload <u>of replacements</u> has been sent <u>to Kingston</u>.

3. <u>With her luck</u>, she will soon be named head <u>of the department</u>.

4. He worked <u>for our company</u> <u>about two years ago</u>.

5. You will not be included <u>in our benefits program</u> <u>during our training period</u>.

In the following exercises, underline the correct pronoun:

6. Send the memo to Sandra and he/<u>him</u>.

7. The red sports car belongs to who/<u>whom</u>?

8. I hope they award the contract to <u>us</u>/we.

9. This information is just between you and I/<u>me</u>.

10. They asked for help from Don and <u>her</u>/she.

In the following exercises, cross out unnecessary words and prepositions that are in the wrong place and insert prepositions where they are required:

11. Where was your argument leading ~~to~~?

12. I wish he would get off ~~of~~ the phone.

13. This is a project ~~into which~~ you can sink your teeth _into_

14. The Mercantile Bank must become aware _of_ and sensitive to its customers' concerns.

15. We are responsible for aircraft safety in the air, _in_ the hangars, and _on_ the runways.

In the following exercises, insert the correct words:

16. Dr. Namaguchi will be talking ___*to*___ the marketing class on Tuesday, but she won't have time to answer students' questions.

17. Matters like this are decided after thorough discussion ___*among*___ all seven department managers.

18. Do you agree ___*to*___ this proposal?

19. We can't wait ___*for*___ their decision much longer.

20. CanCorp would ___*have*___ been in a good position if it had not diversified so soon.

21. Someone should try to reason ___*with*___ him.

22. Who is responsible ___*for*___ ordering sporting goods?

23. Their computer is similar ___*to*___ ours.

24. This model is different ___*from*___ the one we ordered.

25. She got her chair ___*from*___ the person who quit.

Lesson 10
Parts of Speech: Conjunctions

Conjunctions connect the parts of a sentence: words, phrases, and clauses. You are probably most familiar with the following conjunctions:

And	for	or	yet
but	nor	so	

In these sentences, the conjunctions are underlined:

That model is old <u>and</u> unpopular, <u>but</u> it should not be scrapped.
<u>Either</u> you <u>or</u> Gretchen should go.
<u>Because</u> she is out of town, she can't attend the meeting.
The report was late; <u>therefore</u> we haven't made a decision yet.

Notice in the following examples that conjunctions may be used to connect clauses (which have both a subject and a predicate) with other clauses, to connect clauses with phrases (which do not have both a subject and a predicate), and to connect words with words:

Words with words: We sell designer clothing <u>and</u> linens.
Clauses with phrases: Their products are expensive <u>but</u> still appeal to value-conscious consumers.
Clauses with clauses: I will call her on the phone today, <u>or</u> I will visit her office tomorrow.

In the following exercises, underline the conjunctions and write in each blank a code for the type of grammatical elements they join *(W-W* for word to word, *P-C* for phrase to clause, or *C-C* for clause to clause):

1. _____ She was not pleased, nor was she easy to reassure.

2. _____ The new model is sporty yet economical.

3. _____ We are proud of your accomplishments and of your reputation in the community.

4. _____ You promised but apparently forgot to send me the documents.

5. _____ We would cancel the order, for we have not vet sold the items already in stock.

Some conjunctions are used in pairs:

both . . . and	neither... nor	whether... or
either... or	not only... but also	

In the following sentences, take special note of both the underlined conjunctions and the italicized words:

They <u>not only</u> *are* out of racquets <u>but also</u> *are* out of balls.
They *are* <u>not only</u> out of racquets <u>but also</u> out of balls.
They are *our of* <u>not only</u> racquets <u>but also</u> balls.

With paired conjunctions, you must be careful to construct each phrase in the same way. In other words, if you write *not only are out of racquets,* you cannot write *but also out of balls;* you must include the verb *are* after *but also.* But if you write *are not only out of racquets,* with the verb before the conjunction, you should not include the verb *are* after *but also.* The same need for parallelism exists when using conjunctions to join the other parts of speech, as in these sentences:

> He is listed in <u>either</u> *your* roster <u>or</u> *my* roster.
> He is listed <u>neither</u> *in* your roster <u>nor</u> *on* the master list.
> They <u>both</u> *gave* <u>and</u> *received* notice.

In the following exercises, cross out and insert words to make parallel the pairs of conjunctions and the other parts of speech that go with them:

6. She is active in not only a civic group but also in an athletic organization.

7. That is either a mistake or was an intentional omission.

8. The question is whether to set up a booth at the convention or be hosting a hospitality suite.

9. In both overall sales and in profits, we are doing better.

10. She had neither the preferred educational background, nor did she have suitable experience.

In all the previous examples of using conjunctions to join clauses, the clauses have been essentially equal. A different type of conjunction is used to join clauses that are unequal—that is, to join a main clause to one that is subordinate to or dependent on it. Here is a partial list of conjunctions used to introduce dependent clauses:

although	before	once	unless
as soon as	even though	so that	until
because	if	that	when

The dependent clause in each of the following examples is italicized, and the conjunction that links each one to the main clause is underlined:

> Send your check now <u>so</u> *that you will not miss this offer.*
> <u>Until</u> we have seen the new personnel guidelines, *we cannot offer any raises.*
> *We have stopped shipping that item,* <u>because</u> we have discovered problems with its safety mechanism.

Can you see that the italicized part of each of these sentences is indeed subordinate to or dependent on the part that is not italicized?

Some of the conjunctions used to introduce dependent clauses, such as *before,* may also be used as prepositions. If a phrase follows such a word, the word is working in the sentence as a preposition; but if a clause follows it, the word is working in the sentence as a conjunction:

> Preposition (phrase):   <u>Before</u> giving up, she tried calculating an acid-test ratio.
> Conjunction (clause):   <u>Before</u> she gave up, she tried calculating an acid-test ratio.

In the following exercises, circle the conjunctions and underline the main clauses:

11. After making this phone call, I intend to leave.

12. He has already asked for a promotion, even though he started working here only a month ago.

13. Be sure to sign this document before you send it back.

14. If I show you how to use the spreadsheet program, will you show me how to use the word-processing program?

15. She'll jump at this once-in-a-lifetime opportunity when she finds out about it.

Some conjunctions function as adverbs. Here are some of them (and related transitional phrases):

also	in fact	on the other hand
as a result	indeed	otherwise
consequently	instead	still
even so	meanwhile	that is
furthermore	nevertheless	therefore
however	next	thus

These words and phrases link clauses—and sometimes sentences—that are essentially equal. However, unlike other kinds of conjunctions, they may fall either at the beginning of a clause or somewhere within it. Observe the relationship of the conjunctions (underlined) to the verbs they modify in the following sentences:

They are, <u>in fact</u>, here today. (modifies *are*)
<u>Therefore</u>, we will send a replacement. (modifies *will send*)
The deadline has passed; <u>however</u>, we will accept your application. (modifies *will accept*)

Circle the conjunctions working as adverbs in the following exercises, and underline the verbs they modify:

16. The factory was shut down for two weeks; consequently, our stocks of Part C-118 are low.

17. It is indeed a fine example of cooperation.

18. Her experience is limited; on the other hand, her technical skills are excellent.

19. Ask him if he wants it; otherwise give it to me.

20. Meanwhile, they will be preparing the proposal.

In the final exercises for this lesson, underline all words working as conjunctions:

21. After your half-day presentation to management, you were undoubtedly tired but happy to have survived.

22. Send us a lightweight motor, two pulleys, and a winch.

23. Although you could perhaps find a substitute, you would have a hard time finding one.

24. We ask our credit customers to provide either a spotless credit record or substantial collateral.

25. The company nevertheless plans to distribute dividends equal to last year's.

You can learn more about conjunctions by looking up the following topics in a grammar book:

adverbial conjunctions   dependent clauses
conjunctive adverbs   independent clauses
coordinating conjunctions   subordinating conjunctions
correlative conjunctions

You may also wish to refer to Sections 1.6.2, "Conjunctions, Articles, and Interjections," 1.7.2, "Longer Sentences," 1.7.3, "Sentence *Fragments,*" 1.7.4, "Fused Sentences and Comma Splices," and 4.4, "Transitional Words and *Phrases,*" in The "Handbook, Fundamentals of Grammar and Usage," in *Excellence in Business Communication.*

Lesson 10: Check Your Answers

1. __C-C__   She was not pleased, nor was she easy to reassure.

2. __W-W__   The new model is sporty yet economical.

3. __P-C__   We are proud of your accomplishments and of your reputation in the community.

4. __W-W__   You promised but apparently forgot to send me the documents.

5. __C-C__   We would cancel the order, for we have not vet sold the items already in stock.

In the following exercises, cross out and insert words to make parallel the pairs of conjunctions and the other parts of speech that go with them:

6. She is active in not only a civic group but also ~~in~~ an athletic organization.

7. That is either a mistake or ~~was~~ an intentional omission.

8. The question is whether to set up a booth at the convention or ~~be hosting~~ *to host* a hospitality suite.

9. In both overall sales and ~~in~~ profits, we are doing better.

10. She had neither the preferred educational background, nor ~~did she have~~ suitable experience.

In the following exercises, circle the conjunctions and underline the main clauses:

11. (After) making this phone call, I intend to leave.

12. He has already asked for a promotion, (even though) he started working here only a month ago.

13. Be sure to sign this document (before) you send it back.

14. (If) I show you how to use the spreadsheet program, will you show me how to use the word-processing program?

15. She'll jump at this once-in-a-lifetime opportunity (when) she finds out about it.

Circle the conjunctions working as adverbs in the following exercises, and underline the verbs they modify:

16. The factory was shut down for two weeks; (consequently) our stocks of Part C-118 are low.

17. It is (indeed) a fine example of cooperation.

18. Her experience is limited; (on the other hand) her technical skills are excellent.

19. Ask him if he wants it; (otherwise) give it to me.

20. (Meanwhile,) they will be preparing the proposal.

In the final exercises for this lesson, underline all words working as conjunctions:

21. After your half-day presentation to management, you were undoubtedly tired but happy to have survived.

22. Send us a lightweight motor, two pulleys, and a winch.

23. Although you could perhaps find a substitute, you would have a hard time finding one.

24. We ask our credit customers to provide either a spotless credit record or substantial collateral.

25. The company nevertheless plans to distribute dividends equal to last year's.

Lesson 11
Parts of Speech: Modifying Elements

You have already learned that adjectives and adverbs work in sentences as modifiers. Phrases and clauses may also work as modifiers. Often, however, they are misplaced or misused. To keep meaning clear, you should place these modifying elements (underlined in the following examples) as close as possible to the word or phrase that they modify (italicized):

The *engineer* <u>with the microchip</u> said nothing was wrong.
The engineer said nothing was *wrong* <u>with the microchip</u>.
The *secretary* <u>who quit</u> left a note for the staff accountant.
The secretary left a note for the staff *accountant* <u>who quit</u>.
<u>During the meeting</u>, they *learned* of the disturbance.
They learned of the *disturbance* <u>during the meeting</u>.

Some phrases and clauses modify, in effect, nothing. Therefore, they are called dangling modifiers:

<u>Instead of introducing a new service</u>, existing services were improved.

The modifying phrase in this sentence does not refer to anything; nothing in the sentence is capable of introducing a new service. Therefore, the sentence must be changed so that the modifier clearly refers to something that makes sense (italicized in the following sentence):

<u>Instead of introducing a new service</u>, *they* improved existing services.

In the revised sentence, *they* are capable of introducing a new service.

Here is another example that makes no sense:

<u>Although a superb speaker</u>, the organization did not invite her to make a presentation.

An organization cannot be a superb speaker. After a simple change, however, the sentence makes sense:

<u>Although she was a superb speaker</u>, the organization did not invite her to make a presentation.

In the following exercises, underline the modifying elements that are not in the right place and do not make sense:

1. Hampered by a slow economy, dropping the weakest product line seemed reasonable.

2. The typing went quickly, pausing only to get a cup of tea.

3. Because I was unable to make the figures add up, the senior accountant helped me complete the balance sheet.

4. Completely depleted, we must restock the warehouse.

5. While writing the proposal for them, my clients gave me all the information I needed.

6. Obviously a good worker, we should give him a raise.

7. The industry, pressured by imports, suffered losses.

8. Having multiple product lines, poor sales of one won't hurt them.

9. Joel wrote the report in two weeks overwhelmed with other work.

10. With a new batch of products in the warehouse, all orders can be filled next week.

11. Grasping the tab firmly, pull it toward you.

12. Without a single hat in the store, you cannot buy one.

13. Customers get priority service who have maintenance contracts.

14. Exhausted after a long day, sleep seemed the only cure.

15. Despite careful preparation, the proposal was not accepted.

Another sign of careful English is the proper use of *that* and *which*. To use them properly, you must understand the difference between restrictive and nonrestrictive modifiers. A restrictive modifier is essential to the sentence and cannot be omitted without changing its meaning; a nonrestrictive modifier, on the other hand, can be omitted without changing the sentence's essential meaning. Notice the difference:

> Restrictive: The proposal <u>that they submitted</u> will be accepted.
> Nonrestrictive: The proposal, <u>which they submitted far in advance</u>, will be accepted.

In the first sentence, the restrictive clause tells us an important fact about the proposal being discussed; without it, we would not know which proposal is meant. But in the second sentence, the essential meaning (*The proposal will be accepted*) is not affected by the nonrestrictive clause—only modified by it.
As you can see, *that* is used to introduce restrictive modifiers, with no commas separating such a modifier from the rest of the sentence. *Which* is used to introduce nonrestrictive modifiers, which are set off from the rest of the sentence with commas.

The difference between restrictive and nonrestrictive modifiers also applies to sentences that do not use *that* or *which*:

Restrictive: The programmer <u>who designed the subroutine</u> will get a promotion. (identifies one of several programmers)
Nonrestrictive: The programmer, <u>who designed the subroutine</u>, will get a promotion. (gives additional information about the only programmer)

In the following exercises, insert and delete words and commas so that restrictive and nonrestrictive modifiers are used correctly:

16. The one audit which I was working on is for Sparks, Ltd.

17. Anyone, who wants to advance, should develop job skills.

18. DeLora Johnson the director of planning is out of town.

19. Send your resume to the following address that is the address of our personnel office.

20. The carpeting, which you ordered, is not in stock.

21. We will offer the job to John Gates who has the most experience in our industry.

22. My desk that sits under the air conditioner needs to be moved.

23. Nobody wants to use the desk which sits under the air conditioner.

24. All employees, who carpool regularly, are entitled to half a day of paid vacation per year.

25. Tammy while gathering her materials from the lectern added a few last words on third-quarter profits.

If you want to learn more about modifying elements, consult a grammar book on these topics:

appositives	nonrestrictive modifiers	relative pronouns
dangling modifiers	parallelism	restrictive modifiers
misplaced modifiers		

You may also wish to consult Section 1.7.6, "Misplaced Modifiers," in The "Handbook, Fundamentals of Grammar and Usage," in *Excellence in Business Communication.*

Lesson 11: Check Your Answers

In the following exercises, underline the modifying elements that are not in the right place and do not make sense:

1. <u>Hampered by a slow economy</u>, dropping the weakest product line seemed reasonable.

2. The typing went quickly, <u>pausing only to get a cup of tea.</u>

3. Because I was unable to make the figures add up, the senior accountant helped me complete the balance sheet.

4. <u>Completely depleted</u>, we must restock the warehouse.

5. <u>While writing the proposal for them</u>, my clients gave me all the information I needed.

6. <u>Obviously a good worker,</u> we should give him a raise.

7. The industry, pressured by imports, suffered losses.

8. <u>Having multiple product lines</u>, poor sales of one won't hurt them.

9. Joel wrote the report in two weeks <u>overwhelmed with other work.</u>

10. <u>With a new batch of products in the warehouse,</u> all orders can be filled next week.

11. Grasping the tab firmly, pull it toward you.

12. <u>Without a single hat in the store</u>, you cannot buy one.

13. Customers get priority service <u>who have maintenance contracts</u>.

14. <u>Exhausted after a long day</u>, sleep seemed the only cure.

15. <u>Despite careful preparation</u>, the proposal was not accepted.

In the following exercises, insert and delete words and commas so that restrictive and nonrestrictive modifiers are used correctly:

16. The one audit ~~which~~ *that* I was working on is for Sparks, Ltd.

17. Anyone ʃwho wants to advance ʃshould develop job skills.

18. DeLora Johnson ↑the director of planning ↑is out of town.

19. Send your resume to the following address ~~that~~ *which* is the address of our personnel office.

20. The carpeting ʃ~~which~~ *that* you ordered ʃis not in stock.

21. We will offer the job to John Gates↑who has the most experience in our industry.

22. My desk ↑~~that~~ *which* sits under the air conditioner↑needs to be moved.

23. Nobody wants to use the desk ~~which~~ *that* sits under the air conditioner.

24. All employees ʃwho carpool regularly ʃare entitled to half a day of paid vacation per year.

25. Tammy↑while gathering her materials from the lectern↑added a few last words on third-quarter profits.

Lesson 12
Punctuation: The End of the Sentence

Sentences end with one of only three marks of punctuation: a period, a question mark, or an exclamation point. These marks can sometimes be used, however, in other parts of the sentence.

Most frequently, sentences end with periods. All of the following types of sentences use them:

Statement: Their services are in great demand among wealthy retired people.
Expression that stands for a complete sentence: Perhaps. Perhaps not.
Command: Make three copies of this document for tomorrow's meeting.
Polite request: Please make three copies of this document for tomorrow's meeting.
Indirect question: He wanted to know what we plan to do about upgrading our office computers.
Polite request worded like question: Could you please return this copy with your corrections by
   November 1.

One way to tell whether to use a period of a question mark at the end of a polite request worded like a question is to determine the type of answer you expect. If you expect action to be taken, use a period; if you expect a verbal response, use a question mark.

When a complete sentence is enclosed in parentheses, the period should fall within the closing mark. But if the parenthetical statement is merely a part of a sentence, the period should not be inside the closing mark. For example:

(Consult me later about the third-quarter sales figures.)
We should probably consult later (to talk about the third-quarter sales figures).

With quotations, you should always place the final period inside the closing marks—even if the quotation is not a complete sentence:

She said, "Employees work better when they feel secure."
She said that employees work better "when they feel secure."

Periods are also used with abbreviations, such as *etc.* and *a.m.* However, periods are frequently omitted in common abbreviations that refer to organizations, countries, and well-known people and things, such as JFK, wpm, and USSR. You should also omit periods from shortened forms of some words: *math, 3d,* and *memo,* for instance. A dictionary can tell you when to use periods with abbreviations. Periods should not be doubled at the end of a sentence that finishes with an abbreviation.

Like periods, question marks also have several uses:

Direct question: Where did you put the new merchandise that arrived yesterday?
Question at end of statement: You've already applied, haven't you?
Question within sentence: The solution—can you believe it?—was within reach all along.
Quoted question within sentence: "What color would you prefer?" the clerk asked.
Expression that stands for complete question: Why not?
Statement subject to uncertainty: On January 14, 1957 (?), the industry was born.

Never use a comma or a period immediately after a question mark:

"Should I transfer the files?" she asked.
She asked, "Should I transfer the files?"

Exclamation points are seldom used in business writing—except in advertising copy and sales letters. They are used only to express or generate strong emotion:

I can't believe he has taken a job with our competition!
Don't forget!
Can you believe this price!
Now!

As with question marks, exclamation points should never be followed immediately by a comma or a period.

In the following letter, add periods, question marks, and exclamation points wherever they are appropriate.

For your convenience, each line of the letter is numbered:

1.   Dr Eleanor H Hutton

2.   1358 N Parsons Avenue

3.   Waterloo ON N2J 3D4

4.   Dear Dr Hutton:

5.   Your request for information on TaskMasters, Inc has

6.   been passed on to me We truly appreciate your asking

7.   TaskMasters has been in existence for three years,

8.   and in that time we have experienced a phenomenal growth

9.   of 800 percent That qualifies us as a rapidly growing

10. new company, don't you think

11. Our company's president, Daniel Gruber, is a CA On

12. your behalf, I asked him why he started at TaskMasters His

13. initial response: "Why does Dr Hutton want to know

14. Maybe she plans to become a competitor" (He was

15. joking, of course He knows all about your research)

16. Mr Gruber started the company because so many of his

17. regular accounting clients were disorganized Now they

18. can hire us to take care of all their paperwork

19. Is this the sort of information you wanted If you

20. still have questions, you can call me here before 3 pm

21. I have a request for you too Would you possibly mind

22. filling out the enclosed questionnaire We are

23. currently conducting a survey on clients' and potential

24. clients' needs And although you are not yet a client, you

25. may be someday

You can learn more about this subject by looking up the following topics in a grammar book:

exclamation points/marks periods question marks

You may also wish to refer to Sections 2.1, "Periods," 2.2, "Question Marks," and 2.3, "Exclamation Points," in The "Handbook, Fundamentals of Grammar and Usage," in *Excellence in Business Communication*.

Lesson 12: Check Your Answers

In the following letter, add periods, question marks, and exclamation points wherever they are appropriate. For your convenience, each line of the letter is numbered:

1. Dr. Eleanor H. Hutton

2. 1358 N. Parsons Avenue

3. Waterloo ON N2J 3D4

4. Dear Dr. Hutton:

5. Your request for information on TaskMasters, Inc. has

6. been passed on to me. We truly appreciate your asking

7. TaskMasters has been in existence for three years,

8. and in that time we have experienced a phenomenal growth

9. of 800 percent. That qualifies us as a rapidly growing

10. new company, don't you think?

11. Our company's president, Daniel Gruber, is a CA. On

12. your behalf, I asked him why he started at TaskMasters. His

13. initial response: "Why does Dr. Hutton want to know?

14. Maybe she plans to become a competitor" (He was

15. joking, of course He knows all about your research

16. Mr. Gruber started the company because so many of his

17. regular accounting clients were disorganized Now they

18. can hire us to take care of all their paperwork

19. Is this the sort of information you wanted If you

20. still have questions, you can call me here before 3 pm

21. I have a request for you too Would you possibly mind

22. filling out the enclosed questionnaire We are

23. currently conducting a survey on clients' and potential

24. clients' needs And although you are not yet a client, you

25. may be someday

Lesson 13
Punctuation: Commas and Semicolons

Perhaps the most difficult punctuation mark to use correctly is the comma, which indicates a pause—not the full stop indicated by a period. The semicolon, the comma's cousin, indicates a pause greater than a comma but less than a period.

One use for commas is the linking of two independent clauses (sentence parts that contain both a subject and a predicate and can stand along):

We **shipped** the ordered items on November 15, and you **confirmed** receipt on November 20.

The comma is necessary in this sentence because both parts have a subject and a predicate and are equal in importance. Independent clauses like these are joined by the conjunctions *and, but, for, not, or, so,* and *yet.*

Sometimes independent clauses are linked by semicolons instead of commas (no conjunction necessary):

We **shipped** the ordered items on November 15; you **confirmed** receipt on November 20.

But do not use semicolons to link sentence elements that are not equal—such as clause to phrase or independent clause to dependent clause. The use of a semicolon in the following sentence is wrong:

We closed down the warehouse yesterday; because we needed to conduct an inventory·

The clause that begins with *because* cannot stand along and is therefore dependent rather than independent. Semicolons are also used when a transitional expression such as *however, for example,* or *therefore* is used between independent clauses:

We shipped the ordered items on November 15; however, you confirmed receipt on November 20.

Transitional expressions are followed by a comma when they introduce an independent clause—even when it stands alone as a sentence:

In fact, the first shift is understaffed at present.

Modifying elements (clauses and phrases) that introduce a sentence are also followed by a comma. For example:

Because your application reached us after the deadline, you will be considered for a position at a later time.
Judging from your background, I assume that you will be considered for a position at a later time.
Yes, you will be considered for a position at a later time.

However, commas may be left out if the introductory element is a short prepositional phrase (no subject and predicate) and cannot be misread:

With your help we will soon begin.

Be careful not to confuse readers by omitting necessary commas. Can you tell exactly what the following sentence means without backtracking or reading it twice?

Before leaving Ms. Danforth passed out some assignments.

The meaning becomes much clearer if a comma is added after the prepositional phrase:

Before leaving, Ms. Danforth passed out some assignments.

Within sentences, adjectives are sometimes used in combination to modify a single noun. When the order of the adjectives can be switched without affecting the meaning of the sentence, they are separated by commas (never semicolons):

A <u>stale</u>, <u>metallic</u> taste permeates the water.

But leave out the comma if the order of the two adjectives cannot be switched:

The <u>last promising</u> applicant has been interviewed.

Commas are also used to set off a variety of parenthetical words and phrases within sentences, including state names, dates, abbreviations, quotations, transitional expressions, and contrasted elements. Notice in the following examples that the commas are paired if the parenthetical element falls in the middle of the sentence:

Jerry noticed, before anyone else did, that the numbers don't add up.
They were, in fact, prepared to submit a bid.
Tall buildings, reaching for the sky, soon dominated the cityscape.
The best worker in the department is Ken, who jointed the company just a month ago.
Our goal was increased profits, not increased market share.
Service, then, is our main concern.
"The Grant Avenue store," she said yesterday, "is next in line for renovation."
The new factory, has been built in Halifax, Nova Scotia, to take advantage of the labor pool there.
Joanne Dubik, M.D., has applied for a loan from First Savings.
I started to work for this company on March 1, 1989, and soon received my first promotion.
Send the letter to Deborah Schneider, 179 Church Street, Elmhurst, Ontario

Another common use for commas is to separate three or more items in a series. A comma follows every item except the last:

Send us the main unit, all available peripherals, and an operating manual. Go to the personnel office, turn in your forms, and return here by 1:15.

Semicolons should be used to separate the items in a series when one or more of the items includes a comma:

The participants were Everett Johnston, Nagle Corporation; DeLynn Bucklely, Restaurants Unlimited; and Connie Crichton, Tandem Inc.

Insert required commas and semicolons in the following exercises, crossing out unnecessary words:

1. Send us four cases of filters two cases of wing nuts and a bale of rags.

2. Can you help teachers and office workers and sales representatives?

3. Mr. Pechman I hope to see you at our next meeting.

4. Your analysis however does not account for returns.

5. As a matter of fact she has seen the figures.

6. Before May 7 1990 they wouldn't have minded either.

7. You can reach me at this address: 717 Darby Place Hartland New Brunswick E7M 1A9.

8. Transfer the documents from Red Deer Alberta to Moose Jaw Saskatchewan..

9. Sam O'Neill the designated representative is gone today.

10. An outstanding new product has just hit the market.

11. Beginning next week and continuing until January 3 our Cambridge offices will be closed.

12. She may hire two new representatives or she may postpone filling those territories until the spring.

13. After Martha has gone talk to me about promoting her.

14. Stoneridge Inc. will go public on September 9 1999.

15. We want the new copier not the old model.

16. "Talk to me" Sandra said "before you change a thing."

17. This letter looks good that one doesn't.

18. The Zurich airport has been snowed in therefore I won't be able to meet with you before Thursday January 27.

19. Because of a previous engagement Dr. Sroeve will not be able to attend.

20. Send a copy of the memo to Mary Kennedy Vice President of Marketing Robert Bache Comptroller and Dennis McMurphy Director of Sales.

21. She started attracting attention during the long hard recession of the mid-1970s.

22.   We have observed your hard work and because of it we are promoting you to manager of your department.

23.   After we see the outcome of the survey we will choose which product to introduce first.

24.   Yes we will be able to supply you with all you need.

25.   Tolbert & O'Toole is of course a leader in its industry.

To learn more, consult a grammar book on the following topics:

appositives	independent clauses	nonrestrictive modifiers
conjunctions	introductory clauses	parenthetical elements
contrasted elements	introductory phrases	series

You may also wish to consult Sections 1.7.4, "Fused Sentences and Comma Splices," 2.4, "Semicolons," and 2.6, "Commas," in The "Handbook, Fundamentals of Grammar and Usage," in *Excellence in Business Communication.*

Lesson 13: Check Your Answers

Insert required commas and semicolons in the following exercises, crossing out unnecessary words:

1. Send us four cases of filters two cases of wing nuts and a bale of rags.

2. Can you help teachers and office workers and sales representatives?

3. Mr. Pechman I hope to see you at our next meeting.

4. Your analysis however does not account for returns.

5. As a matter of fact she has seen the figures.

6. Before May 7 1990 they wouldn't have minded either.

7. You can reach me at this address: 717 Darby Place Hartland New Brunswick E7M 1A9.

8. Transfer the documents from Red Deer Alberta to Moose Jaw Saskatchewan.

9. Sam O'Neill the designated representative is gone today.

10. An outstanding new product has just hit the market.

11. Beginning next week and continuing until January 3 our Cambridge offices will be closed.

12. She may hire two new representatives or she may postpone filling those territories until the spring.

13. After Martha has gone talk to me about promoting her.

14. Stoneridge Inc. will go public on September 9, 1999.

15. We want the new copier, not the old model.

16. "Talk to me," Sandra said, "before you change a thing."

17. This letter looks good; that one doesn't.

18. The Zurich airport has been snowed in; therefore, I won't be able to meet with you before Thursday, January 27.

19. Because of a previous engagement, Dr. Sroeve will not be able to attend.

20. Send a copy of the memo to Mary Kennedy, Vice President of Marketing; Robert Bache, Comptroller; and Dennis McMurphy, Director of Sales.

21. She started attracting attention during the long, hard recession of the mid-1970s.

22. We have observed your hard work, and because of it, we are promoting you to manager of your department.

23. After we see the outcome of the survey, we will choose which product to introduce first.

24. Yes, we will be able to supply you with all you need.

25. Tolbert & O'Toole is, of course, a leader in its industry.

Lesson 14
Punctuation: Asides and Additions

Some marks of punctuation—colons, parentheses, brackets, and dashes—are used to set off supplementary information from the main part of a sentence.

A colon, for example, calls attention to the words that follow—as if the colon meant "for example" or "that is." Therefore, colons are frequently used to introduce a word, phrase, or sentence of explanation:

> Only one word can describe your proposal: fantastic!
> This, then, is our goal for 1991: to increase sales 35 percent.
> Remember this rule: When in doubt, leave it out.

Colons are also used to introduce lists, although lists that are necessary to complete a thought are not set off by colons. Observe the difference between these two sentences:

> Next year we will have to hire an executive assistant, a bookkeeper, and a receptionist.
> Next year we will have to hire three people: a executive assistant, a bookkeeper, and a receptionist.

In the first example, the list actually serves as the object of the sentence *(What will we have to hire?)* and cannot be separated from the subject and predicate by a colon. But in the second example, the part before the colon could stand on its own as a sentence. It is a complete thought in itself and must be separated from the list.

Colons may also introduce formal quotations:

> Chairman Dana Gerster announced: "Aquatec today acquired the assets of Marine Corp."

Finally, colons have several specialized uses. In letters, of course, they are used with closed or mixed punctuation following the salutation (*Dear Ms. Norden:*); they are used with memo headings (*TO:*); and they are used to separate hours from minutes in time designations (*11:30 a.m.*).

Parentheses are also used to set off information from the main part of a sentence. Some sentences use commas to indicate a supplementary idea; parentheses do much the same thing, but they are used when the idea has little importance to the main part of the sentence. Compare these two examples:

> She drove her own car, a '95 Chrysler, last week.
> She drove her own car (a '95 Chrysler) last week.

The only difference between these two sentences is the degree of emphasis given to the type of car being discussed. Context and judgment should tell you whether to use commas or parentheses in a given situation.

Parentheses themselves are relatively easy to use; what is more difficult is to use other punctuation properly when you're using parentheses. For instance, what kind of punctuation do you use when a complete sentence is embedded in another sentence by means of parentheses? You should never use a period at the end of an embedded sentence, but you can use a question mark or an exclamation point:

> When you hear from her (have you already heard?), call me.

226

Notice that the embedded sentence is not capitalized. Notice also that the comma that would normally be used at the end of the introductory clause is still included, although it follows the parenthetical statement.

Semicolons and colons are also included after the closing parenthesis if necessary to the main part of the sentence.

If the material between the parentheses is a sentence by itself and is not embedded in another sentence, its punctuation is self-contained:

> Our company's profit history is irregular. (See Table 2 for a complete rundown on company profits over the past ten years.)

Brackets, which look similar to parentheses, have a specialized use. In quoted material, they set off the writer's comments from the comments of the person being quoted:

> "In the past seven years [during which Cass has dominated the market], we have exceeded our goals," Dr. Blevins noted.
> "The closest airport of any size," said Carol Nichols, "is about 25 kilometers [15.5 miles] away:"

One other way that you can insert parenthetical material into a sentence is to use dashes (which are typed as two hyphens with no extra spaces between or on either side). Dashes give inserted material more emphasis than either commas or parentheses and should be used sparingly.

Compare these sentences and note the weight given to the parenthetical thought by the three types of punctuation:

> Model 7-103, the latest in our line of quality conveyors, will be introduced at the convention in Chicago.
> Model 7-103 (the latest in our line of quality conveyors) will be introduced at the convention in Chicago.
> Model 7-103—the latest in our line of quality conveyors—will be introduced at the convention in Chicago.

Abrupt interruptions to the main thought are also set off by dashes:

> The file on Marian Gephardt—yes, we finally found it—reveals a history of late payments.

Dashes or parentheses, not commas, are used when the parenthetical statement itself contains commas: Three qualities—speed, accuracy, and reliability—are desirable in any data entry persons employed by our department.

Dashes are also used when a sentence begins with a list and then finishes with a summarizing statement: Speed, accuracy, and reliability—these are the qualities we look for in any data entry persons employed by our department.

In the following exercises, insert colons, parentheses, brackets, and dashes wherever necessary:

1. Only one thing increased productivity will save us.

2. Stealth, secrecy, and surprise those are the elements that will give us a competitive edge.

3. The clients were most interested in income statements, balance sheets and payroll statements.

4. Her response see the attached memo is disturbing.

5. His motivation was obvious to get Meg fired.

6. Only two firms have responded to our survey J.J. Perkins and Tucker & Tucker.

7. Only two sites maybe three offer the things we need.

8. Sarah O'Roarke an appraiser will be here on Thursday.

9. The assistant the one who just had a baby will have the document ready later today.

10. Kevin Langhans our top sales representative last year is at the bottom of the pile so far this year.

11. Your training kit consisting of a manual, supplementary reading, and product samples has already been shipped.

12. Please be sure to interview these employees next week Henry Golden, Doris Hatch, and George Iosupovich.

13. The new offices will be spacious, well lit, and inviting.

14. The convention kit includes the following response cards, giveaways, brochures, and a display rack with samples.

15. Glenda she's the union representative has been helpful.

16. Professor Pettit had this to say: "We cannot assume a larger market, even with an increase in population. Demographic patterns have changed radically."

17. Send the memo to all the sales reps, the sales managers, and the director of marketing.

18. Ron Franklin do you remember him? will be in town Monday.

19. I want to make one thing perfectly clear: neither of you will be promoted if the sales figures do not improve.

20. Four items ladders, workbench kits, fluorescent light fixtures, and pegboard supplies will go on sale March 1.

21. Service and value those are Krasner's watchwords.

22. We will operate with a skeleton staff during the holiday break December 21 through January 2.

23. Refinements in robotics may prove profitable. More information on this technology appears in Appendix A.

24. Please return it before the deadline January 31, so we may send all the documents to you by the end of February.

25. Lucy has a math background an enormous advantage.

To learn more about these types of punctuation, consult a grammar book on the following topics:

brackets	dashes	parentheses
colons	embedded sentences	parenthetical elements

You may also wish to refer to Sections 2.5, "Colons," 2.7, "Dashes," and 2.11, *"Parentheses," in* The "Handbook, Fundamentals of Grammar and Usage," in *Excellence in Business Communication.*

Lesson 14: Check Your Answers

In the following exercises, insert colons, parentheses, brackets, and dashes wherever necessary:

1. Only one thing increased productivity will save us.

2. Stealth, secrecy, and surprise those are the elements that will give us a competitive edge.

3. The clients were most interested in income statements, balance sheets and payroll statements.

4. Her response see the attached memo is disturbing.

5. His motivation was obvious to get Meg fired.

6. Only two firms have responded to our survey J.J. Perkins and Tucker & Tucker.

7. Only two sites maybe three offer the things we need. *or parentheses*

8. Sarah O'Roarke an appraiser will be here on Thursday. *or parentheses*

9. The assistant (the one who just had a baby) will have the document ready later today.

10. Kevin Langhans our top sales representative last year is at the bottom of the pile so far this year.

11. Your training kit consisting of a manual, supplementary reading, and product samples has already been shipped.

12. Please be sure to interview these employees next week Henry Golden, Doris Hatch, and George Iosupovich.

13. The new offices will be spacious, well lit, and inviting.

14. The convention kit includes the following response cards, giveaways, brochures, and a display rack with samples.

15. Glenda she's the union representative has been helpful.

16. Professor Pettit had this to say: "We cannot assume a larger market, even with an increase in population. Demographic patterns have changed radically."

17. Send the memo to all the sales reps, the sales managers, and the director of marketing.

18. Ron Franklin do you remember him? will be in town Monday. *or parentheses*

19. I want to make one thing perfectly clear; neither of you will be promoted if the sales figures do not improve.

20. Four items—ladders, workbench kits, fluorescent light fixtures, and pegboard supplies—will go on sale March 1. *or parentheses*

21. Service and value—those are Krasner's watchwords.

22. We will operate with a skeleton staff during the holiday break (December 21 through January 2). *or dash*

23. Refinements in robotics may prove profitable. More information on this technology appears in Appendix A.)

24. Please return it before the deadline (January 31) so we may send all the documents to you by the end of February.

25. Lucy has a math background—an enormous advantage.

Lesson 15
Punctuation: Quotations

You may often want to use someone else's words in your business writing, especially in reports and persuasive sales letters. Quotation marks are indispensable for reporting what someone else has said:

Dan Hurtig said, "Only five companies will remain after the coming shakeout in our industry."
According to Inez Castro, the hospital supply department is "coping heroically under difficult circumstances."
"Where there's a will, there's a way," she remarked.

Notice that the first word of a quotation is capitalized only when the quotation begins a sentence (as in the third example) or is itself a sentence and is preceded by a word like *said* (as in the first example). When the quotation is only part of a sentence and serves as the object of the sentence, the first word is not capitalized (as in the second example).

Direct quotations, whether spoken or written, should always be put between quotation marks and attributed to the person who originated them. Indirect quotations, however—paraphrased statements—-do not require quotation marks. In the following sentence, the introductory word *that* is a clue that the quotation is indirect:

Alice Montero said that few of the new employees have opted for day-care benefits.

Quotation marks are also used to set off words and phrases that are being treated with irony or are being used in a special context.

The "benefits" of working for him include frequent criticism and scant praise.
A "request for proposal" is a government notice that proposals will be accepted.
When you are defining a word, put the definition in quotation marks:
The abbreviation *etc.* means "and so forth."

Quotation marks are also used in reference notes to set off the titles of articles, book chapters, and other small works or parts of larger works:

Did he find "Seeking Profits in the Nineties" in *Business Today*?

Periods and commas always fall within the last set of quotation marks, but semicolons, colons, and dashes always fall after the last set:

"Given their recent performance," she said, "we probably should not risk a large investment." They note "a marked lack of respect"; however, Drake was not working directly for them at that point.
Two things affect "demand curves": price and quantity.
Harry DeLuca—-our plant's "top gun"—-should undertake that project.

In using quotation marks with question marks and exclamation points, however, you must use your judgment. If the quoted passage is itself a question or an exclamation, the punctuation should be placed inside the last set of quotation marks:

"Can you find the source of the problem?" she asked.

He spoke in frustration: "These developers! I wish they would just accept the zoning plan!"

Notice in the first example that no comma is used to set the quoted passage apart from the rest of the sentence. Do not use a comma in combination with a question mark or an exclamation point.

Question marks and exclamation points are set outside the quotation marks when the quoted material is merely part of a sentence that is itself a question or an exclamation:

They themselves drew our attention to these "irregularities"!
Do you know who asked for "bilateral decisions"?

When quoting a long passage (more than three lines), you should set off the material by indenting it on both sides and single-spacing. This treatment makes quotation marks unnecessary.

Sometimes you will find that material you want to quote contains more than you need. In that case, use points of ellipsis to indicate that you have left out words:

"It is in our nature ... to look for advantage."

Ellipses (omissions) are always indicated with only three dots, although a fourth dot—a period—is included when necessary:

"It is in our nature to look for advantage...."

Italics are often used in connection with quotations, for citing a printed source. Use italics for the titles of books, magazines, newspapers, movies, and other inclusive reference materials:

Our ad will appear in The *National Post.*
The Wealth of Nations proposed an early version of this notion.

Italics and bolding are used to mark words used as words and to emphasize (sparingly) words and phrases:

The word *profit* has a variety of meanings.

The **result** of this campaign did not justify the expense.

In the following exercises, insert all necessary punctuation and italics (bolding) in the right places:

1. Be sure to read How to Sell by Listening in this month's issue of Fortune.

2. Contact is an overused word.

3. I don't care why you didn't fill my order; I want to know when you'll fill it.

4. We all make mistakes sometimes, the letter said.

5. Where did you put the Hartnet files? he asked.

6. Do you remember who said And away we go?

7. I can't believe that she doesn't know how to find, as Dr. Frankel puts it, sufficient resources.

8. Whom do you think Time magazine will select as its Man of the Year?

9. Bah! Humbug! said Scrooge.

10. The term up in the air means undecided.

11. As the report that I read concluded, Crown Products' best avenue for growth is the consumer market; I believe we should follow up on this analysis.

12. Susan said that she could not find the source of the error.

13. A computer nerd would have no trouble with it.

14. Professional bookkeepers use the double-entry method.

15. Business is the lifeblood of our country! she exclaimed.

16. Can you see the difference between debits and credits?

17. Only two were listed in the manager's little black book: Cathy Navasitis and Jeff Stamper.

18. Stephen Roussin made this point: The element of surprise would be of little use to us in this case; therefore, we should seek information wherever we can find it.

19. Then she asked, Do you have any disabilities that would prevent you from taking this job?

20. Can you believe that he would say something like We're only here to serve larger corporations?

21. Do you know anything about read-only memory?

22. The SBP'S next conference, the bulletin noted, will be held in Montreal.

23. Sir Wilfrid Laurier proclaimed The twentieth century belongs to Canada.

24. Let's subscribe to Advertising Age.

25. What about taxes? we asked.

If you want to learn more about quotations, consult a grammar book on these topics:

direct quotations	indirect quotations	quotation marks	underscoring
ellipses	italics	reference notes	

You may also wish to consult Sections 2.10, "Quotation Marks," 2.12, "Ellipses," and 2.13 "Underscores and Italics," in The "Handbook, Fundamentals of Grammar and Usage," in *Excellence in Business Communication*.

Lesson 15: Check Your Answers

In the following exercises, insert all necessary punctuation and italics (bolding) in the right places:

1. Be sure to read How to Sell by Listening in this month's issue of <u>Fortune</u>.

2. <u>Contact</u> is an overused word.

3. I don't care <u>why</u> you didn't fill my order; I want to know <u>when</u> you'll fill it.

4. We all make mistakes sometimes, the letter said.

5. Where did you put the Hartnet files? he asked.

6. Do you remember who said And away we go?

7. I can't believe that she doesn't know how to find, as Dr. Frankel puts it, sufficient resources.

8. Whom do you think <u>Time</u> magazine will select as its Man of the Year?

9. Bah! Humbug! said Scrooge.

10. The term <u>up in the air</u> means undecided.

11. As the report that I read concluded, Crown Products' best avenue for growth is the consumer market; I believe we should follow up on this analysis.

12. Susan said that she could not find the source of the error.

13. A computer nerd would have no trouble with it.

14. Professional bookkeepers use the double-entry method.

15. Business is the lifeblood of our country! she exclaimed.

16. Can you see the difference between debits and credits?

17. Only two were listed in the manager's little black book: Cathy Navasitis and Jeff Stamper.

18. Stephen Roussin made this point: The element of surprise would be of little use to us in this case; therefore, we should seek information wherever we can find it.

19. Then she asked, Do you have any disabilities that would prevent you from taking this job?

20. Can you believe that he would say something like We're only here to serve larger corporations?

21. Do you know anything about read-only memory?

22. The SBP'S next conference, the bulletin noted, will be held in Minneapolis.

23. Patrick Henry is supposed to have challenged them with Give me liberty, or give me death!

24. Let's subscribe to <u>Advertising Age</u>.

25. What about taxes? we asked.

Lesson 16
Punctuation: Within Words

The main marks of punctuation used within words are apostrophes and hyphens. Apostrophes are used to indicate omitted letters; hyphens are used to link words or parts of a word into one.

One use for apostrophes is within contractions like the following:

don't	do not	it's	it is
we'll	we will	'98	1998

In the most formal writing, contractions should be avoided. They are acceptable, however, in speech and in informal writing.

Be careful that you do not confuse contractions with possessive pronouns. *It's* (contraction) and *its* (possessive) are often confused, as are *their's* and *theirs* and *they're* and *their*. If you have trouble deciding which one to use, take a moment to remember what words the contraction stands for. If the sentence still makes sense when you substitute those words, you can use the contraction. Otherwise, use the possessive pronoun.

What makes the distinction between contractions and possessive pronouns so confusing to some people is the fact that apostrophes are also used to make words possessive:

Amina's pen   report's cover   employees' wages

Be careful to use the possessive form only when "ownership" is indicated; change the words around and add *of* as a test:

Amina's pen	pen of Amina
report's cover	cover of the report
employees' wages	wages of the employees

It is sometimes hard to figure out where to put the apostrophe when showing ownership. As a rule, you simply add *'s* to the end of any word that does not already end in *s*, whether the word is singular or plural:

Cathy Onishi's letter	children's books
Grady Inc.'s main office	people's needs

If the word is plural and ends in *s* and an *s* sound, you usually add just an apostrophe at the end:

consultants' recommendations	twenty dollars' worth
Morrises' home	companies' plans

You add *'s* to singular words that end in one *s* or *s* sound, an apostrophe along when the word ends in two *s* sounds:

boss's chair	Mr. Sanchez's office

With compound nouns, add the apostrophe to the last word:

mother-in-law's idea   attorney general's opinion

When two or more individuals each own something separately, you should use the apostrophe with both names. But when they own something together, use the apostrophe with only the second name:

Paul's and Sam's offices   Paul and Sam's office

The use of apostrophes in business names can become complicated. For example, some organizations use the apostrophe and some don't:

Harrison's Hardware, Inc.   Friedmann Leasing, Ltd.

There is no hard and fast rule for using apostrophes with the names of organizations. Check the organization's letterhead or a directory.

Nor is there a rule you can consult to decide whether to use an apostrophe in phrases like these:

employee handbook   employees' handbook   employee's handbook

Consult other company documents for guidance in these cases—or use your judgment to figure out the real meaning behind the words you are using.

With most abbreviations, the apostrophe is used to form possessives just as it would be with any other word—although you must be careful to put the apostrophe after the period, if there is one:

CBS's report   R.N.'s schedule

You should not use an apostrophe to indicate plural numbers (for example, 1990s is correct), but you should use apostrophes with letters used as letters (A's and B's).

Test your ability to use apostrophes properly by adding them wherever necessary in the following exercises:

1. Collect every employees timecard on Friday.

2. Is that Tracys or Nicks?

3. The outcome of the test is anyones guess.

4. All the attorneys offices are cleaned every night.

5. Well discuss the mens coat department tomorrow.

6. Mr. Dunne completed the course in the 1960s with all As.

7. Its hard to see how their situation could improve.

8. We might buy a thousand dollars worth.

9. Where did you get IBMs annual report?

10. The electronics industry gives its best wages to Ph.D.s.

The other type of punctuation mark commonly used within words is the hyphen. Hyphens are always used to separate the main part of a word from the prefixes *all, ex,* and *self;* the main part from the suffix *elect;* a prefix from a capitalized word; and a prefix or suffix from numbers or letters:

all-inclusive	ex-athlete	self-controlled
chairperson-elect	non-European	mid-1990s

Adding a prefix to a noun that already has a modifier presents a problem:

ex-prime minister   or ex-prime-minister?

Avoid the issue: former prime minister

Other words that combine parts may or may not use a hyphen. In fact, they may or may not be two separate words:

half hour	half-baked	halfway

The best way to find out whether to use a hyphen in words like these is to look them up in a dictionary. (However, remember that dictionaries take different approaches to hyphenating words.) If the combined word does not appear in the dictionary, it should be written as two separate words.

Hyphens are also used to combine whole words. For example, the following nouns use a hyphen:

programmer-analyst   sister-in-law

However, authorities vary widely on which combinations of nouns require a hyphen. In general, the use of hyphens can improve readability, as in the following situations:

Awkward combinations of letters: re-enact, twist-tie
More than one meaning: The Reform Party has re-formed as The Alliance Party.

Multiple modifiers preceding a noun:

We plan to start a <u>small business</u> publication. (a business publication that is small)
We plan to start a <u>small-business</u> publication. (a publication for small businesses)

Ask the intern to prepare a <u>short term</u> paper. (a term paper that is short)
Ask the intern to prepare a <u>short-term</u> paper. (a paper dealing with the short term)

It is unnecessary to hyphenate combinations of an adjective and a modifier ending in ly—because a modifier that ends in *ly* is an adverb, and clearly modifies the adjective, not the noun: *poorly marketed product, newly hired employee.*

When a sentence contains a series of hyphenated words that are similar, you may shorten it by dropping the repeated word:

We need to order some three- and four-compartment servers.

Insert hyphens only where necessary in the following exercises:

11. A highly placed source explained the negotiations.

12. They're selling a custom designed machine.

13. A bottle green sports jacket is hard to find.

14. How many owner operators are in the industry?

15. You can always count on an all inclusive report from Roberto.

16. Politicians call them fact finding missions; their critics call them junkets.

17. Myrna Talefiero is the organization's president elect.

18. I need a small business loan of $10,000 so I can expand my boutique.

19. How can we possibly please all the higher ups?

20. Try to eliminate your self consciousness.

21. We must carefully limit aid to truly needy residents.

22. High living bureaucrats receive extra scrutiny.

23. Your devil may care attitude affects us all.

24. His new office is well decorated.

25. What decision making processes will the group use?

To learn more about punctuation within words, you may wish to consult a grammar book on the following topics:

apostrophes	hyphens	suffixes
compound words	prefixes	

You may also wish to consult Sections 1.1.3, "Possessive Nouns," 2.8, "Hyphens," and 2.9, "Apostrophes," in The "Handbook, Fundamentals of Grammar and Usage," in *Excellence in Business Communication*.

Lesson 16: Check Your Answers

Test your ability to use apostrophes properly by adding them wherever necessary in the following exercises:

1. Collect every employees timecard on Friday.

2. Is that Tracy's or Nick's?

3. The outcome of the test is anyone's guess.

4. All the attorneys' offices are cleaned every night.

5. We'll discuss the men's coat department tomorrow.

6. Mr. Dunne completed the course in the 1960s with all A's.

7. It's hard to see how their situation could improve.

8. We might buy a thousand dollars' worth.

9. Where did you get IBM's annual report?

10. The electronics industry gives its best wages to Ph.D.s.

Insert hyphens only where necessary in the following exercises:

11. A highly placed source explained the negotiations.

12. They're selling a custom-designed machine.

13. A bottle-green sports jacket is hard to find.

14. How many owner-operators are in the industry?

15. You can always count on an all-inclusive report from Roberto.

16. Politicians call them fact-finding missions; their critics call them junkets.

17. Myrna Talefiero is the organization's president-elect.

18. I need a small-business loan of $10,000 so I can expand my boutique.

19. How can we possibly please all the higher-ups?

20. Try to eliminate your self-consciousness.

21. We must carefully limit aid to truly needy residents.

22. High-living bureaucrats receive extra scrutiny.

23. Your devil-may-care attitude affects us all.

24. His new office is well decorated.

25. What decision-making processes will the group use?

Lesson 17
Mechanics: Numbers

In general, numbers from one to ten are spelled out, and numbers over ten are written in figures. (If your organization has adopted its own style for dealing with numbers, use it.) But when a number begins a sentence, it should always be spelled. You can avoid writing an awkwardly large number (more than two words) at the beginning of a sentence by rewriting the sentence. For example:

Awkward: Five hundred thirty-seven people have signed up.
Better: Sign-ups number 537.
Better: About 540 people have signed up.

Approximate numbers that can be expressed in one or two words are also spelled out (notice the use of hyphens with some numbers):

About twenty-five people have applied for the job.
Over one hundred software titles are in stock.
We're looking for something in the seventy-five-dollar range.

When dealing with numbers over 999, remember to use a comma to separate thousands from hundreds: *2,384*. Numbers in the millions and billions combine words and figures: *7.3 million, 2 billion*.
Usually, however, words and figures should not be combined. In a series of related numbers, spell all (if all are ten or under) or write all in figures:

Please send 12 copies of *Bridge for Beginners,* 6 copies of *Bridge Strategies,* and 3 copies of *Secrets of the Life Masters.*

The general rule about using words and figures may also be ignored when two numbers fall next to each other in a sentence. Regardless of the size of the numbers, use figures for the number that is largest, most difficult to spell, or part of a physical measurement; use words for the other:

I have learned to manage a classroom of 30 twelve-year-olds.
She's won a bonus for selling 24 thirty-volume sets.
You'll need twenty 3-inch bolts.

In money expressions, approximate dollar amounts may be expressed in words: *five dollars*. But specific dollar amounts are written in figures with a dollar sign: *$5.95, $27, $3 million*.
For amounts less than one dollar, use figures and the word *cents: 5 cents*. But if you are writing a series of money expressions and at least one has a dollar sign, all the rest should too. Remember also to include cents with all the numbers if one of them is not an even dollar amount:

The skins retail for $12.00 each; the hole punches, $3.59 each; and the grommets, $0.19 each.

In dates, the month is always spelled out, and the date and year are written in figures: *August 29, 2001*. In foreign, military, and some government correspondence, however, the order of the date and month is reversed: *29 August 2001*. Observe how dates are written when the year is not specified:

29th of August   August 29   the 29th .

References to centuries or decades may be in words or in figures:

twentieth century   20th century,
sixties   1960s

Time expressions that use *a.m.* or *p.m.* should be written in figures, but time expressions that use *o'clock* should be written in words. Compare:

The meeting starts at 9:30 a.m.
The meeting starts at eleven o'clock.

Most other time expressions are spelled out for the numbers ten and under and written in figures for the numbers over ten. The only exception is that figures are sometimes used for emphasis in detailing the terms of doing business:

Your account will be credited within 5 working days.

In addresses, all street numbers except *One* are in figures. So are suite and room numbers and ZIP codes. But what about street names that are numbered? Because practice varies so widely, you should use the form specified on an organization's letterhead or in a reliable directory. All of the following are correct:

One Fifth Avenue   297 Ninth Street
1839 44th Street   11026 West 78 Place

Telephone numbers are always expressed in figures. Usually, parentheses separate the area code from the rest of the number, but a slash or dash may be used instead if the entire phone number is enclosed in parentheses:

(602) 382-8329   (602/382-8329)   (602-382-8329)

Figures are also used for extension numbers: *(602) 382-8329, extension 71.*

Percentages are another type of number that is always expressed in figures. The word *percent* is used in most situations (for example, *27 percent*), but *%* may be used in tables, forms, and statistical writing.

Physical measurements—distance, weight, and volume—are also often expressed in figures (*9 kilometers*).
Ages are usually expressed in words—except when a parenthetical reference to age follows someone's name:

Mrs. Margaret Sanderson is seventy-two.
Mrs. Margaret Sanderson, 72, swims daily.

Ages expressed in years and months do not use a comma: *5 years 6 months.*

Figures are used to designate a great many other things as well, such as parts, forms, pages, and accounts. Even if these numbers have four or more digits, they do not use commas:

Section 7   Serial No. 38293   page 84

When you need to indicate numbered order, spell out ordinals from first to tenth and use the abbreviations *st, d,* and *th* with ordinals over 11th:

fifth grade   first floor
23d day   20th century

Use figures and ordinal abbreviations for editions of books in bibliographies:

2d ed.   4th ed.

Decimal numbers are always written in figures. In most cases, add a zero to the left of the decimal point if the number is less than one and does not already start with a zero:

1.38   .07   0.2

In a series of related decimal numbers with at least one number greater than one, make sure that all numbers smaller than one have a zero to the left of the decimal point: *1.20, 0.21, 0.09.* And express all decimal numbers in a series to the same number of places by adding zeroes at the end:

The responses were Yes, 37.2 percent; No, 51.0; Not Sure, 11.8.

Simple fractions are written in words, but more complicated fractions are expressed in figures or, if easier to read in figures and words:

two-thirds   9/32   2 hundredths

A combination of a whole number and a fraction should always be written in figures. Note that a hyphen is used to separate the fraction from the whole number when a slash is used for the fraction: 2-11/16.

In the following exercises, correct numbers wherever necessary:

1. Let's invite about 20 outstanding college students.

2. Fifty-two computers were purchased.

3. We need to hire one office manager, four bookkeepers, and twelve clerk-typists.

4. They want to spend about $300.

5. The population of Guatemala is almost six million.

6. The agency's report totaled 1835 pages.

7. The 1st person who makes a purchase wins a prize.

8. Our offices are open between 9 o'clock and 5 o'clock.

9. Can you make it on the 7th?

10. We have enclosed checks for $45 and $37.50.

11. Deliver the couch to 1 South Thirty-eighth Avenue.

12. 95 percent of our customers are men.

13. Your measurement appears to be off by .7 centimeter.

14. Over 1/2 the U.S. population is female.

15. Our building is three miles past the intersection.

16. Hanna Hilgersen just turned thirty.

17. You'll find a definition of coverages on page five.

18. Of the fifteen applicants, seven are qualified.

19. Last year I wrote twenty one fifteen-page reports.

20. Set up enough chairs for an audience of at least 100.

21. 50,000,000 Canadians can't be wrong.

22. This is the thirty-fifth request for confirmation.

23. Plan to be here for interviews from 1:00 to 4:30 p.m.

24. We need a set of shelves ten feet, eight inches long.

25. Check the following specifications: A, 2.39; B, .5; C, .09.

To learn more about this subject, consult a grammar book on the following topics:

decimals	hyphenated numbers
fractions	ordinals

You may also wish to consult Section 3.3, "Numbers," in The "Handbook, Fundamentals of Grammar and Usage," in *Excellence in Business Communication.*

Lesson 17: Check Your Answers

In the following exercises, correct numbers wherever necessary:
1. Let's invite about ~~20~~ *twenty* outstanding college students.
2. Fifty-two computers were purchased.
3. We need to hire ~~one~~ *1* office manager, ~~four~~ *4* bookkeepers, and ~~twelve~~ *12* clerk-typists.
4. They want to spend about ~~$300.~~ *three hundred dollars*
5. The population of Guatemala is almost ~~six~~ *6* million.
6. The agency's report totaled 1835 pages.
7. The ~~1st~~ *first* person who makes a purchase wins a prize.
8. Our offices are open between ~~9~~ *nine* o'clock and ~~5~~ *five* o'clock.
9. Can you make it on the 7th? *$45.00*
10. We have enclosed checks for ~~$45~~ and $37.50.

11. Deliver the couch to ~~1~~ *One* South Thirty-eighth Avenue.

12. *About* ~~^~~95 percent of our customers are men.

13. Your measurement appears to be off by ~~1~~ *0.7* centimeter.

14. Over ~~1/2~~ *half* the Canadian population is female.

15. Our building is ~~three~~ *3* miles past the intersection.

16. Hanna Hilgersen just turned thirty.

17. You'll find a definition of coverages on page ~~five~~ *5*.

18. Of the ~~fifteen~~ *15* applicants, ~~seven~~ *7* are qualified.

19. Last year I wrote ~~twenty-one~~ *21* fifteen-page reports.

20. Set up enough chairs for an audience of at least ~~100~~ *one hundred*.

21. ~~50,000,000~~ *Fifty million* Americans can't be wrong.

22. This is the ~~thirty-fifth~~ *35th* request for confirmation.

23. Plan to be here for interviews from 1:00 to 4:30 p.m.

24. We need a set of shelves ~~ten~~ *10* feet, ~~eight~~ *8* inches long.

25. Check the following specifications: A, 2.39; B, ~~.5~~ *0.5*; C, ~~.09~~ *0.09*.

Lesson 18
Mechanics: Abbreviations and Symbols

Abbreviations and symbols provide a short, convenient way to express yourself, but some readers may not know what they stand for. Even if you think that readers will recognize them, you should generally limit their use to tables, graphs, lists, forms, technical documents, and informal memos. In any case, approach the abbreviation decision with this rule in mind: When in doubt, spell it out.

One way to handle an abbreviation that you want to use throughout a document is to spell it out the first time you use it, follow it with the abbreviation in parentheses, and then use the abbreviation in the remainder of the document.

The commonly used abbreviations for most organizations are capitalized and lack periods:

AT&T   UNICEF   NHL   CKNB-TV

Some abbreviations of organizations' names are more than just initials; instead, they are shortened versions of the full name:

Bell Labs   Ryerson Polytech   the Falls

You may use these shortened names only in informal writing.

Abbreviations are also commonly used in addresses. Company names, for instance, often end with Inc., Ltd., Co., or Corp. If the company uses any of these abbreviations in its letterhead or in references to itself, you should use them too. For repeated reference to the same company, however. you may drop such abbreviations and use only the main part of the name.

Compass points (north, south, east, west) are usually not abbreviated when they come before a street name; however, the compass points that sometimes follow a street name NW, NE, SW, SE) are usually abbreviated. Do not abbreviate other parts of the street name such as *Street* and *Avenue*) unless you have very little space.

Most place names are not abbreviated: Fort William, Port Arthur, Mount Pleasant, West Flamboro. The exception is place names that include the word *Saint:* St. John.

Within addresses, use the two-letter postal abbreviations for province names, such as *BC* and *PQ*. If you must abbreviate province names elsewhere but are not using postal codes, you may use such abbreviations as *Ont.* and *Alta.*

The names of countries are usually spelled out, both in addresses and in the body of letters, memos. and reports. The two most common exceptions are *USSR* and *U.S.*

What about the names of people? Do not abbreviate unless a person wants to be known by first and middle initials or by an abbreviated first name (B. J. Brooks, Geo. E Carlisle). Notice that the initials are separated by a space.

Titles are another matter. The abbreviations *Mr., Ms., Mrs.,* and *Dr.* should always be used when they appear before a person's name. (Do not use *Mr., Ms., Mrs., Dr., or Esq.* [Esquire] with any other title.) Other titles that come before a person's name may or may not be abbreviated if they are used with the person's full name but should never be abbreviated if they are used with the last name alone:

Sen. Elizabeth Clarke   Senator Clarke
Capt. Robert Leinert   Captain Leineft
Prof. Patricia Stone   Professor Stone

Another sort of abbreviation comes after a person's full name:

Nathaniel Grob, Jr.   Artis Remer, M.B.A. (or MBA)
Richard Taylor, Esq.   Peggy Klein, D.V.M. (or DVM)

In statistical or technical writing and in tables and charts, you may use abbreviations for units of measurement. For example:

m   km   l   kg   kph   wpm

Notice that metric measures (m, kg) have no period; nor does the abbreviation for words per minute. Some references to time are typically abbreviated:

a.m.   A.D.   CST (Central Standard Time)

The following list shows one way of using periods and capital letters in abbreviations of some business terms; your source may recommend another:

acct.	account	LIFO	last in, first out
A/P	accounts payable	mdse.	merchandise
ASAP	as soon as possible	mfg.	manufacturing
bal.	balance	mgr.	manager
b/l	bill of lading	IT	information technology
cc	carbon copy	mtg.	meeting
CEO	chief executive officer	N/30	net due in 30 days
c/o	care of	no.	number
C.O.D.	cash on delivery	p., pp.	page, pages
CA	Certified Accountant	pd.	paid
cr.	credit	PR	public relations
CRT	cathode ray tube	P.S.	postscript
cwt	hundredweight	R&D	research and development
dept.	department	rm.	room
div.	division	R.R.	railroad, rural route
doz.	dozen	RSVP	please reply
DP	data processing	std.	standard
ea.	each	ste.	suite
e.g.	for example	VIP	very important person
e.o.m.	end of month	WP	word processing
et al.	and others	/	per
etc.	and so forth	#	number
ext.	extension	%	percent
FIFO	first in, first out	@	at
fig.	figure	$	dollar
FOB	free on board	™	trademark

FYI	for your information	¶	paragraph
GDP	gross domestic product	®	registered
GNP	gross national product	©	copyright
i.e.	that is		

For the following exercises, assume that the reader is an "insider," and substitute abbreviations wherever possible:

1. Paul Hansen, Registered Nurse, is joining our staff.

2. The Young Men's Christian Association has a centre here.

3. Send it to Mister H. K. Danforth, Rural Route 1, Wakefield, New Brunswick E7M 1A8.

4. She is a candidate for the master of business administration degree at the University of British Columbia.

5. Call me at 8 in the morning, Pacific Standard Time.

6. The data processing department will work on it as soon as possible.

7. The core sample weighs 1.7 kilograms.

8. The Toronto Stock Exchange sent notice to them.

9. General John de Chastelain chaired the commission.

10. We are sending it cash on delivery, net due in 15 days.

For the remaining exercises, assume that the reader is an "outsider," and spell out abbreviated words wherever possible:

11. The RCMP is based in Ottawa, ON.

12. St. John's, Nfld., is their headquarters.

13. Mr. Geoffrey Finley is the CEO of TrendWell, Inc.

14. Call me at 818-3948, ext. 72, between 10 a.m. and 3 p.m.

15. Send the package to Mr. C. W. Crane, 382 W. Okanagan Rd., Ft. McMurray, AB T9H 1G7.

16. FYI, the Bilbray accts. are past due.

17. I have an M.Sc. degree from UBC.

18. It's 3 km from our office to the nearest restaurant.

19. Over 50% of our engineering staff have Ph.D.s.

20. Christine Jarvis, CA, is joining the mfg. div.

21. The UN is headquartered in NYC.

22. The Hon. Donna Stroeb-Atkins will speak at our meeting.

23. Send your std. #10 envelopes, @ $9.95/box.

24. RSVP ASAP.

25. Capt. Macek et al. participated in the setting up of the MIS.

If you would like to study more about this subject, consult a grammar book under the following headings:

acronyms	names
addresses	periods
capitalization	scientific/technical terms
dates	titles and degrees
measurements	trade names

You may also wish to consult Section 3.2, "Abbreviations," in The "Handbook, Fundamentals of Grammar and Usage," in *Excellence in Business Communication,* Fourth Edition.

Lesson 18: Check Your Answers

For the following exercises, assume that the reader is an "insider," and substitute abbreviations wherever possible:

1. Paul Hansen, ~~Registered Nurse~~ *R.N.*, is joining our staff.

2. The ~~Young Men's Christian Association~~ *YMCA* has a centre here.

3. Send it to ~~Mister~~ *Mr.* H. K. Danforth, ~~Rural Route~~ *R.R.* 1, Wakefield, ~~New Brunswick~~ *NB* E7M 1A8.

4. She is a candidate for the ~~master of business administration~~ *MBA or M.B.A.* degree at the ~~University of British Columbia~~ *UBC*.

5. Call me at 8 ~~in the morning~~ *a.m.*, ~~Pacific Standard Time~~ *PST*.

6. The ~~data processing~~ *DP* ~~department~~ *dept.* will work on it ~~as soon as possible~~ *ASAP*.

7. The core sample weighs 1.7 ~~kilograms~~ *kg*.

8. The ~~Toronto Stock Exchange~~ *TSE* sent notice to them.

9. ~~General~~ *Gen.* John de Chastelain chaired the commission.

10. We are sending it ~~cash on delivery~~ *C.O.D.*, ~~net due in 15 days~~ *N/15*.

For the remaining exercises, assume that the reader is an "outsider," and spell out abbreviated words wherever possible:

11. The ~~RCMP~~ *Royal Canadian Mounted Police* is based in Ottawa, ON.

12. St. John's, ~~Nfld.~~ *Newfoundland*, is their headquarters.

13. Mr. Geoffrey Finley is the ~~CEO~~ of TrendWell, Inc. *Chief Executive Officer*

14. Call me at 818-3948, ~~ext.~~ 72, between 10 a.m. and 3 p.m. *extension*

15. Send the package to Mr. C. W. Crane, 382 ~~W~~. Okanagan ~~Rd.~~, ~~Ft.~~ McMurray, ~~AB~~ T9H 1G7. *West Road Fort Alberta*

16. ~~FYI~~, the Bilbray ~~accts.~~ are past due. *For your information accounts*

17. I have ~~an M.Sc.~~ degree from ~~UBC.~~ *a master of Science University of British Columbia*

18. It's 3 ~~km~~ from our office to the nearest restaurant. *kilometres*

19. Over 50~~%~~ of our engineering staff have ~~Ph.D.s~~. *percent doctorate degrees*

20. Christine Jarvis, ~~CA~~, is joining the ~~mfg. div.~~ *Certified Accountant manufacturing division*

21. The ~~UN~~ is headquartered in ~~NYC~~. *United Nations New York City*

22. The ~~Hon.~~ Donna Stroeb-Atkins will speak at our meeting. *Honourable*

23. Send your ~~std. #~~10 envelopes, ~~@~~ $9.95~~/~~box. *standard number at per*

24. ~~RSVP ASAP.~~ *Please respond as soon as possible*

25. ~~Capt.~~ Macek ~~et al.~~ participated in the setting up of the ~~MIS~~. *Captain and others management information system*

Lesson 19
Mechanics: Capitals

Capital letters are used, of course, at the beginning of sentences. But they are also used at the beginning of other word groups:

Formal statement following colon: She has a favorite motto: Where there's a will, there's a way.
Phrase used as sentence: Absolutely not!
Quoted sentence embedded in another sentence: Scott said, "Nobody was here during the lunch hour except me."
Set-off list of items: Three preliminary steps are involved:
1. Design review
2. Budgeting
3. Scheduling

Capital letters are also used with proper nouns and proper adjectives, such as the following:

Red Green   Victorian mansion

A proper noun is separated from a prefix with a hyphen:

ex-Premier   anti-American

People's titles are capitalized when they are used in addressing a person, especially in a formal context. They are not usually capitalized, however, when they are used merely to identify the person. Observe the difference here:

Address the letter to <u>Chairperson</u> Anna Palmer.
I wish to thank <u>Chairperson</u> Anna Palmer for her assistance.
Please deliver these documents to board chairperson Anna Palmer.
Anna Palmer, chairperson of the board, took the podium.

Titles should also be capitalized if they are used by themselves in addressing a person:

Thank you, <u>Doctor</u>, for your donation.

Titles used to identify a person of very high rank are capitalized regardless of where they fall or how much of the name is included:

the <u>Prime Minister</u> of Canada   the Pope

In addresses, salutations, signature blocks, and some formal writing (such as acknowledgments), all titles are capitalized whether they come before or after the name.

The names of organizations are capitalized, of course; so are the official names of their departments and divisions:

252

Route this memo to <u>Personnel</u>.
Larry Tien was transferred to the <u>Microchip Division</u>.
Will you be enrolled in the <u>Psychology Department</u>?

However, when referring in general terms to a department or division, especially one in another organization, do not capitalize:

Someone from the <u>engineering department</u> at EnerTech stopped by the booth.
Our <u>production department</u> has reorganized for efficiency.
Send a copy to their <u>school of business administration</u>.

Capitalization is also unnecessary when using a word like *company, corporation,* or *university* alone:

The <u>corporation</u> plans to issue 50,000 shares of common stock.

The names of specific products should be capitalized, although the names of general product types should not be:

Compaq computer   Tide laundry detergent

Many writers have trouble with the capitalization of compass directions. For instance, should you use *southern Ontario* or *Southern Ontario, north county* or *North County?* Capitalize when the compass direction is part of a place's name, whether in official or in common use; do not capitalize when referring to a direction or general location. Here are some examples:

the West   the western half of Canada
the South   southern New Brunswick
the Northeast   northeasterners

Another problem that often arises in writing about places is the treatment of two or more proper nouns of the same type. When the common word comes before the specific names, it is capitalized; when it comes after the specific names, it is not. Observe the capitalization here:

Lakes Ontario and Huron
St. Lawrence and Ottawa rivers

The names of languages, races, and ethnic groups are also capitalized: *Japanese, Caucasian, Hispanic.*

In referring to the titles of books, articles, magazines, newspapers, reports, movies, and so on, you should capitalize the first and last words and all nouns, pronouns, adjectives, verbs, adverbs, and prepositions and conjunctions with five letters or more. Except for the first and last words, do not capitalize articles, and do not capitalize conjunctions and prepositions with fewer than five letters. For example:

Economics During the Great War
"An investigation into the Market for Long-Distance Services"
"What Successes Are Made Of"

When *the* is part of the official name of a newspaper or magazine, it should be treated this way too: *The Calgary Herald.*

References to specific pages, paragraphs, lines, and the like are not capitalized: *page 72, line 3.* However, in most other numbered or lettered references, the identifying term is capitalized:

Chapter 4   Serial No. 382-2203   Item B-11

Words for specific markings or instructions on documents are also capitalized:

Stamp this letter "Confidential" before it goes out.

Finally, the names of academic degrees are capitalized when they follow a person's name but are not capitalized when used in a general sense:

I received a <u>bachelor of science</u> degree.
Thomas Whitelaw, <u>Doctor of Philosophy</u>, will attend.

Similarly, general courses of study are not capitalized, but the names of specific classes are:

She studied <u>accounting</u> as an undergraduate.
She is enrolled in <u>Accounting 201</u>.

Remember that the principles described here are well accepted but that your organization may have its own rules for capitalization.

In the following exercises, capitalize wherever appropriate:

1. Yates & co. is in suite 303 of park towers.

2. The luxury of chinese silk is yours.

3. Pat swink said, "my research shows something else."

4. The president of the company has adopted this motto: look before you leap.

5. I'm taking two psychology courses.

6. Let's invite dr. lynne jamison, the director of personnel.

7. See page 143 in chapter 5.

8. We plan to establish a sales office on the west coast.

9. The personnel department has submitted its budget.

10. Do you know how to fix the xerox machine?

11. Check in the *dictionary of occupational titles*.

12. We're at the corner of madison and king streets.

13. Did you see the file labeled "overdue accounts"?

14. The staff at university hospital deserves praise.

15. Address it to art bowers, chief of production.

16. Our new tractor, the sodbuster, has been developed to solve the special problems of western grain farmers.

17. See if you can find "in search of a stable economy."

18. We're forming a partnership with a south american corporation.

19. You could reserve the regency and embassy rooms.

20. New caressa skin cream smooths wrinkles.

21. I have a graduate degree in business administration.

22. She characterized the movie as "an orwellian fantasy."

23. Tell me, professor, do you plan to come?

24. The company is forming a new policies group.

25. Maybe we should consider a location in the deep south.

To learn more about this subject, consult a grammar book on the following topics:

abbreviations	proper nouns
addresses	quotations
bibliographies	titles and degrees
personification	trademarks
place names	

You may also wish to consult Section 3.1, *"Capitals,"* in The "Handbook, Fundamentals of Grammar and Usage," in *Excellence in Business Communication*.

Lesson 19: Check Your Answers

In the following exercises, capitalize wherever appropriate:

1. Yates & co. is in suite 303 of park towers.

2. The luxury of chinese silk is yours.

3. Pat swink said, "my research shows something else."

4. The president of the company has adopted this motto: look before you leap.

5. I'm taking two psychology courses.

6. Let's invite dr. lynne jamison, the director of personnel.

7. See page 143 in chapter 5.

8. We plan to establish a sales office on the west coast.

9. The personnel department has submitted its budget.

10. Do you know how to fix the xerox machine?

11. Check in the *dictionary of occupational titles.*

12. We're at the corner of madison and king streets.

13. Did you see the file labeled "overdue accounts"?

14. The staff at university hospital deserves praise.

15. Address it to art bowers, chief of production.

16. Our new tractor, the sodbuster, has been developed to solve the special problems of western grain farmers.

17. See if you can find "in search of a stable economy."

18. We're forming a partnership with a south american corporation.

19. You could reserve the regency and embassy rooms.

20. New caressa skin cream smooths wrinkles.

21. I have a graduate degree in business administration.

22. She characterized the movie as "an orwellian fantasy."

23. Tell me, professor, do you plan to come?

24. The company is forming a new policies group.

25. Maybe we should consider a location in the deep south.

Lesson 20

Words

One of the greatest sources of trouble for business writers is groups of words that look alike, sound alike, or have special connotations. Note carefully the differences in meaning among the following:

accept	to take, to agree	assure	to personally promise
except	excluding	ensure	to guarantee
		insure	to issue an insurance policy
access	entry, means of approaching		
excess	too much	beside	next to
		besides	other than
adapt	to adjust		
adept	skilled	biannual	twice a year
adopt	to take on	biennial	once every two years
adverse	unfavorable	bloc	group of people
averse	against	block	solid mass, to put up an obstacle
advice	recommendation	born	brought forth by birth
advise	to counsel, to recommend	borne	carried
affect	to change, to have an impact	breath	air inhaled and exhaled
effect	result of action	breathe	to inhale and exhale
aggravate	make a problem worse	capital	money, seat of government
annoy	to bother	capitol:	building used by a legislature
irritate	to cause anger or impatience		
		casual	informal
allusion	reference to	causal	related to a cause
illusion	appearance of		
		cite	to refer to
among	referring to three or more	sight	vision, to see
between	referring to two	site	location
anxious	nervously anticipating	clothes	garments
eager	enthusiastically anticipating	cloths	fabrics
appraise	to estimate a value	coarse	rough
apprise	to inform	course	direction, route
apt	naturally inclined or able	command	order, to order
likely	probable, appropriate	commend	to praise
assistance	help	complement	something that completes or
assistants	helpers	makes perfect,	to make whole
		compliment	expression of praise, to praise, to congratulate

compose	to formulate	envelop	to surround
comprise	to include, to contain	envelope	paper covering for a letter
confidant	person who hears secrets	explicit	clearly stated
confident	self-assured	implicit	unstated, hidden
conscience	sense of right and wrong	farther	more distant
conscious	aware	further	more, additional, to advance
constant	recurring in the say way	feasible	desirable and possible
continual	recurring at frequent intervals	possible	able to likely to happen
continuous	ongoing	practicable	possible given existing conditions
core	center		
corps	group	formally	in a formal manner
		formerly	previously
council	committee		
counsel	adviser, to advise	human	relating to people
		humane	compassionate
deference	submission		
difference	dissimilarity	imitate	to copy
		intimate	personal
dependence	reliance		
dependents	those who rely on someone	imply	to hint
		infer	to interpret
deprecate	to protest, to belittle		
depreciate	to lessen value	incidence	rate of occurrence
		incidents	occurrences
detract	to take away from		
distract	to divert	ingenious	clever
		ingenuous	naïve and innocent
device	mechanism		
devise	to construct	instance	case
		instants	moments
disapprove	to condemn		
disprove	to prove wrong	intense	heightened
		intents	purposes
disburse	to pay out		
dispense	to distribute	intercity	between cities
disperse	to scatter	intracity	within a city
discreet	prudent	its	of it
discrete	separate	it's	it is
elicit	to draw out	later	more advanced in time
illicit	unlawful	latter	item closest to the end
eminent	notable	lead	metal; to show the way
imminent	impending	led	showed the way

lend	to give the use of		
loan	something lent	presence	attendance
		presents	gifts
liable	legally responsible		
libel	written defamation	principal	main, head, capital (money)
		principle	rule
local	of the surrounding area		
locale	place	raise	to lift
		rise	to get up, to go up
loose	unrestrained		
lose	to misplace, to fail to win	role	part
		roll	bread, to throw, to turn over
moral	honest, lesson		
morale	mental condition	set	to put down
		sit	to take a seat
passed	went by		
past	bygone	stationary	in one place
		stationery	paper
pedal	foot lever, to move with the feet		
peddle	to sell	straight	not curved
		strait	narrow waterway, difficult
perquisite	benefit		position
prerequisite	qualification		
		than	compared with
persecute	to harass	then	time past
prosecute	to start legal proceedings		
		their	of them
personal	of the person	there	in that place
personnel	staff, employees	they're	they are
perspective	view	to	opposite of from
prospective	potential, forthcoming	too	overly, also
		two	2
populace	inhabitants		
populous	having many people	vice	immorality
		vise	instrument for gripping
practicable	able to be done		
practical	workable (things), sensible	waiver	abandonment of a right
	(people)	waver	to flicker, to hesitate
pragmatic	hard-headed, realistic		
		who's	who is
precede	to go before	whose	of whom
proceed	to continue		
		your	of you
preposition	a part of speech	you're	you are
proposition	scheme		

Underline the correct word in each of the following exercises:

1. Everyone accept/except Barbara King has registered.

2. The whole debt was born/borne by his parents.

3. We need to find a new security device/devise.

4. They decided to sue for liable/libel.

5. The passed/past few days have been hectic.

6. How much farther/further is the convention center?

7. Just set/sit it on the credenza.

8. Enter the number of dependence/dependents in this box.

9. Were you able to determine their intense/intents?

10. You will be asked to sign a waiver/waver.

11. I assure/ensure/insure you that all will be ready.

12. From my perspective/prospective, this is a bad move.

13. The moral/morale is this: Expect the worst.

14. Your experience is a good complement/compliment to my enthusiasm.

15. I'd like a later/latter appointment.

16. Scientists have established a direct casual/causal relationship between sunburn and skin disorders.

17. He didn't mention it outright, but his need for a decision was explicit/implicit.

18. This month's balance is greater than/then last month's.

19. Can you appraise/apprise us of her qualifications?

20. Look up their/there/they're address.

21. We can't let outside events detract/distract us now.

22. The study group will compose/comprise all the analysts.

23. I'd like to precede/proceed my remarks with a question.

24. An ambitious person will raise/rise above challenges.

25. Dr. Khoury is an eminent/imminent chemist.

If you need help in using words correctly, you may wish to consult a grammar book on the following topics:

diction	usage
homonyms	vocabulary
idioms	

You may also wish to consult Sections 4.1, "Frequently Confused Words," 4.2, "Frequently Misused Words," and 4.3, "Frequently Misspelled Words," in The "Handbook, Fundamentals of Grammar and Usage," in *Excellence in Business Communication*.

Lesson 20: Check Your Answers

Underline the correct word in each of the following exercises:

1. Everyone accept/<u>except</u> Barbara King has registered.

2. The whole debt was born/<u>borne</u> by his parents.

3. We need to find a new security <u>device</u>/devise.

4. They decided to sue for liable/<u>libel</u>.

5. The passed/<u>past</u> few days have been hectic.

6. How much <u>farther</u>/further is the convention center?

7. Just <u>set</u>/sit it on the credenza.

8. Enter the number of dependence/<u>dependents</u> in this box.

9. Were you able to determine their intense/<u>intents</u>?

10. You will be asked to sign a <u>waiver</u>/waver.

11. I <u>assure</u>/ensure/insure you that all will be ready.

12. From my <u>perspective</u>/prospective, this is a bad move.

13. The <u>moral</u>/morale is this: Expect the worst.

14. Your experience is a good <u>complement</u>/compliment to my enthusiasm.

15. I'd like a <u>later</u>/latter appointment.

16. Scientists have established a direct casual/<u>causal</u> relationship between sunburn and skin disorders.

17. He didn't mention it outright, but his need for a decision was explicit/<u>implicit</u>.

18. This month's balance is greater <u>than</u>/then last month's.

19.   Can you appraise/<u>apprise</u> us of her qualifications?

20.   Look up <u>their</u>/there/they're address.

21.   We can't let outside events detract/<u>distract</u> us now.

22.   The study group will compose/<u>comprise</u> all the analysts.

23.   I'd like to <u>precede</u>/proceed my remarks with a question.

24.   An ambitious person will raise/<u>rise</u> above challenges.

25.   Dr. Khoury is an <u>eminent</u>/imminent chemist.